RADICAL DOCTOR SMOLLETT

Radical
Doctor Smollett

DONALD BRUCE

HOUGHTON MIFFLIN COMPANY BOSTON

The Riverside Press Cambridge

1965

To
ANNE BRUCE

CONTENTS

Section II The Reciprocal Influence.
Influence of mind on body as presented by Smollett. Subjectivity. The nerves. Effects of terror, violent emotion and frustration. Emotionally induced illness.
Section III An Involuntary Instinct.
Smollett's examination of the human personality and of the part played in its manifestations by the association of ideas, by self-interest, by nervous impulse and by brute instinct. The balance of the passions.

PREFACE

This book is intended for the well-informed but not necessarily studious reader who dreads and avoids tedium. It is hoped that the scholar too, though fastidious, will not altogether disdain the sometimes staccato exposition and the occasional small asides with which in my simplicity I have tried to beguile him. The book was conceived and carried out as an attempt to do justice to one of our older novelists. Though the achievement has been little enough, I may at least boast that the intention was a worthy one.

My gratitude is due to Dr. L. Haddakin of University College, London, who first saw me safely embarked on my circumnavigation of Smollett, and to all those who have encouraged and sustained me during it, in particular Mr. John Strudwick, J.P., and Mrs. Strudwick and, above all, my wife Erika Bruce. Amongst those who have lent me the advantage of their special knowledge I would like to single out Dr. F. Poynter of the Wellcome Library of the History of Medicine, who obligingly read through and commented on the draft of the second chapter; Mr. A. Trubshaw, M.A., who taught me History when I was a boy at Sutton Grammar School and also when I was a master there; Mr. Douglas Jones, B.A., Lecturer in History and Philosophy at Coventry Training College, who helped me find my way around Hume; and Miss Dorothy Roberts of Maria Grey College, Twickenham, who told me about Vanbrugh's Gothic lapses and other points of architectural interest.

My final acknowledgement is both respectful and cordial. It is ironical that this book owes so much to one of the most notable upholders of the reputation of Pope and Fielding, and I hope that what I have written about them will meet with the same patient indulgence as Professor James Sutherland has always shown me. Without the help, benign but never intrusive, of Professor Sutherland, this book would never have taken its present shape.

I would like to add that none of the kindly people whom I have mentioned is answerable for any statement made in the opinionated and contentious work to which I now resign the reader's attention.

D. B.

Maria Grey College, Twickenham
April, 1964

CHAPTER I

A LAUREL AT HIS TOMB

Between the gentlemanly biography by Sir Walter Scott and the more professional one by Professor Louis Knapp, few serious appreciations of Smollett were attempted. The scholars, particularly the American scholars, gave much of their time to such harmless games as finding out how much rent Smollett paid during the composition of *Peregrine Pickle*. The critics used the words *low, coarse and brutal* in various combinations and then went on to Fielding. Perhaps they did so because they were convinced that the authority of Hazlitt, one of the first and certainly the most eminent of Smollett's detractors, is absolute. Yet the portrait of Smollett which they copied so faithfully from Hazlitt was crooked in its conception and raw in its execution.

It should be remembered that Hazlitt and, later, Thackeray were, as popular lecturers on Smollett, facing the ticket-holding public of an officiously genteel age. Hazlitt voiced his distaste for the open discussion of the indelicate. This distaste had, no doubt, occasioned his flight from the Lake District some time previously after trying to ravish a Cumberland peasant girl. Anyway, the audience at the Surrey Institution, which had already put up with a great deal from Hazlitt, was hardly likely to tolerate the open discussion of the indelicate. Thackeray's observations on Smollett were disconnected and awkward, because the role of hypocrite was unfamiliar to him. Succeeding critics were surer of themselves. The convention among them was like the one about Swinburne at Eton, that if they came near Smollett they kicked him and if they saw him at a distance they threw something.

Smollett had started off with considerable acclaim. The first three editions of *Evelina*, with a sale of 2,300 copies, made Fanny Burney a conspicuous literary figure. The first three editions of *Roderick Random* sold nearly three times as well. Not only was this so, but shortly after the appearance of *Roderick Random* the story of Mrs. Williams was reprinted in the *Gentleman's*

Magazine as a reinforcement of Dr. Cobden's sermon, *A Persuasive To Chastity*, with the comment:

> Of this wretched state (prostitution) a most lively and striking picture is exhibited in *Roderick Random*, which we have copied as a warning to one sex and a remonstrance against t'other.[1]

Up to the late 1760's such unfriendly criticism of Smollett as was made at all was confined to the trivial and the peripheral. His chapter headings were tedious. He gave the story away in advance. The hero of *Ferdinand, Count Fathom* was a rogue. The friendly criticism was hardly more discerning, as when the Gothick sub-plot of Rinaldo and Monimia and the character of Don Diego in *Count Fathom* were singled out for praise.[2] It was the laboured and apocryphal extravagance, *The Adventures of An Atom*, which first attracted to Smollett the imputations of being indecent and obscene, made by the same *Gentleman's Magazine* which twenty years earlier had thought him to be so very much on the side of chastity. Having made up its mind about Smollett, the *Gentleman's Magazine* went on to say, in 1771, that *Humphry Clinker* was often prurient. In the same year (that of Smollett's death) the *Monthly Review* accused Smollett of "grossness and ill-nature".[3] In 1773 he was reproached in the *Monthly Ledger* for failing to provide "virtuous examples to follow".[4]

Such were the views of inconsiderable critics. It is significant that the first misgivings about Smollett on the part of a person of any distinction were expressed by Dr. Charles Burney. He observed that Smollett's novels "are so damned gross that they are not fit reading for women with all their wit".[5] Dr. Burney was a member of Mrs. Thrale's little circle at Streatham, about which more will be said later, and was thus entrenched in all the mercantile "refinement" which Smollett so vividly disliked. Smollett was more pleasing to the ribald old aristocracy, if Lady Mary Montagu can be taken as its representative. Although she never met Smollett, she refers to him in a letter on 1 January, 1755, as "my friend Smollett", saying that she is sorry that he "loses his time in translations". On 3 October, 1758, she regrets that "my dear Smollett disgraces his talents by writing those stupid romances commonly called history". Lady Mary was all for novels.

Most of the major English writers of the early nineteenth century were Smollett-lovers. Lamb, Hunt, Hazlitt, Carlyle and Dickens have all left autobiographical passages in which they

associate Smollett's novels with their boyhood and a lyrical
first acquaintance with books.[5] At the age of sixteen Macaulay
wrote a letter in defence of Smollett to the *Christian Observer*.[6]
Keats imagines, in a letter of 1819, a nonsensical continuation of
Humphry Clinker. Coleridge instances "the exquisite humour"
of the characters Strap, Bowling, Morgan and Bramble.[7] De
Quincey mentions that Wordsworth delighted in "the ability of
the execution" of the eighteenth-century novelists, whom the
dissident De Quincey considers "so disgusting by their moral
scenery and the whole state of vicious society in which they keep
the reader moving".[8] Although Wordsworth thought that the
Scotch historians of the eighteenth century "did infinite mischief
to style", he excepted "Smollett, who wrote good pure English".[9]
Wordsworth was the recipient in 1801 of an unusually fierce
letter from Charles Lamb, which contains what is possibly the
shrewdest remark ever made about the morality of Smollett's
novels and about moral purpose in fiction generally. Objecting
to the direct expostulations in the *Lyrical Ballads*, Lamb wrote:

> An intelligent reader finds a sort of insult in being told, I will
> teach you how to think upon this subject. This fault, if I am
> right, is in a ten-thousandth worse degree to be found in Sterne
> and many novelists and modern poets, who continually put a sign
> post up to show where you are to feel. They set out with assuming
> their readers to be stupid. Very different from *Robinson Crusoe,
> The Vicar of Wakefield, Roderick Random*, and other beautiful
> bare narratives. There is implied an unwritten compact between
> author and reader; I will tell you a story, and I suppose you will
> understand it.

In spite of the value placed upon Smollett by these great men,
by nobody more generously or more justly than by Sir Walter
Scott, the Streatham point of view predominated. The refined
middle class was more powerful even than in Mrs. Thrale's time
and socially more subtle. Dr. Burney's host brewed beer. John
Ruskin's father imported sherry. Dr. Burney growled about Smollett's "damned grossness". Ruskin gave little falsetto screams over
Smollett's "innuendoes of abomination", protesting against the
coarseness of *Humphry Clinker* in imagery a great deal more disgusting than anything Smollett himself ever wrote.[10]
Yet this was a book which the ethical Dr. Arnold of Rugby
liked so much that he told Dean Stanley it was not too much to
say that he had read it through fifty times.[11] Anthony Trollope,
in his discussion of the eighteenth-century novel, asserts that

Smollett, like Juvenal, was a "most lascivious writer" and doubts whether "he does much service to morality". How seriously Trollope is to be taken is suggested by his previous comment on Richardson's *Clarissa* :

> Against the horrors to which his heroine was subjected it is not necessary to warn our girls in this safer age—or to speak of them.[12]

R. L. Stevenson mentions portions of *Roderick Random* "over which the reader passes lightly and hurriedly, like a traveller in a malarious country", as if the conditions aboard ship in the eighteenth century were Smollett's own fault.[13] Smollett was also unfortunate in his editors. Alexander Chalmers placed Smollett's poems before the public with the words : "Nor has he scrupled to introduce, with more than slight notice, those vices which are not fit to be named".[14] Saintsbury introduced Smollett as "admittedly one of the nastiest writers in English". Henley displayed so open a dislike for Smollett that two of the reviewers of the time wondered why he had agreed to edit him. Henley truthfully remarks in his introduction, "I have said what I believe to be the worst that can be said for Smollett".[15] This is not how other people are edited. It is not surprising that, presented in this way, Smollett works were banned from public libraries in the early years of the present century.[16]

The Victorian critics lived in Mayhew's London, at a time when Nathaniel Hawthorne wrote in a letter to America :

> I offer it as a serious conviction, from what I have been able to observe, that the England of today is the unscrupulous old England of Tom Jones and Joseph Andrews, Humphry Clinker and Roderick Random; and in our refined era, just the same as at that more free-spoken epoch.[17]

It would have been more to the credit of the critics if, instead of bemoaning Smollett's want of refinement, they had protested against the infamy of their own streets, done something about the indigence and unrelieved sickness which, all around them, led their fellow men to uneuphemistic deaths. It would have harmed nobody if they had spoken up in language as direct as Smollett's. Smollett, always ready to denounce social wickedness and "fix the brand of infamy on vice",[18] was a great deal more moral than they were. It is not until the air has been cleared of much late nineteenth-century cant that Smollett can be discerned in his true form. His large intellect, his manliness, his unusual honesty and penetration, all his qualities cry out for recognition and justice.

Hazlitt as a critic deserves more respect than Hazlitt as a moralist, but he is often insensitive when his enthusiasm has not been touched off. Smollett never won him over. He considers that Smollett "seldom probes to the quick or beneath the surface". Smollett's humour arises from "the situation of the person or the peculiarity of their external appearance". Fielding has "a superior insight into the springs of character".[19]

Partisanship in literary criticism is seldom rewarding to the reader, and the discussion of Fielding and Smollett's comparative merits is not only banal but unprofitable. But perhaps for once a little may be said, fairly belligerently, on Smollett's side. Fielding's aristocracy is both his asset and his limitation. By experience and character he was confined to the common opinions of an eighteenth-century gentleman. Smollett was classless and unconfined. It is true that he took considerable pride in his family, which he described to an American admirer as "reputable",[20] and about the antiquity of which he speculated in a letter to one of his cousins, conjecturing that "we were originally Malet or Molet and came from Normandy with the Conqueror".[21] Yet he spent his boyhood in near-penury, barefooted, subsisting on oatmeal, occupied in grooming horses. The combination of distinguished antecedents and an impoverished youth was probably responsible for his personal bearing, as it appears in the *Travels*. Whilst he was emphatic about being treated by the bourgeois with the respect due to a person of standing, he was on easy and complaisant terms with the working class. Severe on inn-keepers, he would listen attentively, and making joking comments, to a postillion's life-story.

Inquisitive, adaptable and penniless, he was exposed to every possibility of eighteenth-century life. He carried his Scotch learning from the cockpit of the H.M.S. *Chichester* to Downing Street, from Downing Street to prison, he carted it picaresquely around Europe with his silver and his table-linen. He pamphleteered and inveighed, qualified between novels as a physician, and edited three magazines. He prepared a tragedy for the stage, wrote a treatise on bathing, and contributed the preface to a work on midwifery. He translated Lesage and Cervantes. He annotated Voltaire. He laboured at a series of vast compendia. He brought out a History of England from the Roman Conquest to the Treaty of Aix la

Chapelle; then continued it up to the year of publication. The extent of his reading for pleasure can be judged by the books which he took with him on his travels in France, the detention of which at Boulogne "deprives me of an amusement which I can very ill dispense with".[22] They included editions of Juvenal, Tibullus, Shakespeare, Congreve and Voltaire. In the letters from Italy, which are largely given up to the denunciation of the Ancient Romans, he reveals what nimble reconnaissances he has made into enemy territory by quoting Virgil, Horace, Ovid, Persius, Juvenal, Martial, Pliny and Suetonius in the original Latin. He was equally conversant with Raphael's frescoes, the manners of the inhabitants of Greenland, Boerhaaven's system of anatomy, the merits of the different methods of vine-growing, the ingredients of Ancient Roman pickles and the domestic arrangements of Dr. Johnson. His life of hard work, a life of only fifty years, was spent amongst the distractions of ill-health, endless financial difficulty, constant travel, frequent changes of house and a large correspondence. At any time from 1749 to 1754 he could conceivably have been brought before Henry Fielding, magistrate. At any time during the same five years he could conceivably, as a physician, have administered to Henry Fielding's mortality.

The diversity of Smollett's experience made him intellectually broader and deeper than Fielding. In the eighteenth century the study of Man by observation had concluded in a perplexed re-assessment of moral and religious ideas. It was a time of half-formulated doubts and misgivings. Fielding never doubted. Urbane, harmonious, he takes his ease, Olympian, in good fellowship with Homer and Horace. Smollett, with the anxious pragmatism of his time, investigates "the operations of the animal oeconomy". He has more than an insight into the springs of character. He has the will to find out what winds them up. Two events in his early life brought the whole organisation of eighteenth-century English society under his scrutiny. These were the Battle of Carthagena in 1741 and the Battle of Culloden in 1746, two moves in what he was later to call "a cruel game of blood".

Smollett set out as a surgeon's mate on board the H.M.S. *Chichester* in 1741, on an expedition of doubtful morality, to take away by force the trading rights which the Spaniards had preserved in the West Indies. The navy at this time was notorious for its corruption, both at the Admiralty and on board ship.

Because of the understandable aversion caused by the injustice and ill-treatment with which the ordinary seamen were treated, large numbers of them had to be recruited by the press-gangs. As a contemporary admiral said, the fleet was "first manned by violence and maintained by cruelty".[23] In the naval episode of *Roderick Random*, which is at least partly autobiographical, Smollett describes how Random is turned away when he presents his qualification as second-mate at the Navy Office. He later discovers that this is because he has failed to bribe the secretary:

> We went down stairs, and conferred together on our expectations, when I understood that each of them had been recommended to one or other of the commissioners, and each of them promised the first vacancy that should fall; but that none of them relied solely upon that interest, without a present to the secretary, with whom some of the commissioners went snacks. For which reason each of them had provided a small purse; and I was asked what I proposed to give? This was a vexatious question to me, who, far from being in a capacity to gratify a ravenous secretary, had not wherewithal to purchase a dinner.[24]

Whilst the commissions are filled by influence and bribery, there is plenty of room in the ranks, as Random discovers when he takes an ill-advised walk on Tower Wharf, where he is seized and with great brutality carried on board ship by the press-gang. Once on board, however, he finds an old friend, now in a position of authority, who is able to redress Random's wrongs:

> And this was not the only satisfaction I enjoyed; for I was, at the request of the surgeon, exempted from all other duty than that of assisting his mates in making and administering medicines to the sick. This good office I owed to the friendship of Mr. Thomson, who had represented me in such a favourable light to the surgeon that he demanded me of the lieutenant to supply the place of his third mate, who was lately dead.[25]

By accident coupled with the advantage of a well-placed acquaintance, Random obtains one of those vacancies for which his honest qualifications were not enough. Very dearly he wins the privilege of witnessing, like Smollett, the callous ineptitudes of the attack of Carthagena.

The mission of H.M.S. *Chichester*, even from the practical point of view, was from the start bedevilled by the frequency with which the troops which it was carrying, victims of bad organisation, fell sick. There were deaths almost daily.[26] The living conditions were unhealthy, the medical facilities were managed in the same casual manner as that which enabled Random so promptly to be made third mate, and the food was rank. For example, the ship was bearing 1,895 lb. of putrefied cheese through the tropics. After Carthagena had been taken with great loss of life, the army was·forced to abandon it because of an epidemic brought on by bad provisions, a shortage of clean water and the lack of medical attention. In the epidemic three thousand men died. In this respect the expedition to Carthagena anticipated the Seven Years War, during the course of which eighty-eight English soldiers died of disease or ill-treatment for every one who was killed in action.[27] It was not even a profitable inhumanity. Most of the victims of the Carthagenan expedition were new recruits, since, Smollett suggests, the veteran regiments "refused to embark in such a dangerous and precarious undertaking".[28] The commander of the expedition, Admiral Vernon, made a considerable fortune out of the war and, after having received the freedom of the city from the London merchants, retired to a directorship of the New Herring Fisheries.

The whole affair was an epitome of what was wrong with eighteenth-century England. An incompetent and oligarchic administration dispensing offices as bribes to creatures who used the offices as a means of obtaining more bribes; ability kept down by these means, to the country's great harm; the productive youth of the land squandered in the blundering pursuit of commercial interest; the cost in terms of human suffering entirely disregarded —it all affronted not only the pronounced sense of decency but also the powers of reasoning of the twenty-year-old surgeon's mate. He was later to write two separate long accounts of this formative voyage. Meanwhile, further evidence of the undesirability of the existing social order presented itself in the peeved viciousness with which the families of the '45 rebels were persecuted after the Battle of Culloden. In an overflow of grief and indignation Smollett wrote *The Tears of Scotland*:

> Yet, when the rage of battle ceased,
> The victor's soul was not appeased;
> The naked and forlorn must feel
> Devouring flames and murdering steel.

He rapped out six stanzas at one sitting, then, warned that his poem would give offence, swiftly added a seventh more pugnacious than the others:

> While the warm blood bedews my veins,
> And unimpair'd remembrance reigns,
> Resentment of my country's fate
> Within my filial breast shall beat
> And, spite of her insulting foe,
> My sympathizing verse shall flow :
> "Mourn, hapless Caledonia, mourn
> The banish'd peace, the laurels torn."

Apart from his unlucky tragedy, *The Tears of Scotland* was his earliest work, so that from the start his utterance was one of outrage and protest, the voice of the first of the great British reforming novelists.

Smollett gave his definition of the novel in *Ferdinand, Count Fathom* :

> A novel is a large diffused picture, comprehending the characters of life, disposed in different groups, and exhibited in various attitudes, for the purposes of a uniform plan and general occurrence, to which every individual figure is subservient.[29]

Now surely the *uniform plan* of *Fathom* is not the achievement of recognitions and surprises. Shakespeare shows how it is possible to be true to life within a convention of disguises and pat marriages which in itself is not so, but accepted for the sake of form. Smollett accepted a convention that a novel is a history of someone, with peripety and a wedding. He involves his intellectual complexity in the further complexity of rococo intrigue. Detached from the Renaldo-Monimia story, and written in another idiom, *Fathom* would be considered a strikingly realistic study. Moreover, the rhetoric is present only in the dialogues. In the actual narration Smollett's diction is, as always, tough and economic, nice in its respect for etymology, exact in the timing of the periods. Nobody could question the largeness or diffusion of a picture which takes in Hungary, Austria, France and England, and recruits from those countries a total of 110 figures. Hogarth himself could hardly have devised a composition complex enough to include, as *Fathom* does, a wounded Turkish aga stabbed to death by a vivandiere in Marlborough's army; an old woman acting as a decoy for two assassins; a Westphalian count, a Bolognese marquis, a French abbé and a Dutch colonel, all participant in a bawdy-house brawl; a punctilious and disguised Spaniard who has been obliged to kill his wife and daughter in order to conform to the sentiments of honour; a corpulent

Quaker and a Wapping landlady; Lords Grizzlegrin and Tromp-
ington; the king of Corsica; a sentimental Jewish money-lender;
the rich daughter of a London soap-boiler; a "very sanguine"
widow called Muddy; and a merchant's daughter running at
high speed away in a hearse with her father's foul-mouthed
clerk, who is dressed up as a clergyman. There are plenty of
different groups and attitudes here. The subservience of the
groups and the structual dominance of the hero are maintained
by the fact that the group is seldom larger than a trio, of which
the hero is usually one member. Each group contributes to the
rise and fall of this gifted but unscrupulous adventurer, who,
starting from nothing, twice makes his fortune and is twice
cheated out of it. This is Smollett's large diffused picture, but,
as we all know nowadays, a picture should be more than a mere
representation. The story of *Fathom* could not have been invented without a knowledge of, an opinion about, the nature of
society. What Smollett in fact planned was a coherent exposition
of that knowledge and that opinion. To some extent he proceeds
by direct statement, but in the main by the accumulation of
significant examples.

Perhaps it was as a tart comment on his machinery that he
makes one of his characters observe, of a particularly far-fetched
encounter, "that such a meeting could not be effected without
the immediate and miraculous interposition of Heaven". The
least of Smollett's functions was to make up a plausible story.
By letting the "vicissitudes of life appear in their peculiar circumstances", he was working towards a definition of the nature
of Man. It was because of this serious but artistically concealed
purpose that from the start Smollett was tacitly acknowledged to
be inimitable. Richardson, Fielding and Sterne were all followed
by literary imitators (Sterne by at least twenty-three of them)
but Smollett was recognised as possessing some distinctive im-
ponderable.[30] Perhaps it was this quality that Hazlitt had in mind
when he pointed out how "modern" Smollett seemed, compared
with the other eighteenth-century novelists. Literary art of the
highest order, such as, let us say, the conversational pleasantry
at the beginnings of Plato's dialogues, often gives an impression
of "modernity" because of its universal consonance.

Since Smollett is a novelist, not a philosopher, he does not present his conclusions systematically. Holding the same opinion as
Charles Lamb, Smollett regards moralising in the course of an

imaginative narrative as "an impertinent anticipation of the peruser's own thoughts" :

> I might here, in imitation of some celebrated writers, furnish out a page or two, with the reflections he made upon the instability of human affairs, the treachery of the world, and the temerity of youth; and endeavour to decoy the reader into a smile, by some quaint observation of my own, touching the sagacious moraliser : but, besides that I look upon the practice as an impertinent anticipation of the peruser's thoughts, I have too much matter of importance upon my hands, to give the reader the least reason to believe that I am driven to such paltry shifts, in order to eke out the volume.[31]

He has other ways of labouring in the cause of truth :

> Of all kinds of satire, there is none so entertaining and universally improving, as that which is introduced, as it were, occasionally, in the course of an interesting story, which brings every incident home to life.[32]

In the manner of Horace Wiseman's treatises on surgery, with which Smollett was well acquainted, he presents definite items for the reader's consideration and own further judgement— items such as the irritability of Matthew Bramble or the seductions of Ferdinand, Count Fathom—and proceeds by instances. In order to get at the essentials of human character, Smollett often selects examples from low life, "where the humours and passions are undisguised by affectation, ceremony or education".[33]

To what conclusions did Smollett come and to what extent did he share the disquiet of his age? To answer these questions we must first know something of his intellectual setting (politically, socially, philosophically, medically, in all the branches of his thought), and then examine his novels as closely as we can. Such an examination will show that Smollett's comment on Count Fathom was equally true of himself : "He had studied mankind with incredible diligence."

CHAPTER II

THE ANIMAL ECONOMY

I HOPE IT WILL not be found wearisome if, in an attempt to
fix Smollett's intellectual position, we suppose a title page engraved in the Baroque manner so dear to the eighteenth century.
The reader will be so indulgent as to contemplate an allegory
somewhat in the style of a Parnassus by Verrio or Thornhill—
a thing of attributes and tutelary circles. The central figure,
Smollett, who is represented as spoiled in his fortune and
thwarted in his invalid body, holds a looking glass. In it he
discerns, not his own person, but the stone man of Condillac on
the dissecting table of William Hunter. Smollett is sponsored by
a group of modest-looking men in perukes who bear, however, in
their hands the instruments of heresy and revolution. Informing
all, an improbable Jupiter on a cloud above, sits Sir Isaac
Newton. The allegory, in accordance with eighteenth-century
taste, spills into every corner with significant bric-à-brac. This is
not lacking in a life so varied as Smollett's.

Now for the meaning of the allegory. Dr. Giovanni Gentili,
who attended Smollett during his last illness, described him as
"a man of pronounced talents exposed to all the outrages of
human life and almost a misanthrope... asthmatic, suffering
from colic, chronic diarrhoea and convulsive fever".[1] The justified concern for his own health which is a characteristic of
Smollett's letters to his friends, made him examine himself. What
he saw, or what he thought he saw, when he looked inward, was
partly determined by the medicine and the philosophy of his
time.

With eighteenth-century medicine he had every reason to be
conversant. During a period of Scottish superiority in medicine[2]
his acquaintance was amongst the most prominent of the Scottish
doctors. He himself practised, first as surgeon's mate and later
as physician, for at least eleven years, and Dr. John Moore was
of the opinion that Smollett's "learning, diligence and natural
acuteness would have rendered him eminent in the science of
medicine"[3] if he had not given it up.

It was quite usual for students in the newly instituted Faculty of Medicine at Glasgow University to serve an apprenticeship, as Smollett did, in an apothecary's shop.[4] Smollett's master, John Gordon, was more than an apothecary. He taught at the University, and his shop should be thought of as a kind of rudimentary out-patients' department. Smollett certainly did not spend all his time in running errands and preparing poultices. "During his apprenticeship Smollett attended the anatomical and medical lectures at the University."[5]

The setting up of this Faculty at Glasgow was a considerable event in British medical history. The advances in experimental science which had been made by Newton's generation lured on, because of their half-evident possibilities, the careful burghers of Glasgow. On the raw Glaswegian slopes the course of medicine changed.[6] Galen and Avicenna had already been put to one side. The doctrines of the four humours and the influence on the body of the stars had become antiquarian studies, the terms of the preposterous old learning being retained only in their secondary meanings. In medicine the age of authority was over.[7] In the new Faculty everything proceeded by observation and experiment. It was during the Faculty's first intense pullulation, which threw off such men as Cullen and the Hunters, that Smollett attended the lectures.

From the first the Faculty had a materialist outlook. Its tendency was always to explain life in terms of the fascinating new sciences of Chemistry and Physics. Cullen, for example, considered that life was no more than a manifestation of nervous energy and that nerve was a continuation of muscle.[8] Whilst the Faculty did not go to the same extreme as Descartes, who located the soul in the pineal gland, there was a marked endeavour to explain life in mechanical terms.[9] Crab, the illiberal apothecary in *Roderick Random*, is contemptuous of the results of the new system—young fools who think that they can "account for muscular motion and explain the mystery of the brain and nerves".[10] For many years the books which Smollett read, and the men with whom he associated, were directly concerned with those problems. When he took his M.D. (no longer an easy acquisition) it was in such studies that he was examined.

In the early eighteenth century the population of Edinburgh was 31,000 and of the whole of Scotland less than a million, whilst that of London was 630,000, with one accredited physician to every 7,500 citizens. The number of Scotsmen who had

laboriously attained medical qualifications was out of proportion
to the population of their country. Because of this excess of
talent, it was natural enough that the Scottish doctors should
move to the metropolis in search of a living. The London contingent was headed by two of the most able men of science of the
age : William and John Hunter. With both of these Smollett was
closely acquainted. William Hunter, who introduced scientific
surgery into England, lodged with Smollett in Downing Street,
lent Smollett money, kept up a long correspondence with him
when he was abroad, and showed the most affectionate concern
for his failing health. He was the doctor who ordered Smollett
south to the Mediterranean. John Hunter (who is referred to as
"Jock" in Smollett's correspondence) also wrote Smollett letters
of guidance about his health. For his part Smollett used the
Critical Review, of which he was editor, to ward off attacks on
William Hunter. During his stay abroad he collected rare books
for John Hunter, and proposed to bequeath his body to Hunter's
anatomical collection.

The Hunters were, like Smollett, Glaswegians. William started
his medical career, first as the pupil, and later as the partner, of
the eminent William Cullen, afterwards Professor of Medicine at
Edinburgh, with whom he maintained a lifelong friendship. He
arrived in England to find that surgeons were so little esteemed
that they were bundled in with the barbers as a joint company.
In 1743 he launched a series of lectures on anatomy and two
years later, after the surgeons had dissassociated themselves from
the now-bewildered barbers, he embarked on his annual London
campaign of lectures in which he scoured the whole field of
medicine, from an initial have-at-you with Chemistry to a final
tidying-up of the rare diseases. He was a stylish speaker who, at
one time, had thoughts of turning author. In 1770, on the site
of the Windmill Theatre, he built an anatomy theatre of a more
sombre kind than the present-day one. Both his life and his death
were singularly even and harmonious, his last words being, "If I
had enough strength to hold a pen, I would write how pleasant
and easy a thing it is to die".[11]

Noting "the necessity or advantage" of all parts of the body,
he regarded his anatomical findings as evidence for religious belief. "Who can know and consider the thousand evident proofs,"
he asked, "of the astonishing art of the Creator in forming and
restraining an animal body such as ours without feeling the most

pleasing enthusiasm?" He considered the mind to be an "immaterial part" which is "placed in a corporeal fabric, to hold a correspondence with other material beings by the intervention of the body".[12] These were certainly not the views of his brother John, or of the rest of the Hunterian circle. Like his brother's friend, Cullen, John Hunter insisted that Man is distinct from vegetable life and the inanimate only because of a difference of structure. Cullen's view was that Life is merely an emanation of nervous energy (from which he concluded that disease is largely a matter of nervous disorganisation). Cullen did not consider the mind to be immaterial: "We cannot doubt that the operations of the intellect always depend on some motions taking place in the brain."[13] There is every evidence that John Hunter was in full agreement with Cullen. In that respect his views derived from the same school of thought as those of Smollett.

Originally a cabinet-maker, John Hunter's only formal qualification was his apprenticeship in his brother's surgery. At the age of seventeen he could neither read nor write, and indeed never seems to have become fully literate, or at least coherent. So great was his difficulty in expressing himself clearly, and such was the revulsion he felt from speaking in public, that he used to take laudanum before giving his lectures. Because of his difficulties with expression he relied excessively on his secretary. This was unfortunate, since the secretary destroyed many of the notes which Hunter left behind at his death. It has been suggested that the notes had an irreligious tendency, like the strictures on the Book of Genesis which he had published during his lifetime. Whether this was so or not, destroyed they certainly were.

In 1755 he became partner in William Hunter's anatomy school, obtaining by underhand means bodies for his more elegant brother's dissecting room. With the coarse energy and unremitting diligence which were his chief characteristics, John Hunter made his own way, refusing his brother's offer to send him to the University. In 1760 he quarrelled with William (an event which made Smollett attempt the unfamiliar role of peacemaker) and became an army surgeon. Convinced that he could cure syphilis, he injected himself, in a mood of obstinate assertion, with the disease. He did indeed cure himself of the primary effects of syphilis, but was unaware of the secondary ones, which later caused his death. With the proceeds of a growing reputation he bought a vast plain house in Earls Court, which became the repository of such fancies as a pool, decorated with skulls, in which he bred oysters. Here he collected a large number of animals, alive and dead, one of his pastimes being to wrestle with a pet bull. Grotesquely parodying the fashionable doctor's chariot and pair, he used to drive into town in a coach drawn by two buffaloes. Roughly, almost grudgingly, with a surliness which bordered on outright misanthropy, he conferred considerable benefits upon suffering humanity, initiating methods of treatment which are used to this day. His more urbane colleagues thought him mad. This was an ungenerous estimate, although in the freaks and enormities of his conduct one finds little trace of any wish to conform to the ways of other men.

Cullen had lectured concurrently on Medicine and Chemistry, and it is with Chemistry that John Hunter began his researches— with Chemistry and the assembly of a vast collection of facts. Using the inductive methods of Bacon and the Royal Society, he found that some of these facts operate upon each other. These he patiently grouped, trying to classify animals (as Linnaeus had classified plants) by organs and structure, and working slowly towards an accurate understanding of the relationship between form and function. He has been described at work, poised with his forceps, still as a statue except for his right hand, standing for hour after hour dissecting those nerves which Cullen had said were the implements of Life, obstinately and delicately seeking out the truth to which he had dedicated himself. It is in this figure, rigid in its fascinated perplexity, that we recognise the true John Hunter, liberated from the need to express himself, doggedly finding things out; the John Hunter who could not write a letter of personal sympathy to his jilted pupil, Jenner, without including various speculations about the hedgehog. In Science he reached the same conclusions as Hume did in Philosophy, observing that "all the causes of things cannot be seen, because they appear to depend on circumstances which are unknown, or appear to be accidental".[14]

Two other members of the little clan of expatriate doctors are of special importance to us, since they were Smollett's closest friends. These were John Armstrong and John Moore.

John Armstrong, described in *Humphry Clinker* as "an excellent writer" was probably introduced to Smollett by William Hunter. Their acquaintance dates from 1748. Anderson, an early biographer of Smollett, describes Armstrong as living "on the most intimate terms of private friendship" with Smollett.

Almost certainly he helped Smollett conduct the *Critical Review*.
Twelve years Smollett's senior, he lived to write the inscription
for Smollett's monument at Leghorn. Yet his long life was also
a bitter one. After a roundabout course of study, including an
apprenticeship similar to the one which Smollett underwent, he
qualified as a Scotch M.D. in 1732. He had been obliged to
fight against the most humiliating poverty in order to win this
qualification. For example, his matriculation at Edinburgh
was deferred, not because he did not know enough but because
he had to go away to earn enough money to pay the small
fee.

Unable to find employment in Scotland, he went to London,
where, in spite of the shortage of doctors, the College of Physicians refused to recognise his Scotch degree. For this reason he
was not allowed to practise (except on needy fellow Scots) and his
hard-won honours were rendered useless. He wrote for a living,
offering up an occasional and unavailing dedication to some
dignitary of the College of Physicians. In 1736 he published the
Economy of Love, a strange work in which sniggers and high
seriousness, exhortation and bawdry are jumbled together; a
medico-rakish combination of a manual for those about to marry
with an art of love of the Ovidian type. In the following year
he looked at the blacker side of his subject by publishing a
Synopsis of the Venereal Diseases. His dedications coming to
nothing, he accepted a post as an army doctor and retired as
soon as possible on half-pay. A splenetic, disappointed man, he
described himself as saying every evening, "Thank heavens! The
day is done!" In a letter on the death of his friend, the poet
Thomson, he wrote: "I think him greatly to be envied, to have
got fairly rid of this rascally world."[15]

The Economy of Love begins with an examination of puberty,
the stage at which:

> stung with keen desire
> The maddening boy his bashful fetters bursts;
> And urged with secret flames, the riper maid,
> Conscious and shy, betrays her smarting breast[16]

Referring to the different phases of sexual development, Armstrong recommends that:

> It boots thee much
> To study the complexion, much the clime
> And habitudes of life[17]

In his view it is external compulsion which determines conduct.
He finds no reason to reproach the prostitute who :

> with Fortune's smiles
> And fair example, might have graced thy bed,
> A virtuous mate, in every charm complete.[18]

He regards what he calls love as a nervous effect, especially of
the tactile nerves which "thrill to" the brain. He advises young
men to :

> shun the soft embrace,
> Emasculant, till twice ten years and more
> Have steeled the nerves.[19]

Old men too must take account of their nervous condition
before attempting the sacrifice to Venus :

> Cease, reverend fathers, from those youthful sports
> Retire, before unfinished feats betray
> Your slackened nerves.[20]

It is not merely Armstrong's remark on the death of Thomson
which has the ring of Smollett about it. Although there is a
certain degree of simple lechery in the *Economy of Love*, much
of it is a serious attempt to explain behaviour (in this case
sexual behaviour) in the light of current medical theory. When
we examine Smollett's work later on we shall see that nervous
impulse, and even romance as a form of nervous impulse, are
important in his explanation of conduct. Again, Smollett shares
Armstrong's Montesquieu-like concern for "the complexion,
clime and habitudes of life". Such a concern is most conspicuous
in Smollett's study of foreign society in the *Travels*. The history
of Mrs. Williams in *Roderick Random* is a fable to which Armstrong's lines about the prostitute could very adequately serve
as a moral. A third although incidental interest which Smollett
and Armstrong have in common is in the social implications of
homosexuality. Dealing with the recent prevalence of unnatural
vice in England, Armstrong writes that in such a chaste clime it

> Cannot but by forced cultivation thrive.[21]

In *Advice: a Satire*, his first published work, Smollett suggests
that this forced cultivation is extensive :

> Eternal infamy his name surround,
> Who planted first that vice on British ground !
> A vice that, spite of sense and nature reigns,
> And poisons genial love, and manhood stains !

Let Chardin with a chaplet round his head,
The taste of Maro and Anacreon plead,
"Sir, Flaccus knew to live as well as write,
And kept, like me, two boys array'd in white."
Worthy to feel that appetence of fame
Which rivals Horace only in his shame!
Let Isis wail in murmurs, as she runs,
Her tempting fathers, and her yielding sons.[22]

In *Roderick Random* the first two homosexual characters in
English fiction, Earl Strutwell and Captain Whiffle, are portrayed. Thus both Armstrong and Smollett show a willingness to
consider all aspects of human behaviour, although in this instance they do so with fierce subjectivity.

Moore, who like Smollett had served an apprenticeship under
Gordon, was the neurologist of the Scottish contingent. The
account of the nervous system in Moore's *Medical Sketches* is
a Glaswegian one. Wholly mechanist, it corresponds with the
psychology of David Hartley. Moore defines the nerves as "the
organs of sense and motion" and "the organs of the will".[23] He
is certain that "we can examine the structure of the brain and
the nerves ... and have the strongest proofs that they are the
immediate organs of perception, sensation and motion".[24] He
considers the physical basis of thought:

"A long exertion of thought is apt to create a headache, just
as an excessive exertion of arms and legs is to produce uneasiness in those members. . . . Whatever confines or injures the brain,
disturbs thought. A blow on the head has rendered a man of
acuteness stupid during the remainder of his life. The brains of
madmen are generally found of an unusual hardness or
weight. . . . Every sentiment of the mind has particular parts of
the body in correspondence with it and affected by it."[25]

John Armstrong and John Moore between them gave the
doctrine of the nerves, as laid down by Cullen, its final form.
It is in that final form that the doctrine appears in Smollett's
novels, as part of his presentation, in applied terms, of the
Glaswegian argument.

CHAPTER III

MANY INGENIOUS TREATISES

SMOLLETT, TIDYING UP the reign of George II in his *History of England*, states that "many ingenious treatises on Metaphysics and Morality appeared during the course of this reign, and a philosophic spirit of enquiry diffused itself".[1] The enquiry was very similar to that being made, with different equipment but from the same principles, by the Glaswegian group of doctors. Smollett was in a sense the middleman between the doctors and the philosophers. The hand which shook John Hunter's also shook David Hume's. Smollett refers in a letter of 1768 to the "friendly intercourse" which he has "maintained with one of the best men and undoubtedly the best writer of the age".[2] In his *History* he pays his more public respects to "the ingenious, penetrating and comprehensive Hume".[3] We shall see what the ingenious, penetrating and comprehensive Hume had to say about the nature of Man, and therefore about the image which Smollett saw in the looking glass of his malady.

In Smollett's novels, as in Smollett's life, Hume and Hunter come together.

One is struck again and again by the regularity with which Smollett was on the spot where changes were being made in the intellectual life of the eighteenth century. Sometimes it was intentionally, more often by chance, but the wry, deprived face, resembling that of a ravaged macaw, appeared at every turn. Modern medicine began in his familiar circle. Modern liberalism begins with Voltaire, and it was under Smollett's editorship that Voltaire first appeared in English. Hume, the master of Hartley and the most influential British philosopher of the time, was Smollett's close acquaintance. Smollett was in Paris with John Moore in 1750, at the close of a decade which had brought forth Condillac's *Essai sur l'Origine des Connaissances Humaines* and Montesquieu's *Esprit des Lois*, at a time, that is to say, when the physical origins of human understanding, and the economic foundations of human institutions were, as Goldsmith testifies, the stock topics of educated conversation :

A man of fashion at Paris, however contemptible we may think him here, must be acquainted with the reigning modes of philosophy as well as of dress, to be able to entertain his mistress agreeably. The sprightly pedants are not to be caught by dumb show, by the squeeze of the hand, or the ogling of a broad eye; but must be pursued at once through all the labyrinths of the Newtonian system, or the metaphysics of Locke. I have seen as bright a circle of beauty at the chemical lectures of Rouelle as gracing the court of Versailles. And indeed wisdom never appears so charming, as when graced and protected by beauty.[4]

At the end of Smollett's career he was to be found, with his grief on one side and his reluctant certainties on the other, explaining, combining, hard at work on the great body of learning which had emerged during his life-time. Sixty volumes of a Universal History under his immediate direction![5] It is no wonder that he too felt that he was working in the direction of Science.

The discoveries of the Natural Philosophers of the seventeenth century and the work of the Royal Society had made the Universe seem a larger place in which Man looked proportionately small. Pope, in his *Essay on Man*, returns again and again to the theme of humanity's insignificance. Dealing with those who complain of Man's disabilities, he asserts that these disabilities have their place in the general scheme of things, and asks:

> All this dread order break—for whom? for thee?
> Vile worm! Oh madness, pride, impiety![6]

The Universe is not man-centred:

> Has God, thou fool! worked solely for thy good,
> Thy joy, thy pastime, thy attire, thy food?[7]

Psychological materialism was bound to follow Newton's notion of a clockwork Universe wound up by God. Celestial and terrestial mechanics implied the further mechanics of the human body and mind. Hume was in fact to compare the principle of association in psychology to the principle of gravity in Physics. Newton himself first speculated on nervous action in the *Principia*, although he did not go so far as Cullen in suggesting that life is the mere product of nervous energy. The search for effective causes in the human machine was taken up by Locke, who at one time projected a universal history of the mind, to be written

on the model of Newton's principles of Natural Philosophy. Like
so many other grand projects, this one came to nothing.

Locke was made a member of the Royal Society in 1668, eight
years after its foundation. He had studied medicine thoroughly
for a considerable time, and his post with the Shaftesbury family
was originally that of physician. In his *Essay on the Human
Understanding* he takes on the Cambridge Platonists, denying
the existence of innate ideas. Like a true physician, he concludes
that, since our direct contact with the world is limited to that
of our sensations, all understanding derives from physical experience. Instead of the theory of innate ideas he suggests a
psychology of knowledge.

The Cambridge Platonists were a hapless and well-meaning
little group who were subjected not only to Locke's diligent
undermining, but also to the battering-ram of Smollett's scorn.
They had adopted the doctrines of Plato's *Symposium* and
Phaedrus as expounded by the third-century Egyptian philosopher Plotinus. Plotinus thought that Plato had a systematic
philosophy and that the answers to all philosophical questions
were to be found in the Dialogues. Speaking and spelling Greek
badly, capable of explaining a point for three days continuously
(sweating gently as he did so), Plotinus was relentlessly serious and
lacked any appreciation of Plato's civilised nonchalance. Thus
he came to build a system from detached passages of Plato considered out of their context. In the *Symposium* Plato records
Socrates as speaking of Eros, a daemon, neither mortal nor immortal, but something intermediate communicating between
divine and human things "so as to bind together, by his own
power, the universe of things".[8] Socrates goes on to say, "The
bodies and the souls of all human beings are alike pregnant with
their future progeny, and when we arrive at a certain age, our
nature impels us to bring forth and propagate".[9]

It is in the *Phaedrus* that Socrates suggests that there is a
means of communication between the binding force and the
individual mind. That means is inspiration. Listening to a speech
recounted by Phaedrus, he is thrown into an ecstasy, and says
that he is moved to deliver a speech himself. "Now that I could
have invented none of it I am confident, as I am no stranger
to my own stupidity."[10] He compares himself to a pitcher which
has been filled by some foreign force. "By the way, dear
Phaedrus," he asks, "do I appear to have been speaking to you
under some divine influence?" Phaedrus replies that certainly an

unusual fluency has descended upon Socrates. In the course of his argument Socrates postulates some kind of oversoul, which "roams the upper air and regulates the entire Universe". Like Spinoza, he deduces that "the thing which moves another and is by another moved, as it may cease to be moved ceases to live. It is only that which moves itself, inasmuch as it never quits itself, that never ceases moving, but is to everything else that is moved a source and beginning of motion". This is the Absolute. In the *Symposium* Socrates describes the soul as being engaged in the pursuit of the beautiful, which culminates in the perception of Absolute Beauty, "simple, pure, uncontaminated with the intermixture of human flesh and colours, and all idle and unreal shades attendant on mortality".[11]

Yet what were the circumstances in which Socrates spoke? How much of the dialogue of the *Symposium* is pleasantry? A group of Athenians meet to celebrate the success of Agathon's latest play. They have all been very drunk the night before and for this reason decide to drink "only for pleasure, not in order to become tipsy". Aristophanes tells a ridiculous tale which he claims will explain Love. We were all originally egg-shaped but cut in two and twisted about by a malevolent god. For this reason we wander about looking for our other halves. Later Socrates expounds the same subject, and our problem is: at what point does he start to be serious? Alcibiades comes in drunk, and there is a great deal of good-humoured shuffling between Socrates and Alcibiades about who shall recline next to Agathon. Alcibiades and Socrates drain the wine-cooler in turn. The narrator falls asleep and awakes at cockcrow to find Socrates still discoursing, this time on the fundamental similarity of tragedy and comedy.

Again, in the *Phaedrus,* the speech recounted by Phaedrus ("something which will appeal to you, Socrates") is an amatory speech to be made to a beautiful boy. The speech is of a paradoxical nature. Socrates interjects that the speech would be truly delightful and public-spirited if it gave preference to the claims of age and poverty "and all the other properties which belong to myself in common with the bulk of mankind".[12] And the transports into which Socrates is thrown are caused, according to himself, by the sight of Phaedrus' rapture-glowing face. How faint irony can become over the course of twenty-three hundred years! Is it not even possible that Socrates, in the Symposium when he speaks of the intellectually beautiful propagating itself in the physically beautiful, is suggesting, with a reprehensible gallantry, a suitable relationship between himself and Agathon? One would wish to have seen the expression on Socrates' face.

Certainly Plotinus thought that it was a serious one. Upon this section of the Platonic Dialogues he built first a metaphysical system, the main contention of which is that the soul is impregnated and illuminated by God, and secondly a discipline, the aim of which was to attain union with God by contemplation and ecstasy. Plotinus' marvellous phrase for this is "the flight of the Alone to the Alone". He advocated withdrawal from the world so far as one's social obligations admit. One must wait patiently in unbroken contemplation for the illumination of God to come, not chase after it. Four times, his disciple Porphyry records, Plotinus achieved a union "in an unspeakable actuality" with the God who "is neither shape nor any intelligible form, but is throned above intellect and all the intelligible".[13]

With the Renaissance, at the merging of the old Romance with the new classicism, when Apollo re-awoke in a troubador's rose-arbour and Venus sauntered again but this time on a daisy-spotted greensward, when ermine-stoled ruffians wore engraved jewels which informed that part of the populace which could read Greek that, alas, they longed for Julia, the philosophy of the Ancients was wedded, although uneasily, to the precepts of the Christian religion. There is a tale of the period about a bridegroom who, at his wedding feast, for some reason placed his ring on the finger of a statue of Venus. The finger closed on the ring so that it could not be removed and ever after the bridegroom desired only the goddess. This is what happened to the Christian Neo-Platonists. The priest Marsilio Ficino, who first translated Plotinus, always kept a lamp burning in front of a bust of Plato. The purification, enlightenment and ecstasy of the Neo-Platonic discipline became the three stages of the Mystic Way.[14] Professor A. H. Armstrong, the translator of Plotinus, describes Neo-Platonism as a "learned, serious and bookish philosophy". Was Platonism? At any rate, by the time of Whichcote (1609–1683) and the other Cambridge Platonists, Socrates' exposition of the precognisant soul in the *Phaedrus* had developed into the doctrine in innate ideas. Cathedral churches reverberated with statements, a little distorted because of the Gothic acoustics, first expressed so many years ago at that famous banquet given in honour of Agathon, or alongside the brook Ilissus whilst the grasshoppers filled the Greek air with their less pertinent chatter. Let us consider John Smith, the Cambridge Platonist, and his statement of the doctrine of innate ideas. Do we not discern, beneath the churchly cassock and bands, the considerable bulk of an Attic figure, that figure which Alcibiades once compared to a terracotta satyr? God, Smith writes:

> is not only the eternal Reason, that almighty Mind and Wisdom which our understandings converse with; but he is also that unstained beauty and supreme good to which our wills are perpetually aspiring. And wheresoever we find true beauty, love and goodness, we may say here or there is God. And as we cannot understand anything of an intelligible nature but by some primitive idea we have of God whereby we are able to guess at the elevation of its being and the pitch of its perfection, so neither do our wills embrace anything without some latent sense of him, whereby they can taste and discern how near anything comes to that self-sufficient good they seek after. And indeed, without such an internal sensating faculty as this is, we should never know when our souls are in conjunction with the Deity, or be able to relish the ineffable sweetness of true happiness.[15]

Less diffusely, Whichcote had said, "Reason is the divine governor of Man's life, the very voice of God".

To give a summary of the philosophy of John Locke is outside the scope of the present work, and most likely outside the capacity of its author. Our only concern here is with these aspects of it related to the Determinist psychology which Smollett accepted. Locke asserts, in opposition to the Cambridge Platonists, that men "may arrive at certainty without any original notions or principles".[16] He describes how: "Our observation, employed either about external sensible objects, or about the internal operation of our minds perceived and reflected upon by ourselves, is what supplies our understanding with all the materials of thinking."[17] But here Locke takes the agency of thought for the power, and we may quote against him the remark made by Leibniz: "There is nothing in the intellect which did not proceed from the senses, *except the intellect itself.*" Equipped with an unequalled knowledge of the structure of the brain, the modern neurologist Sir Charles Sherrington has stated that "the energy-pattern which is the brain" is no more than the (admittedly indispensable) medium of the mind[18] and that "oversimplified conceptions, such as to ascribe to separate pieces of the roof-brain . . . separate items of highly integrated behaviour" are reminiscent of old-fashioned phrenology.[19] Moreover, an interpretation of reality through sensation, limited to the five available modes of sensation and the state of those modes, cannot be adequate. Whose interpretation of reality is to be accepted, the one made by the man who has taken some such drug as mescalin or the one made by the man who has not, the one made by the cheerful man or the one made by the splenetic? They are not likely to be the same. "It is possible to see purple by taking a certain quantity of Santonin and thus it becomes a simple matter for anyone to change the colour of his walls without touching the walls themselves."[20] Man is in fact like a sailor who can fathom the ocean as far as his line can go.

In comparing the child's mind to a little cabinet in which the outside world stores its impressions, Locke attributes an action to two entities which are by his own definition passive. Nor does he allow for the process of selection which arises from curiosity and interest:

> Pour l'enfant, amoureux de cartes et d'estampes,
> L'Univers est égal a son vaste appétit.

Locke does, however, acknowledge a second source of ideas in what he calls reflection. This is the perception of the operation of our own minds within us, which presents us with a set of ideas which could not be obtained from outside things. "This source of ideas which every man has wholly within himself" provides, for example, "the satisfaction or uneasiness arising from any thought".[21] Locke's more materialistic followers forgot that he allowed for Reflection as well as Sensation. Indeed Locke's divergence from Plato may derive from a mistaken interpretation of the nature of innate ideas. Locke thinks that they imply a repository of useful information. It is fairly certain that this is not what Plato or the Platonists had in mind. What they meant is, surely, that "sense of something far more deeply interfused" which is so evident in the work of such writers as Vaughan, Traherne and Wordsworth.

Stating that nine men out of ten are what they are because of their education, Locke held that even character and inclination are the effects of circumstance. Locke's own pupil, Shaftesbury, must have been the tenth man, since he was to become his old tutor's most impressive opponent. Displeased by the spreading Materialism, Shaftesbury brought out, in 1711, his *Characteristics,* ramshackle but eloquent quartos of rhapsodies and convictions. The representation of Shaftesbury which has come down to us shows him reclining, with a gentlemanly negligence, on the works of Plato and Xenophon. This fixes his position nicely. His philosophy was in fact the ultimate flamboyant exposition of Neo-Platonism. Genteelly irked, he resists the contention that man's nature is determined by his sensory mechanism. Scornfully but with moderation he dismisses the view that generous conduct to one's fellow-men is a matter of expediency, or a response to the bribe of a happy after-life.[22] He acclaims, as an innate moral sense, *amor non mercenarius* (non-mercenary love). Whatever the miseries of the world (and Shaftesbury had his full share of them) everything tends towards the universal good, under the direction of God, the intelligent but impartial driving-force of Nature.

Pope's *Essay On Man*, the standard statement of eighteenth-century optimism, was written almost in collaboration with Bolingbroke, who was a friend of Shaftesbury and derived most of his ideas from that source. Lord Bathurst said that Bolingbroke gave Pope an actual draft in prose of the propositions to be elaborated in the *Essay*. Voltaire is of the same opinion, remarking that Bolingbroke engaged Pope to versify what he calls "cette mauvaise plaisanterie". Certainly the *Essay On Man* can be considered a line on which Bolingbroke played the caught but feinting salmon, Pope, ever drawing him nearer to his own dubious doctrines and the extinction of Pope's pietistical beliefs. Dazzled and dangled by the dangerous Bolingbroke, for whose company he had an "inordinate zeal", poised in the strain of trying to reconcile incompatible contentions, Pope is pathetically inconsistent. He begins by saying that God is a concept, not an anthropomorphic image, yet throughout the poem he speaks of God in anthropomorphic terms. He claims that God invariably acts for the best, but does not explain what the best is. Bolingbroke considered that God was beneficent to Man only in the sense of having made Man "a happiness-seeker who was capable of obtaining much happiness and relatively little pain if he chose the appropriate means".[23] This is the gospel of success on a cosmological plane.

In some parts of the *Essay* we can discern a dimly understood Pantheism :

> All are but parts of one stupendous whole
> Whole body Nature is and God the soul . . .
> He fills, he bounds, connects and equals all.[24]

The order of the Universe derives from the perfection of God. From God a hierarchy of beings proceeds, and since everything rests upon the perfection of the deity, whatever is, is right (a thought which struck Pope so powerfully that he expresses it twice, with typographical emphasis, in the course of the *Essay*). Furthermore, whatever is, is in the right place and should not be disturbed. Thus,

> The rich is happy in the plenty given,
> The poor contents him in the care of Heaven.[25]

God invariably acts for the best in the sense that everything tends, in a general sort of way, towards what is good, although Pope does not follow Socrates in asking : "Good for what and to whom?" Partial ill is universal good, so that the sufferings of individuals are conductive to the welfare of the creation as a whole. Virtue does not necessarily bring good fortune :

> But sometimes virtue starves, while vice is fed.
> What then? Is the reward of virtue bread?[26]

Happiness does not depend on externals, Humility does not need a coach and pair. The reward of virtue is "the soul's calm sunshine". In the meantime,

> Order is Heaven's first law; and this confest,
> Some are, and must be greater, than the rest.[27]

In this way Optimism became a statement of extreme conservatism, so becoming doubly offensive to such minds as Smollett's, which were bent on reform.

Thus, whereas Fielding's Parson Adams consoles Joseph Andrews when Joseph's beloved Fanny has been carried off by bandits, with the notion of Providence, Smollett's Cadwallader Crabtree rallies Peregrine Pickle, whose financial schemes have ended in disaster, with the precepts of Stoicism. Smollett displays his impatience with what he considered to be the futility of the Methodists' professed submission to Providence in an incident in *Humphry Clinker*. Clinker, likely to be hanged for a crime which he did not commit,

> turning up his eyes . . . ejaculated, "The Lord's will be done! If it be my fate to suffer, I hope I shall not disgrace the faith of which, though unworthy, I make profession!"[28]

Commenting on the invalids at Bath "who have acted honourable and distinguished parts in the great theatre", Smollett writes that Nature seems to have intended them for better purposes than to spend their days playing whist and reading the newspapers. Boswell, having described a wrinkled old unemployed day-labourer who was forced to sleep in the street in the January of 1763, when the Thames was iced over and two sentries were frozen to death on duty, remarks: "Why such a wretched being subsists is to me a strange thing. But I am a weak creature. I submit to God's will, I hope to know the reason of it some time."[29] Boswell's problem is implicit in Chapter 16 of Smollett's *Continuation of the History of England,* which opens, curiously, with an account of the suicide of the whole family of a bookseller imprisoned for debt in the King's Bench prison. The husband and wife left several letters. In one they asked their landlord to be kind to their cat and their dog. In another they set forth their reasons for suicide:

> They declared that they withdrew themselves from poverty and rags, evils that through a train of accidents had become inevitable . . . Almighty God, the fountain of goodness and beneficence, could not possibly take delight in the misery of his creatures. They therefore resigned up their lives to him . . . These unfortunate suicides had been always industrious and frugal, invincibly honest and remarkable for conjugal affection.

Smollett observes that although suicide, which is so common in England that it has been much spoken of abroad, may generally be considered the effect of lunacy, "in some few instances it seems to have been the result of cool deliberation". In connection with the invalids at Bath, Smollett speaks of "the lottery of life", a lottery of which he takes the same view as Gibbon:

> The far greater part of the globe is overspread with barbarism or slavery. In the civilised world, the most numerous class is condemned to ignorance and poverty; and the double fortune of my birth in a free and enlightened country, in an honourable and wealthy family, is a lucky chance of an unit against millions.[30]

Pope's exposition of Optimism was a muddled compromise. That of Leibniz was a piece of awkward intransigence. Leibniz became a scholastic influence too early in life and formulated impossible first principles from which he could not later retreat. He was unable to say, with John Locke, "And so I thought when I writ it". It is a sad prospect, that of the dignified professor at Altdorf, with his aggressive nosey pout and his alert but uncomprehending eyes, spending his life in an attempt to reinforce arguments from which he could not secede, but the fallacy of which he must at times himself have recognised. He was primarily a mathematician, and played with language without observing subtle distinctions of meaning. By one misunderstanding he forced himself into a position of extreme fatalism, shored up by current orthodoxy and an appeal to revelation. He took the axiom of scholastic logic, "In a true proposition the predicate is always included in the subject". Confusing the actuality of an object (which is definable in a proposition) with its usage (which is not) he denied the interaction of substances. (The table at which Leibniz was writing did not include in its definable qualities at the time when it became a table the fact that Leibniz would one day write at it, though Leibniz evidently thought so.) Since substances do not interact, the mind is unaffected in its growth by anything outside itself and is brought into being pregnant with its own future. This is, of course, a direct contradiction of Locke. The human understanding, in Leibniz's opinion, is an irreducible unity under the immediate direction of God. In a noble phrase he refers to it as the "living mirror of God". Since there is no causation except that of God, and since God is perfect, this world must necessarily be the best of all possible worlds. In this extreme and distorted version of Shaftesbury's philosophy, Leibniz makes God immediately answerable for everything which happens. Leibniz is the original of Dr. Pangloss in Voltaire's *Candide*, a work which illustrates the full and considerable absurdity of his views.

> A man who wishes to learn something about his own existence, and who has no time to waste, is quite embarrassed. He is impelled simultaneously to read Hobbes, Spinoza, Bayle who wrote against them, Leibniz who disputed with Bayle . . . Cudworth who thinks himself above them because he is understood by nobody. One would die of old age before having worked through the hundredth part of these metaphysical romances.

So wrote Voltaire in the article on a Library in his *Philosophical Dictionary,* and perhaps by now the reader of the present chapter is in full sympathy with Voltaire. In a letter to Frederick the Great, Voltaire made the further observation that all metaphysics contains two things : what all sensible men know already and what they will never know. Yet Voltaire, flippant though he was, inconstant in his beliefs, holding an endless debate with himself, tripping from one contention to another, played a great part in the great eighteenth-century controversy between Deism and Determinism. It is in his important notes to his translation of

Voltaire (where he peers between the colossal legs and adds his approval to what is being said) that Smollett makes his only direct statements, apart from a few slighting references elsewhere to the Neo-Platonists, of his attachments.

In his article on Atheism in the *Philosophical Dictionary* of 1764, Voltaire points out that the Universe is an admirable machine. All living bodies conform to the laws of physics, and the solar system itself operates "by virtue of the most profound mathematical laws". When we see an efficient machine we say that there must be a good engineer. Therefore, since the Universe is an admirable machine, there must have been an admirable intelligence somewhere to devise it. He further deduces the existence of God from the fact that in this Universe there are intelligent beings, "and it would be impossible to show that the operations of chance alone could produce understanding". He takes up Bayle's argument that it is better to disbelieve in God than to believe in Him and think Him capable of evil. "For a long time it has been asked why there are so many snakes and so many wicked men worse than snakes. If flies could reason, they would complain to God of the existence of spiders." Partial ill is universal good, and Evil is a subjective thing. He considers that an intelligent creative cause which "is as evident in the vilest insect as in the stars", must necessarily animate the Universe.

By the time he reached the letter P in his dictionary Voltaire had become less devout. In the article on Power he portrays a God who, limited in his power by the laws of Nature, makes the world the least bad that is possible. Finally, after the earthquake at Lisbon, came the period of disillusion and scorn for the notions of Leibniz, after which he rounded on the optimists:

> Those who have stated that all is well are charlatans. Shaftesbury, who started off this story, was a very unfortunate man. I have seen Bolingbroke corroded by bitterness and rage, and Pope, whom he engaged to put this bad joke into verse, was one of the men with the most to complain of whom I have ever known: deformed in body, of intemperate disposition, always ill, always a burden to himself, harassed to the very end by a hundred enemies.[31]

The translations from Voltaire in which Smollett had a hand are mainly of works from the period of disillusion.

Meanwhile in England the Rev. John Gay, in his influential *Dissertation Concerning the Fundamental Principle of Morality* (1731) had reaffirmed what Locke had said on the subject, and

denied that "this moral sense or these public affections are innate, or implanted in us". Instead, "they are acquired either
from our own observation or the imitation of others". Eight years
later came Hume's weighty *Treatise on Human Nature*. With
Hume, Determinist philosophy takes a more despondent turn.
Locke had accepted Reason, if nothing else, as an Absolute. He
was willing to acknowledge the truth of, for example, mathematical propositions. Hume contends that all deductive reasoning is based on the acceptance, by mediocre human faculties, of
premises which may not be correct, since all that one can do is
to note the connection between cause and effect, and assume
that there is a permanent possibility of the same cause being
followed by the same effect. The recorded sequence will not necessarily be repeated and the recorder, Man, is fallible. Man's pitiful mental processes can be reduced to elements of simple sensation. Indeed, human behaviour and all the sentiments which
prompt it, should properly be studied as branches of physical
science. Everything is open to doubt, nothing is absolute, nothing
has a value in itself. Ethics are an accident of social circumstances, and vary with varying circumstances.[32] This philosophy
culminates in Hartley's doctrine of the vibratiuncles and Condillac's astonishing fancy of a statue which is brought to life
sense by sense. In Smollett's novels it converges with Glaswegian
medicine to become an interpretation of Man's existence. Hume
states that he has taken up his position as an act of intellectual
honesty, in spite of the despair which it has created in his own
mind. It is indeed a cheerless philosophy, which places mankind
in a cosmic waiting room waiting for nothing, just noticing that
there appear to be schedules. There are serious arguments against
it, but these will be considered later. For the present it is enough
to remark that Hume, in drawing these extreme conclusions,
made use of confessedly inadequate equipment.

It was with the same protestations as Hume, the same dis-
mayed attentiveness of a physician in a hopeless case, that
Hartley recorded his *Observations on Man* in 1749, the year
after *Roderick Random* was published. Hartley had intended to
become a priest but, his faith being shaken by Gay's *Dissertation*,
he took up medicine instead. Hartley goes further than to say
that intellectual activity is a development of simple sensation.
Thought itself, in his view, is physical. It consists of minute
vibrations or vibratiuncles, as he calls them, in the brain. Although his speculations are aligned to modern findings on the

subject, Hartley, like Locke, mistakenly identifies the agency of thought with thought itself. Hartley's theory corresponds with the Glaswegian doctors' account of the nerves, as expressed by Cullen and Moore.

Condillac, in his *Essai sur les Connaissances Humaines* of 1746, had largely anticipated Hartley. In order to dispute the contention that ideas are innate, he makes a careful analysis of ideas, singling out the elements of sensation of which they are composed. This *Essai* was the preliminary statement of a theory which he expands in the *Traité des Sensations,* where he lists the different types of ideas under sense-headings. "Le principal objet de cet ouvrage est de faire voir comment toutes nos connaissances et toutes nos facultés viennent des sens, ou, pour parler exactement, des sensations."[33] What follows is the bizarre philosophical fable of a statue which is granted, one by one, the five senses. By combining the pieces of information supplied by the senses, and applying them to practical situations, the statue acquires understanding. It is thereupon thrust out into society, where it learns a working arrangement for living with others called morality, which differs from one society to another.

Between Condillac's introductory *Essai* and his final exposition in the *Traite,* Montesquieu had brought out his *Esprit des Lois* (1748), Montesquieu relates government, law and social conduct to geographical and economic environment. The famous opening sentence of the *Esprit des Lois* reads: "Les Lois, dans la signification plus entendue, sont les rapports nécessaires qui dérivent de la nature des choses." It is indeed arresting to think of the effects of physical chance on civilisation. When the Romans levelled the temple at Jerusalem the Jews, absolved from their obligation to present themselves at it regularly, dispersed and became an international race. Nestorius, expelled from the Western Church by the Council of Ephesus, fled to Persia. As a result he was able to convert the people of Persia and Syria and send Bishops of his own to India and China. (The Nestorian Church, kindled by one accident, was extinguished by another, the Tartar invasion. Because of the physical intervention of the Tartar war-lords, the mighty Asiatic Church became the eccentric group of modern times.) If Boswell had not been unsuccessful as a barrister, he would never have had time to write the *Life of Johnson,* with which he fought off melancholia in his empty chambers. If Byron had not had a club foot, the whole Romantic Movement might have taken a different turn. Such

writers as Sir James Frazer have collected evidence which has
proved again and again how right Montesquieu was. Yet to say
that human affairs, those glimpsed transitory surfaces of an
evolutionary force, are subject to chance is one thing. To deny
that mankind has latent possibilities, including that of resisting
and dominating circumstances, is another. To what comical
extremes Montesquieu's doctrines can be pursued is to be seen
in Taine's *History of English Literature*, where he says, for example, that the English, gluttonous because of the cold, brutally
drunken, kept much at home by the bad weather, of cold temperament and dilatory in making love, were predisposed, because of
their gloom, to Christianity.

Where does Smollett stand? The external evidence may be
briefly restated. He was an intimate of those eighteenth-century
doctors who were so concerned with "the mystery of the brain
and nerves". His best friend was Dr. John Moore, who was convinced that thought has a physical basis in the operations of the
neuro-cerebral system. He was an avowed admirer (and he
avowed admiration for very few people) of Hume. The direct
internal evidence is to be found in the notes to Voltaire, various
passages in *Peregrine Pickle*, a letter to John Wilkes and certain
comments in the *Travels*.

Smollett's contempt for Leibniz and for Leibniz's attitude of
conservative optimism is shown in a note to *Candide*, where he
refers to Pangloss as "an imposter and corruptor of youth". He
points the moral of *Candide* in a further note :

> The moral of this piece seems to be that nothing is so absurd as
> to believe that Providence hath ordered everything for the best;
> that nothing is more ridiculous than the exercise of reason; that
> nothing is more futile and frivolous than the cultivation of
> philosophy; that mankind is a species of savage, who devour one
> another; and that true contentment is nowhere to be found, but
> in cultivating a few acres of ground in Turkey, where the most
> brutal despotism reigns, and there is no sort of security for
> property or life.[34]

He gives his approval to Voltaire's exposition of Locke's account
of sensory perception, observing that it is "expressly the doctrine
of Aristotle. The soul has no knowledge but that which it acquires
through the senses."[35]

Into that large and bulging carpet-bag, *Peregrine Pickle*,
Smollett packs a great deal of satire upon the Neo-Platonists and

the theory of innate ideas. Much of it is concentrated in the character of the pedantic doctor, a notable admirer of Shaftesbury, whom Smollett calls "that frothy writer". The inaction, the giving-way to injustice, which a belief in Providence engenders, is illustrated by the doctor's refusal to intervene when Pickle and Pallet are imprisoned by the French :

> You shall see now that Mr. Pickle and my friend Pallet will fall a sacrifice to the tyranny of lawless power; and, in my opinion, we shall be accessary to the ruin of this poor enslaved people, if we bestir ourselves in demanding or imploring the release of our unhappy countrymen; as we may thereby prevent the commission of a flagrant crime, which would fill up the vengeance of Heaven against the perpetrators, and perhaps be the means of restoring a whole nation to the unspeakable fruition of freedom.

Gracefully turning aside an invitation, in a letter to that not very spiritual personage, John Wilkes, Smollett alludes once more to the Neo-Platonists. He cannot come, although he longs to see Wilkes' house at Aylesbury "as much as ever Akenside or Gilbert Cooper or any other wrong-headed Platonist longed to visit the groves of Academus". The joking reference would have little point if Smollett had not discussed such matters with Wilkes on some previous occasion, and discovered a common opinion.[37]

It is not likely that Smollett ever adopted a formal system of philosophy. He was apt to be impatient with such things. It was not his style to ponder over a problem. He tackled it instead with a quick astringent certainty. For this reason the internal evidence of his novels is even more important than our knowledge of his associates and his sparse polemic utterances. Choosing to argue from vivid instances, Smollett puts forward the materialist psychology of his time : Locke's evaluation of the effects of upbringing and worldly circumstance, Hume's informed scepticism, Hartley's study of the mechanics of emotion and conduct, Montesquieu's awareness of the force of climate and situation. Hume and Hartley were materialists under protest. So was Smollett. It is our purpose to examine Smollett's materialism, and to decide in what terms his protest was made.

CHAPTER IV

THE MECHANISM AND NECESSITY
OF OUR NATURES

I. TELL IT TO YOUR PHYSICIAN

S ATIRISING S MOLLETT AS the copiously grumbling Smell-fungus, Laurence Sterne records the following exchange in *A Sentimental Journey*:

"I'll tell it," cried Smellfungus, "to the world."
"You had better tell it," said I, "to your physician."

Nobody was so well aware as Smellfungus himself of the justice of Sterne's reply. In a letter of 1767, Smollett explained why his recent trip to Scotland had given him no pleasure. "Had I been as well in summer, I should have exquisitely enjoyed my expedition to Scotland, which was productive of nothing to me but misery and disgust."[1] Smollett's interest in the correspondence between body and mind was an immediate one. He was both doctor and invalid, and could well say with Matthew Bramble:

I have had an hospital these fourteen years within myself, and studied my own case with the most painful attention.[2]

Wherever he mentions his own sickness Smollett records its mental effects:

In consequence of a cold caught a few days after my arrival in France, I was seized with a violent cough, attended with a fever, and stitches in my breast which tormented me all night long without ceasing. At the same time I had a great discharge by expectoration, and such a dejection of spirits as I never felt before.[3]

Vespere febris exacerbatur. Calor, inquietudo, anxietas et asthma per noctem grassantur.[4]

Three years after he wrote the letter to Moore, Smollett began a novel with the significant words,

Doctor, the pills are good for nothing; I might as well swallow snowballs to cool my reins. I have told you over and over, how hard I am to move; and at this time of day, I ought to know something of my own constitution.[5]

Nearly all the characters of *Humphry Clinker* are afflicted to some degree with ill-health, which conditions their behaviour, and the interplay of their distressed sensibilities accounts for much of the action. They are Dr. Smollett's travelling clinic. Their afflictions are matched with, and even conducive to, their temperaments. Bramble's general sourness and the "morbid excess of sensation" which leaves him pained, equally by a foul smell or a foolish act, are brought about by his many and intricate ailments. He knows it well himself, and writes to his doctor in these terms:

> The inconveniences which I overlooked in the high-day of health, will naturally strike with exaggerated impression on the irritable nerves of an invalid, surprised by premature old age, and shattered with long-suffering.[7]
>
> Yet I cannot help thinking, I have some right to discharge the over-flowings of my spleen upon you, whose province it is to remove those disorders that occasioned it.[8]

Harsh Mrs. Tabitha suffers from an abrasive intestinal disorder which her purges aggravate. Laeticia, delicately yearning, has the vapours. The gadding Winifred Jenkins is hysterical. The Bath scenery of the gouty, the consumptive and the disabled, with quack doctors in attendance, widens the novel at this point into a panorama of the victims and the profiteers of the flesh.

Smollett's disturbing biological attitude to personality is present from the beginning of his work. In *Roderick Random*, Narcissa's aunt displays the characteristic freaks of the dropsy which in the end kills her. One of Peregrine Pickle's most savage jests as a boy is to lure his aunt, Mrs. Trunnion, into taking an over-dose of jallop, with this effect:

> She was brought home in a torture, which was a little assuaged when the dose began to operate; but such was the excess of evacuation which she sustained that her spirits were quite exhausted, and she suffered a succession of fainting fits which reduced her to the brink of the grave.[9]

Peregrine Pickle also contains an account of:

> an old officer, whose temper, naturally impatient, was, by repeated attacks of the gout, which had almost deprived him of the

use of his limbs, sublimated into a remarkable degree of virulence and perverseness.[10]

Smollett's physiological interests are carried over into his *History of England*. In the "characters" with which old-fashioned biographies always conclude, he lists medical details, noting, for example, that William III "was subject from infancy to an asthma and continual cough".[11] Smollett is of the opinion that illness can not only impair, but at times improve, the understanding :

> A seasonable fit of illness is an excellent medicine for the turbulence of passion. Such a reformation had the fever produced in the economy of his thoughts, that he moralised like an apostle and projected several prudential schemes for his future conduct.[12]

Disease and a low diet make Fathom's grasping hands slacken. Disease and the fear of death bring about the repentance of the usurping Count Trebasi. It is one of the refinements of Smollett's satire on what he considers to be the mean physical condition of mankind, that he relates virtue to ill-health. The reader is reminded of the comment which Hartley makes on the mental effects of indigestion :

> Thus it may appear that there ought to be a great reciprocal influence between the mind and the alimentary duct.[13]

Deformity is a bodily ill which has more obvious psychological consequences. What is it which causes the difference between the wild Peregrine Pickle and his vicious younger brother, except that Peregrine's body is straight, whilst his brother's is an object of detestation? Both are aggressive and uncomprising, quick to take offence and impetuous in action. Miss Snapper (in *Roderick Random*) is obliged to develop her intellectual possibilities, and her menacing wit, so that she can defend herself against the contempt of others for her deformed person, and sustain her self-esteem against the slights she receives.

In his frequent prison scenes Smollett illustrates how necessary a state of physical well-being is to the preservation of civilised values. Random, destitute in the Marshalsea, falls into brutish and nasty ways. Pickle's imprisonment operates on his mind in the form of extreme dejection, which emaciates his body and diminishes his self-respect. All that is left of his previous bearing is "a certain ferocity" in his eyes :

He knocked softly at the door, and when it was opened, started back with horror and astonishment : the figure that presented itself to his view was the remains of his once happy friend; but so miserably altered and disguised, that his features were scarce cognisable. The florid, the sprightly, the gay, the elevated youth, was now metamorphosed into a wan, dejected, meagre, squalid spectre; the hollow-eyed representative of distemper, indigence, and despair; yet his eyes retained a certain ferocity, which threw a dismal gleam athwart the cloudiness of his aspect, and he, in silence, viewed his old companion with a look betokening confusion and disdain.[14]

The deprivations and restricted scope of the prison in *Ferdinand, Count Fathom* make nonsense of the most exalted aspirations. Fathom encounters a king in a woollen night-cap, a major in a blanket, and a chevalier who is reduced to borrowing a pound of sausages :

True it is, this presence-chamber was not so superb, nor the appearance of the kings so magnificent, as to render such an honour intoxicating to any person of our hero's coolness and discretion. In lieu of tapestry, the apartment was hung with half-penny ballards, a truckle-bed without curtains supplied the place of a canopy, and instead of a crown his majesty wore a woollen night-cap.[15]

The complex relation of body to mind is cunningly explored in the account of Peregrine Pickle's career as a writer :

The approbation of the public, which he had earned or might acquire, like a cordial often repeated, began to lose its effect upon his imagination; his health suffered by the sedentary life and austere application; his eyesight failed, his appetite forsook him, his spirits decayed; so that he became melancholy, listless, and altogether incapable of prosecuting the only means he had left for his subsistence.[16]

This sudden change from his former way of life agreed so ill with his disposition that, for the first time, he was troubled with flatulencies and indigestion, which produced anxiety and dejection of spirits, and the nature of his situation began in some measure to discompose his brain.[17]

Voltaire remarked in a letter of 1727 that even the weather can condition a man's state of mind, "tant nous sommes machines, et tant nos âmes dépendent de l'action des corps".[18] Smollett

makes the same point, both in his own person and in that of
Matthew Bramble:

> The truth is, I was that day more than usually peevish, from
> the bad weather, as well as from the dread of a fit of the asthma,
> with which I was threatened.[19]

> Perhaps you are partly in the right; for I have perceived that
> my opinion of mankind, like mercury in the thermometer, rises
> and falls according to the variations of the weather.[20]

The understanding itself is at the mercy of physical happenings.
Smollett gives two examples of how shock can take away the
power to comprehend. Pickle's acquaintance, Pallet, tries a
particularly highly flavoured Roman dish:

> And the painter being certified of his approbation, lifted the
> spoon to his mouth without scruple; but far from justifying the
> eulogium of his taster, when this precious composition diffused
> itself upon his palate, he seemed to be deprived of all sense and
> motion, and sat like the leaden statue of some river god with
> the liquor flowing out at both sides of his mouth.[21]

Roderick Random is wrongfully arrested:

> I had no sooner recovered the use of my reflection, which had
> been quite overthrown by this accident, than I sent for
> Thomson.[22]

Shock can displace the reason and, judiciously used, can restore
it too. The quality of which Man is most proud can be obtained
by prescription:

> He, (Fathom) had now retrieved the use of his perception by
> the operation of the blisters, which began to torture him
> severely.[23]

The turbulent Pickle is brought under control by similar means:

> His faithful valet, having waited two whole hours, in hope of
> seeing this gust of passion overblown, and perceiving that the
> paroxysm seemed rather to increase, very prudently sent for a
> physician of his master's acquaintance, who, having considered
> the circumstances and symptoms of the disorder, directed that he
> should be plentifully blooded, without loss of time, and .pre-
> scribed a draught to compose the tumult of his spirits.[24]

The effect of strong waters on the well-ordered seat of the
intellect intrigued Smollett. That he deplored it as well would

not be apparent to those who see no more in Smollett than his subject matter, but in his *Travels* he states his belief that all "fermented liquors are pernicious to the human constitution". *The Essay on the External Use of Water* also deals with the virtues of water when internally applied:

> Pure water is certainly of all others the most salutary beverage.... These admirable qualities inherent in simple water are clearly evinced by the uninterrupted health, good spirits and longevity of those who use nothing else for their ordinary drink.[25]

In the drinking bout between Random and Narcissa's brother— the humour of which is in keeping with *a satire on mankind*— Smollett demonstrates the stages by which the understanding succumbs to the chemical actions of the alcohol. Always specific, he notes that each fermented drink has its own effect. Wine stupefies, spirit inflames:

> "Suppose," he (the adulterous Fathom) said to himself, "this brutal German, instead of being stupefied with wine, should come home inflamed with brandy, to the use of which he is sometimes addicted, far from feeling any inclination to sleep, he will labour under the most fretful anxiety of watching, every irascible particle in his disposition will be exasperated; he will be offended with every object that may present itself to his view; and, if there is the least ingredient of jealousy in his temper, it will manifest itself in riot and rage.[26]

The motive for drinking, Smollett finds, is to increase confidence and bring about a gay carelessness of normal restraints. Pickle attempts, by country dancing and wine, to warm Emilia's blood for his seduction of her. The more diffident Pallet takes a glass too much himself in the hope of bringing himself up to the pitch which he feels is required of him:

> The painter saw, and was offended at this correspondence, which he considered as an insult upon his misfortune, as well as an evident preference of his rival; and conscious of his own timidity, swallowed an extraordinary glass, that his invention might be stimulated, and his resolution raised to the contrivance and execution of some scheme of revenge.[27]

Alcohol brings about Celinda's "wild irregular sallies" in the lascivious hands of Ferdinand, Count Fathom. Indeed, it does not lull, but increases any disturbance of the mind. The frightened ship's chaplain gets drunk at the Battle of Carthagena:

The fumes of the liquor, mounting into the parson's brain, conspired with his former agitation of spirits, to make him quite delirious.[28]

Elinor, who has had all her money stolen, is given a glass of wine:

The cordial she swallowed, far from calming, increased the disturbance of her thoughts, and produced an intoxication, during which she talked in an incoherent strain, laughed and wept by turns, and acted other extravagances, which are known to be symptoms of the hysterical affection.[29]

Alcohol brings out the meridional violence of the people of Nice:

Even here, when the peasants quarrel in their cups, (which very seldom happens) they draw their knives, and the one infallibly stabs the other. To such extremities, however, they never proceed, except when there is a woman in the case; and mutual jealousy co-operates with the liquor they have drank, to inflame their passions.[30]

It can invoke imaginings, even in the ordered Hanoverian mind of Peregrine Pickle's tutor:

The opium which had been given to Jolter, together with the wine he had drunk, produced such a perturbation in his fancy that he was visited with horrible dreams, and among other miserable situations, imagined himself in danger of perishing in the flames.[31]

What is so original about Smollett, considered as an eighteenth-century novelist, is his insistence on the sympathy between body and mind. His psychological view of life accounts for much which has alarmed the fastidious. It is clear that he regretted that Man's captivity begins with his captivity in the flesh. Much of Smollett's work could be regarded as a hopeless protest against that fact. Smollett's two earlier heroes—dangerous friends and intractable enemies—are hooligans, young male animals undisciplined by life. That he makes them his heroes does not mean that he likes them. Moreover, the practical jokes in which Roderick Random and Peregrine Pickle delight bring their victims' physical nature, physically expressed, into play. Brutal though these jokes may seem nowadays, they are not out of place in *Roderick Random*, which, though entitled "a satire on mankind", is really a savage romp at the expense of man's physical needs. In *Peregrine Pickle*, the grimly accomplished Crabtree is used as instrument of Smollett's protest. Crabtree diverts Peregrine's practical jokes—in themselves the product of mere animal vitality—towards moral exposure, and so gives them an ethical justification.

It is significant that Humphry Clinker enters the novel which he dignifies with his name posteriors foremost—those posteriors, bared by poverty, which were so offensive to the carnally disordered Tabitha Bramble, and so naïvely white to the indiscreet nubility of Winifred Jenkins. A physical aspect of Clinker makes an impression on two physically conditioned natures, and the reason for it all is cruel circumstance.

II. THE RECIPROCAL INFLUENCE

So Condillac's statue, gifted with senses, has come to life, and its understanding is formed and conditioned by the impact of physical experience upon the feeling nerves. But there is a further complexity. The formed mind in its turn has a qualifying effect on the experience, twitching the sensory lines which lead up to it. As Condillac says in his *Essai*, "Soit que nous nous elevions, pour parler metaphoriquement, jusques dans les cieux: soit que nous descendions dans les abimes, nous ne sortons point de nous memes: et ce n'est jamais que notre proper pensée que nous apperçevons".[32]

The different temperaments of the characters in *Humphry Clinker* are responsible for the disparate effects which such places as Bath and London make upon them. The distempered Matt. Bramble sees disorder and infection everywhere at Bath. He faints because of the stench of the crowd, later complaining that his companions must be very insensitive to have escaped the same fate. Jerry Melford comments: "For my part, I am very thankful for the coarseness of my organs, being in no danger of falling a sacrifice to the delicacy of my nose."[33] Jerry, fresh from college and the only healthy person in the whole party, regards Bath as a microcosm of the big surprising world of affairs. Lydia, young, enthusiastic (her head aches for excess of joy) and anxious to impress the school-friend to whom she is writing, writes descriptions so greatly at variance with those of her uncle that one would hardly think that Bramble's Vauxhall and Lydia's Vauxhall were the same place. To Bramble it is a composition of baubles, to Lydia a variety of beauties. Bramble's "unnatural assemblage of objects" is Lydia's "wonderful assemblage of the most striking and picturesque objects". Lydia extolls the way in which "the whole is illuminated by an infinite number of lamps". Bramble grumbles that "a few lamps glimmer like so many farthing candles". Lydia's visitors "sup on cold collations", Bramble's "devour sliced beef and swill port". Both see crowds, Bramble of "noisy people, sucking up the nocturnal rheums of an aguish climate", Lydia of "the gayest company, ranging through those blissfull shades". Lydia tells us that Bramble was caught in the rain, a fact which Bramble does not mention himself, though it probably has some bearing on his account of the dangers of Vauxhall:

> When I see a number of well-dressed people, of both sexes, sitting on the covered benches, exposed to the eyes of the mob, and, which is worse, to the cold, raw, night air, devouring sliced beef, and swilling port, and punch, and cider, I can't help compassionating their temerity, while I despise their want of taste and decorum; but when they course along those damp and gloomy walks, or crowd together upon the wet gravel, without any other cover than the cope of heaven, listening to a song which one half of them cannot possibly hear, how can I help supposing they are actually possessed by a spirit more absurd and pernicious than anything we meet with in the precincts of Bedlam? In all probability, the proprietors of this and other public gardens of inferior note, in the skirts of the metropolis, are, in some shape, connected with the faculty of physic, and the company of undertakers; for, considering that eagerness in the pursuit of what is called pleasure, which now predominates through every rank and denomination of life, I am persuaded that more gouts, rheumatisms, catarrhs, and consumptions are caught in these nocturnal pastimes, sub dio, than from all the risks and accidents to which a life of toil and danger is exposed.[34]

As Lydia later points out, "People of experience and infirmity, my dear Letty, see with very different eyes from those such as you and I make use of".[35] Jerry makes much the same point when, with reference to his friend Barton, who has obtained a place in the government, he remarks with unusual sententiousness:

> Without all doubt, the fumes of faction not only disturb the faculty of reason, but also pervert the organs of sense; and I would lay a hundred guineas to ten that if Barton, on one side, and the most conscientious patriot in the opposition on the other,

were to draw, upon honour, the picture of the K(ing) or
m(inistry), you and I, who are still uninfected and unbiassed,
would find both painters equally distant from the truth.[36]

That Bramble's comments on Bath ("a compound of villainous
smells") are intended to illustrate the condition of Matt. Bramble
rather than the condition of Bath, can be seen from Smollett's
own account of the city in *The Present State of all Nations*,
which, whilst not in total agreement with Lydia's judgement that
"all is gaiety, good humour and diversion", is friendly enough.
Much of *Humphry Clinker* is a bland statement of the subjectivity of human outlook, and, since it allows for the variations
of prejudice and opinion, the book is all the more valid as a
survey of England in the late eighteenth century. More than
once Smollett in his own person unconsciously illustrates human
subjectivity. In the *Travels* it is amusing to compare his abuse of
England in the first letter with his praises in the last, written when
he was refreshed and restored to some degree of good health, and
perhaps a little softened by his long absence.

The power of the mind to superimpose itself on reality is
depicted in the episode of Fathom's escape from the bandits. His
terror mounts into active illusion:

Never had our hero spent a moment in such agony as he felt
during this operation; the whole surface of his body was covered
with a cold sweat, and his nerves were relaxed with a universal
palsy. In short, he remained in a trance that, in all probability,
contributed to his safety; for, had he retained the use of his senses,
he might have been discovered by the transports of his fear. . . .
His spirits were agitated into a state of fermentation that produced a species of resolution akin to that which is inspired by
brandy or other strong liquors, and, by an impulse that seemed
supernatural, he was immediately hurried into measures for his
own preservation. . . . The first steps he had taken for his preservation were the effects of mere instinct, while his faculties
were extinguished or suppressed by despair; but now, as his
reflection began to recur, he was haunted by the most intolerable
apprehensions. Every whisper of the wind through the thickets
was swelled into the hoarse menaces of murder, the shaking of
the boughs were construed into the brandishing of poniards, and
every shadow of a tree became the apparition of a ruffian eager
for blood. In short, at each of these occurrences he felt what was
infinitely more tormenting than the stab of a real dagger. . . .
After he had continued in this progress through a succession of
groves, and bogs, and thorns, and brakes, by which not only his

clothes but also his skin suffered in a grievous manner, while every nerve quivered with eagerness and dismay, he at length reached an open plain.[37]

Smollett often describes the paralysis of the nerves which can result from violent emotion. One of his most whimsical passages concerns Roderick Random's courtship of Narcissa:

> I studied many pathetic declarations, but when I attempted to give them utterance, my tongue denied its office; and she sat silent, with a downcast look, full of anxious alarm, her bosom heaving with expectation of some great event. At length I endeavoured to put an end to this solemn pause, and began with, "It is very surprising, madam—" Here the sound dying away, I made a full stop—while Narcissa starting, blushed, and, with a timid accent, answered, "Sir?" Confounded at this note of interrogation. I pronounced with the most sheepish bashfulness, "Madam!" To which she replied, "I beg your pardon—I thought you had spoke to me."[38]

Most frequently this paralysis takes place as the result of either fear or shock:

> When Tom told him (Pallet, who is fighting a duel) that they had faced about, and admonished him to advance, the nerves of his arm refused their office, he could not hold out his pistol, and instead of going forward, retreated with an insensibility of motion.[39]

Don Diego rediscovers his daughter, whom he thought dead:

> His nerves were too much overpowered by this sudden recognition, to manifest the sensation of his soul by external signs. He started not, nor did he lift a hand in token of surprise; he moved not from the spot on which he stood.[40]

There are a number of passages where Smollett deals with other forms of nervous disarrangements. Peregrine Pickle's nerves thrill at the mention of Emilia's name, "which he never heard pronounced without agitation". Waiting to join Serafina in bed braces Renaldo's nerves "to such a degree of impatience, that human nature could not long endure the tension".[41] In its intensest form, this nervous excitement throws the senses out of gear. Roderick Random remeets Narcissa after a long absence:

> Good Heaven! what were the thrillings of my soul at that instant! my reflection was overwhelmed with a torrent of agitation! my heart throbbed with surprising violence! a sudden mist

overspread my eyes! my ears were invaded with dreadful sound! I paused for want of breath, and in short, was for some moments, entranced![42]

Peregrine Pickle is overwhelmed by sexual jealousy:

> In a word, his endeavours to conceal the situation of his thoughts were so violent, that his constitution could not endure the shock; the sweat ran down his forehead in a stream, the colour vanished from his cheeks, his knees began to totter, and his eyesight to fail; so that he must have fallen at his full length upon the floor, had not he retired very abruptly into another room, where he threw himself upon a couch, and fainted.[43]

This is plainly Moore's doctrine of the nerves, adapted to Armstrong's assertion that romance is a by-product of nervous function.

It takes little out of the ordinary to cause nervous transports in Strap:

> When our mutual caresses were over, I sat down again to be shaved; but the poor fellow's nerves were so discomposed by this unexpected meeting, that his hand could scarcely hold the razor, with which, nevertheless, he found means to cut me in three places, in as many strokes.[44]

Such are the processes by which emotion is converted into sweat and trepidation. In the gambling scene in *Peregrine Pickle*, Smollett pays close attention to the physical effects of strong feeling:

> Godfrey collected his whole art and capacity and augmenting his core to number ten, indulged himself with a view of the whole fraternity. The visages of these professors had adopted different shades of complexion at every hazard he had taken; from their natural colour they had shifted into a sallow hue; into a mahogany tint; and now they saw seventeen hundred pounds of their stock depending upon a single stroke, they stood like so many swarthy Moors, jaundiced with terror and vexation. The fire which naturally glowed, in the cheeks and nose of the player, seemed utterly extinct, and his carbuncles exhibited a livid appearance, as if a gangrene had already made some progress in his face; his hand began to shake, and his whole frame was seized with such trepidation, that he was fain to swallow a bumper of brandy, in order to re-establish the tranquillity of his nerves.[45]

The detailed observation of this passage is suggestive of Darwin's book on the expression of the emotions in man and animal.

Sometimes the roused body half-subjugates the will:

> He accepted the invitation; and I betook myself to the field, though not without feeling considerable repugnance to the combat, which frequently attacked me in cold sweats, by the way : but the desire for revenge, the shame of retracting, and hope of conquest, conspired to repel these unmanly symptoms of fear; and I appeared on the plain with good grace.[46]

> Yes, he (the imprisoned Fathom) had no sooner committed his effects to the care of this triumvirate, than his fancy was visited with direful warnings, which produced cold sweats and palpitations, and threw him into such agonies of apprehension as he had never known before.[47]

Revulsed and terrified, Pallet makes his escape from the Bastile with "each particular hair crawling and twining like an animated serpent".[48]

Even more dramatic effects are caused by Pallet's mistaken notion that he has eaten tom-cat:

> Before this sentence was uttered, Pallet's belly seemed to move in contact with his backbone, his colour changed, no part but the whites of his eyes were to be seen, he dropped his lower jaw, and fixed his hands in his sides, reached with such convulsive agonies, as amazed and disconcerted the whole company; and what augmented his disorder was the tenacious retention of his stomach, which absolutely refused to part with its contents, notwithstanding all the energy of his abhorrence, which threw him into a cold sweat, and almost into a swoon.[49]

In *Humphry Clinker* a young clothier from Leeds, discovering that the crafty lawyer Micklewhimmen's bottle labelled "Stomachic Tincture" contains Bordeaux, jokingly drinks up the contents. Micklewhimmen is able to persuade him that the Bordeaux contained a powerful infusion of jallop:

> "In truth, mester what-d'-ye ca'um," replied the lawyer, "your wit has run you into a filthy puddle—I'm truly consarned for your waeful case. The best advice I can give you in sic a dilemma, is to send an express to Rippon for Dr. Waugh without delay; and, in the meantime, swallow all the oil and butter you can find in the hoose, to defend your poor stomach and intastines from the

villication of the particles of the jallap, which is vara violent, even when taken in moderation."

The poor clothier's torments had already begun. He retired roaring with pain, to his own chamber; the oil was swallowed, and the doctor sent for; but before he arrived the miserable patient had made such discharges upwards and downwards that nothing remained to give him farther offence. And this double evacuation was produced by imagination alone; for what he had drank was genuine wine of Bordeaux, which the lawyer had brought from Scotland for his own private use. The clothier, finding the joke turn out so expensive and disagreeable, quitted the house next morning, leaving the triumph to Micklewhimmen, who enjoyed it internally, without any outward signs of exultation; on the contrary, he affected to pity the young man for what he had suffered and acquired fresh credit from this show of moderation.[50]

Not only fear but also frustration can express itself palpably :

while, I seeing my money melt away, without any certainty of deliverance, and, in short, all my hopes frustrated, grew negligent of life, lost all appetite, and degenerated into such a sloven, that during the space of two months I was neither washed, shifted, nor shaved; so that my face rendered meagre with abstinence, was obscured with dirt, and overshadowed with hair, and my whole appearance squalid and even frightful;[51]

An intervention saves Roderick Random, so that his misery does not have a lasting physical effect. The sage in *Peregrine Pickle*, whose face "was a lively portraiture of that rancorous discontent which follows repeated damnation", was not so lucky. Nor was Smollett.

Since emotion can operate through the nerves on the body, it is not surprising that it can cause sickness. As Smollett remarks in the *Essay on the External Use of Water*, "That fancy operates with great power on the human body is so evident in all hypochondriac and hysteria disorders that it would be idle and superfluous to call in the evidence in support of a truth so well known".[52]

In his *Travels*, Smollett refers to a gentleman with "a most dreadful nervous asthma". Roderick Random's nose is liable to bleed with vexation. The agitation of Mrs. Williams' thoughts during her pregnancy produces first a fever, which then brings on a miscarriage. Another example is to be found in the case book of the quack Doctor Fathom. A certain Miss Biddy, who has been thrown into a frenzy and a subsequent coma by the defection of her lover, is instantly cured by the news that his elopement with another woman has not been successful:

> It would be superfluous to observe that these tidings operated like an admirable specific on the spirits of the young lady, who, while she affected to pity the squire, was so much overjoyed at his disappointment, that her eyes began to sparkle with uncommon vivacity, and in less than two hours after the last of those terrible attacks, she was restored to a better state of health than she had enjoyed for many weeks.[53]

The penitent and ailing adultress in *Ferdinand, Count Fathom* recovers because of her husband's forgiveness:

> So saying, he approached her bedside, and embraced her in token of his sincerity. Whether this generous condescension diffused such a composure upon her spirits as tended to the ease and refreshment of nature, which had been almost exhausted by disease and vexation, certain it is, that from this day she began to struggle with her malady in surprising efforts, and hourly gained ground, until her health was pretty well re-established.[54]

The stages of emotionally induced illness are well illustrated by the account of Monimia's decline when she thinks she has lost the affections of Renaldo. Weakened by "a severe fever which was the consequence of her disappointment and despondence", she sought out a quiet place,

> where she could, unmolested, dwell upon the wretched comparison between her past and present condition, and paint every circumstance of her misery in the most aggravating colours, that they might make the deeper impression upon her mind, and the more speedily contribute to that dissolution for which she ardently wished, as a total release from her woe.
>
> Amidst these pinings she began to loathe all sustenance.[55]

Even when, by some pat reversal of fortune, sorrow and disappointment is banished, it leaves its marks on the body which it has ravaged. "Is it possible," says Sophy, "that the gay Mr. Pickle should be so much altered in such a short space of time!"[56] When Smollett revisited Scotland in 1755, his mother did not at first recognise him.

Like so many of Smollett's comic passages, the descent of Lismahago in a blanket is more than comic. The mind is at work on the body, every toe denotes terror. It is also a quiet mockery of the similar descent of Winifred Jenkins, which was to make such an impression on the affections of Humphry Clinker. Winifred is smoother and plumper than Lismahago, but, as in Rembrandt's painting of *Susanna and the Elders* at Vienna, the old man and the girl have the same basic humanity, the same tissues and needs, the same disturbed flesh. The distinction between them lies rather in Humphry Clinker's eroticism than in their own substance.

III. AN INVOLUNTARY INSTINCT

The dramatists of the Renaissance have accustomed us to the figure of the plotter who uses impersonations, masks, forgeries and poisons. The successes of Ferdinand, Count Fathom, are due to subtler means. He works by observation and the slightest possible interventions in the course of events. He always understands what can be made out of an existing situation. His unprincipled application of a knowledge of human nature is a weapon far more potent than the webs and daggers of the Machiavellian stage. Naturally, the "uncommon capacity" of Fathom is backed by the uncommon capacity of his creator. The mechanics of conduct, to which Smollett gave so much thought during the composition of the earlier novels, are exploited by Fathom to the full. Nowhere is Smollett's psychology defter, nowhere are his ironical twists and turns more skilful, than in this sombre novel. Nowhere is it clearer that Smollett's purpose is the study of the human personality, its origins and the compulsions which it must bear.

As Monimia is about to leave Renaldo's house for ever, she encounters his dog, a reminder of happier times and meetings :

> As Fathom led her to the door, she was met by Renaldo's dog, which had long been her favourite; and the poor animal fawning upon her as she passed, her heart was overwhelmed with such a gush of tenderness, that a flood of tears streamed down her cheeks, and she had well nigh sunk upon the floor.[57]

In this incident, which has the despairing compassion of Rembrandt's picture of Hagar in tears quitting Abraham, Smollett has given colour and form to the theory of association. He does so once more in his moving story of the blacksmith's widow, in *Humphry Clinker*.

The association of ideas makes human purpose a fortuitous thing. A dog, a well-known sound, a dream, a momentary recollection—all these can upset the precarious balance, causing the sudden flow of tears, the saving tenderness, the averted retribution :

> I, (Mrs. Williams, who has plotted Lothario's murder) dreamed Lothario appeared before me, pale, mangled, and bloody, blamed my rashness, protested his innocence, and pleaded his own cause so pathetically, that I was convinced of his fidelity, and waked in a horror of remorse.[58]

> There are certain considerations that strike upon the mind with irresistible force, even in the midst of its distraction; the momentary recollection of some particular scene, occasioned by the features of the devoted victim, hath often struck the dagger from the assassin's hand.[59]

Commodore Trunnion was once fined a swingeing sum in a law court, and so sweats with agony at the sight of an attorney. Every carriage which passes Pickle in the street mortifies him by recalling to him the details of his former prosperity. Renaldo tries to take his mind off his woes by drawing portraits, but some chance feature in his sketches always reminds him of one of the angry faces of his creditors.

Smollett states in *Ferdinand, Count Fathom*, that his own "notions of human excellence are not quite so sublime" as those of the modern Platonists (such as Shaftesbury) who ascribe good actions to the innate virtue and generosity of the human heart. His notions come nearer those of Gay and Hartley. Self-interest (although often in a refined or projected form) is the motive power of human nature. The only things which arouse Man's affections are those which he associates with his former pleasures. The death of a father who has treated him badly does not distress Pickle in the least :

> and he took the road to the garrison, in the most elevated transports of joy, unalloyed with the least mixture of grief at the death of a parent, whose paternal tenderness he has never known. His breast was absolutely a stranger to that boasted . . . instinct of affection, by which the charities are supposed to subsist.[60]

It is his benefactor, Trunnion, who is the object of Pickle's affections.

The structural necessity for Trunnion to adopt Pickle is employed to an additional and psychologically just end. Smollett could not make Pickle the son of Trunnion, because that would have embedded the hero in the burlesque element of the novel. Besides, Pickle would naturally have inherited some of Trunnion's characteristics, and this would not have been consistent with the suave belligerence of Pickle's role. On the other hand, it was necessary for Pickle to be given the indulgent and eccentric education which only Trunnion could provide. Smollett settles the difficulty with his usual quick sureness. He also takes advantage of the opportunity of a hasty peripheral skirmish with Shaftesbury.

Hume put forward the view that although Man would seem to have powers of reasoning, they are usually set in motion irrationally, by a merely animal impulse. In Smollett's characterisation these impulses are of the greatest importance. Strap is Smollett's answer to Shaftesbury's ready-made man. Strap, like Pallett and Clinker, lives very close to his animal responses. These three characters are composed of the very stuff of nervous reaction. They are illustrations of the animal economy under stress, studies in the processes of joy and fear:

> During the recital, my friend was strongly affected, according to the various situations described. He started with surprise, glowed with indignation, gaped with curiosity, smiled with pleasure, trembled with fear, and wept with sorrow, as the vicissitudes of my life inspired these different passions.[61]

It is significant that Strap's voice, heard in the dark, "is like that of a baboon when he mews and chatters".[62] Strap's master can hardly be called more rational. Random, crossed in love, goes home "in the condition of a frantic Bedlamite" and vents his fury on Strap.[63] In the same way, Peregrine Pickle, incensed on one occasion by Pipes' insubordination, fires a pistol into his face.

Smollett records the features of irrationality in some detail:

> He pulled off his woollen night-cap, pummelled his bare pate, beat the floor alternately with his feet, swore his people had betrayed him, and cursed himself to the lowest pit of hell, for having admitted such a cocktrice into his family.[64]

Often the brute instinctive prompting comes from the sight of blood. The Swiss Chevalier who wishes to fight a duel with Fathom is swiftly discouraged when he sees that Fathom's hand is smeared with blood, "as if he had just come from the slaughter of a foe".[65] Pickle, fighting a duel with Gauntlet,

was transported with rage at sight of his own blood, and returned the assault with such fury and precipitation, that Gauntlet,
loth to take advantage of his unguarded heat, stood upon the
defensive.[66]

The abbé in *Fathom* is likewise enraged by the sight of his own
blood :

finding his hand besmeared with his own blood, he began to
caper about the apartment, in a transport of rage and vexation.[67]

Sometimes the instincts are saving ones. Pallet does not drown
when he falls in the Maese, although his senses have forsaken
him, because his hands fasten involuntarily on the cable of a
ship. Don Diego in distress takes measure for his safety "in consequence of an involuntary instinct, that seems to operate the
animal machine, while the faculty of thinking is suspended".[68]
At other times the instinct produces, not redoubled activity, but
inaction. Commodore Trunnion, thrust into marriage with Mrs.
Grizzle, sits silent and broils with vexation.[69] Random, having lost
all his money, is amazed to find himself so much at ease. It is
not until the next morning that he understands he has mistaken
his stupor for resignation. When things in *Humphry Clinker* are
at their worst, Matthew Bramble, commonly very articulate, sits
silent with a sour, knowing smile on his face.

Even on the conscious level, conduct is seldom determined by
reflection. It is the balance of the passions which is important. At
times the poise is all too fine, resulting in standstill, as when the
fire alarm is given at the College of Authors :

Several members of the college followed his example, and happily
accomplished their escape : the chairman himself, being unwilling
to use the same expedient, stood trembling on the brink of
descent, dubious of his own agility, and dreading the consequence
of such a leap.[70]

More often, the opposing forces of the emotions keep the person
who finds himself between them upright and steady. Monimia,
after her mortal part had lost its chance, "encouraged no discourse but that which turned upon her immortal part".[71] Emilia
Gauntlet's love of gaiety, by occupying her imagination, serves
to protect her from the deeper sensations of sorrow. Resentment,
a state of mind well known to Smollett, he depicts as one of those
passions which swallow up passion. When Renaldo is near prostration because of the death of Monimia, it is the desire for

vengeance which revives him, making his blood circulate with new vigour.[72] Motives of resentment help Pickle to bear his disappointment in love. He vows to make up for Emilia's disdain by possessing the first woman who will have him.[73] "What would become of the unfortunate," Smollett asks,

> if the constitution of the mind did not permit them to bring one passion into the field against another? Passions that operate in the human breast like poisons of a different nature, extinguishing each other's effect.

It is interesting to compare Matthew Bramble, as a type of benevolence, with Fielding's Mr. Allworthy. Allworthy is an ideal figure, with a gift for improving on every occasion which he carries to the length of preaching a whole sermon on chastity that the author happened to have by him. Bramble is a creature of frailties, but his weakness and his strength are affiliated to each other in a way that is generally productive of good. His morbid excess of feeling, for example, places him militantly against cruelty and injustice. Thus his strategically placed weaknesses are of greater moral value than his strength. Similarly, Trebasi, the bully in *Fathom*, is brave because of his brutal insensibility towards danger. Applying this notion of the balance of the passions to real life, Smollett, asserts that, had the painter Raphael not lacked fire, then he would instead have lacked the serenity which characterises him.[74]

Amongst the most powerful of the instincts is the gregarious one, the dumb warmth which men feel in the mere presence of their fellows. Random notices at the Battle of Carthagena how the sailors are "encouraged by society and behaviour of each other", and compares this with the terrors of his own isolation. His grief was the more penetrating "because there was nobody on board to whom I could communicate my sorrows".[75] Fathom asks Don Diego the reason for his distress:

> Ali, thus solicited, would often shake his head, with marks of extreme sorrow and despondence, and, while the tears gushed from his eyes, declared that his distress was beyond the power of any remedy but death, and that, by making our hero his confidant, he should only extend his unhappiness to a friend, without feeling the least remission of his own torture. Nothwithstanding these repeated declarations, Ferdinand, who was well enough acquainted with the mind of man to know that such importunity is seldom or never disagreeable, redoubled his instances, together

with his expressions of sympathy and esteem, until the stranger was prevailed upon to gratify his curiosity and benevolence.[76]

Fathom is indeed "well enough acquainted with the mind of man". The disdainful cadences with which Smollett describes Fathom's deceptions are not without a touch of malice for the foolish victims. There is no doubt that Smollett enjoyed, with a wry Scottish delight, the spectacle of the world at work. His enjoyment must certainly have been heightened by the sense of analytical verve and moral *furor* which speeded him along. But even his most comic passages are more than comical. Satire is always present in his work, but so is pity, and so is indignation over Man's miserable dependence on the flesh.

CHAPTER V

THE ECONOMY OF LOVE

SMOLLETT'S EXAMINATION OF Love is that of an eighteenth-century savant: pragmatic, encyclopaedic, Newtonian. From a study of the evidence he concludes that Love, like all other human activities, is promoted by a whole tangle of first causes: the nerves and the tissues of the body, the social situation, the ambiguities of motive and the variations of Chance. Such a conclusion was far from acceptable to the sexual romanticism of the nineteenth century, and this is one of the reasons why Smollett was treated with little respect by the Victorian critics. They compromised with known material facts, whilst Smollett recorded his repugnance for them in puritanical detail. His disdain for his hero, Roderick Random, is never so complete as in his account of the apish maraudings at the apothecary's shop, and of the graceless episode in France, when Random shares a peasant-girl with an evil-smelling friar who afterwards shrives her.

There is both compassion and contempt for human necessity in Smollett's description of how indecorously even a Methodist can fall in love:

> This maiden was just as she had started out of bed, the moon shone very bright, and a fresh breeze of wind blowing, none of Mrs. Winifred's beauties could possibly escape the view of the fortunate Clinker, whose heart was not able to withstand the united force of so many charms; at least, I am much mistaken, if he has not been her humble slave from that moment.[1]

Thomas Pipe responds to the stirrings of the tender sentiment with all the intelligence of a probed mollusc:

> But Thomas, notwithstanding his irony appearance, was in reality composed of flesh and blood. His desire being titillated by the contact of a buxom wench, whose right arm embraced his middle as he rode, his thoughts began to mutiny against his master, and he found it almost impossible to withstand the temptation of making love.[2]

Lydia Bramble's romantic pretensions are hardly accepted by her
uncle, who says that she has been cooped up in a boarding school
so long that she is "as inflammable as touchwood".[3] Most of
Pickle's work has been done for him already by officious Nature
when he sets up

> his throne amongst those who laboured under the disease of
> celibacy, from the pert Miss of fifteen, who, with a fluttering
> heart, tosses her head, bridles up, and giggles involuntarily at
> sight of a handsome young man, to the staid maiden of twenty-
> eight, who, with a demure aspect, moralises on the vanity of
> beauty, the folly of youth, and simplicity of woman, and ex-
> patiates on friendship, benevolence, and good sense, in the style
> of a Platonic philosopher.[4]

According to this Determinist notion, Love becomes a Picaresque jape, sometimes as brutal as the one played out in *Roderick
Random*. Returning disappointed from the bedroom of one of
the maids, whom he has found asleep in the arms of another
man, Roderick by mistake enters the bedroom next to his own,
where his master's daughter, who despises Random, lies waiting
for Captain O'Donnell:

> I did not perceive my mistake before I had run against the bed-
> posts, and then it was not in my power to retreat undiscovered;
> for the nymph being awake, felt my approach, and, with a soft
> voice, bade me make less noise, lest the Scotch booby in the next
> room should overhear us. This hint was sufficient to inform me of
> the assignation; and as my passions, at any time high, were then
> in a state of exaltation, I resolved to profit by my good fortune.
> Without any more ceremony, therefore, I made bold to slip into
> bed to this charmer, who gave me as favourable a reception as I
> could desire. Our conversation was very sparing on my part; but
> she upbraided the person whom I represented with his jealousy
> of me, whom she handled so roughly, that my resentment had
> well-nigh occasioned a discovery more than once.[5]

This unsentimental transaction completed, Random leaves the
young woman, and, content with a successful evacuation, falls
asleep "in the congratulation of my own happiness".

It will naturally be objected that we are not discussing Love
but Lust. Let us consider the seductions of Ferdinand, Count
Fathom. There can be no doubt about which category Fathom's
feelings come into. That potent animal impulse was to be his un-
doing, for all his artifice and cunning. But his victims give in to

him, not because of desire but because of affection. Their affection for him arises from his manipulation of their circumstances. All these women are in a forlorn state when he takes them up, and he is ruthless in his pursuit of the ultimate gratification.

Wilhelmina is at war with her mother and she is grateful for Fathom's help in her solitary campaign. She lacks the experience to withstand his flatteries, which console her for the fact that, within her own family, she is unacceptable. Wilhelmina's mother, with whom Fathom is conducting a parallel amour, fancies quite correctly that her charms are decreasing with the passing years. Hungry for attentions, she is a lady

> who with all the intoxication of unenlightened pride, and an increased appetite for pleasure, had begun to find herself neglected, and even to believe that her attractions were actually on the wane.[6]

Elinor is a naïve country girl who thinks that Fathom has saved her from destitution in a strange place. Having made her drink a large glass of Canary, he takes advantage of her perturbation:

> This is a season which of all others is most propitious to the attempts of an artful lover; and justifies the metaphorical maxim of fishing in troubled waters. There is an affinity and short transition betwixt all the violent passions that agitate the human mind. They are all false perspectives, which, though they magnify, yet perplex and render indistinct every object which they represent. And flattery is never so successfully administered, as to those who know they stand in need of friendship, assent and approbation.[7]

Aided by the joint workings of gratitude and Canary, Fathom "gradually proceeded in sapping from one degree of intimacy to another", until she received him with very marked ardour.[8]

The timorous and friendless Celinda finds Fathom indispensable to her weak nerves. She admits him to her bedroom at nights, so that she may have company "to defend her from the shocking impressions of fear".[9] He profits by this intimacy and by the readiness with which one strong emotion changes to another. The clergyman's wife is in a state of convalescent lassitude, too tired, and too grateful to her apparent saviour, to resist when he enlarges on the intimacies permitted to a physician. His talents are on the wane by the time that he makes his attempt on

Monimia, but he shows his old discernment in seeking to profit by

> that languor which often creeps upon and flattens the inter-
> course of lovers cloyed with the sight and conversation of each
> other.[10]

There is nothing absolute about the love of these women. It is
the excrescence of chance, which Fathom adapts to his own
purposes.

In the attempted seduction of Mlle. Melvil, Fathom, who has
discovered "some marks of inflammability in mademoiselle's
constitution", uses social pressure to direct her general aptitude
for love towards the particular available object, himself. Knowing
Mlle. Melvil to be of studious reflective habits, with few diversions, he conspires with her maid to accustom Mlle. Melvil to
licentious ways of thinking. The maid

> seized all opportunities of introducing little amorous stories, the
> greatest part of which were invented for the purposes of warming
> her passions, and lowering the price of chastity in her esteem; for
> she represented all the young lady's contemporaries in point of
> age and situation, as so many sensualists, who, without scruple,
> indulged themselves in the stolen pleasures of youth.[11]

Fathom reveals himself as a practical exponent of Montesquieu's
contention that individual morality is related to the morality of
the class or the group. Indeed, all Fathom's seductions demonstrate that what appears to be an act of will is really the combination of a material situation with a biological need.

The heroes of *Gil Blas* and *Le Roman Comique* are not
examples of high moral integrity. Fathom is the point at which
the rogue-hero turns thoroughly nasty. He is the wolf-man of
Hobbes living on his wits in a Picaresque setting of travels, inns
and prisons. Fathom's immediate predecessor, Peregrine Pickle,
although only an intermediary, is nasty enough. The attempted
seduction of Emilia, with the aid of wine and a hired room at a
bagnio, is a venture worthy of Fathom himself.

It is unusual for a novelist to isolate, with cruel certainty, the
physical element in the hero's passion for the girl whom he marries in the last chapter. This is what Smollett does in *Peregrine
Pickle*. What attaches Pickle to Emilia, and keeps him constant
in spite of many setbacks and slights to his conspicuous self-
esteem, is "the utmost turbulence of unruly desire". It is the
same "headlong desire" which gets the better of his revengeful
disposition, and decides him in favour of a reconciliation after

the incident at the bagnio.[12] He sets out for Mrs. Gauntlett's house "with the unjustifiable sentiments of a man of pleasure, who sacrifices every consideration to the desire of his ruling appetite".[13] He congratulates himself on his proposed triumph over Emilia's virtue, and begins to "project future conquests among the most dignified characters of the female sex"[14]. A few timely disturbances alter his financial position so that he does not need a rich wife. Emilia, indefatigably chaste, will not admit the pleasurable attentions which he has in mind, unless he marries her. At their wedding Crabtree, the cynical mischief-maker, is loud in his expressions of satisfaction. Smollett ends his novel in the conventional way, but there is something cracked in the sound of the church bells.

Smollett always relates the nature of the sexual motive to the nature of the character. In Pickle's attempts on Emilia Gauntlett an arrogant will to conquer, deviating occasionally into pique at the lack of effect which he is making, predominates. Equally it is Emilia's essential coquetry which enables her to avoid serious involvement with Pickle, except on terms approved by her mother, and incidentally causes her to sustain his propulsive resentment. The bookish Mrs. Williams, in *Roderick Random*, yields to Lothario because she associates him with the heroes of romantic fiction:

> All night long my imagination formed a thousand ridiculous expectations. There was so much of knight-errantry in this gentleman's coming to the relief of a damsel in distress, with whom he immediately became enamoured, that all I had read of love and chivalry recurred to my fancy, and I looked upon myself as a princess in some region of romance, who, being delivered from the power of a brutal giant or satyr by a generous Oroondates, was bound in gratitude, as well as led by inclination, to yield my affections to him without reserve. In vain did I endeavour to chastise these foolish conceits, by reflections more reasonable and severe. The amusing images took full possession of my mind, and my dreams represented my hero sighing at my feet in the language of a despairing lover.[15]

Later, "savaged by her wrongs" at Lothario's hands, in "a delirium of gloomy joy" at the prospect of being revenged upon him, she learns the principle of prostitution (so determining her career) by allowing Horatio the possession of her body as a reward for killing Lothario.

In Roderick Random's attachment to Narcissa there are always

traces of social aspiration and self-esteem. The notion of posing
as a gentleman of fashion in order to hunt his fortune after he
has been reduced to the rank, first of footman in Narcissa's
family and then of private soldier in the French army, appeals
to him "because it flattered my vanity, and indulged a ridiculous hope I began to entertain of inspiring Narcissa with a mutual
flame".[16] Meeting Narcissa after a long parting, he is gratified
by the agitation which he creates in her bosom :

> When I thus encircled all that my soul held dear, while I hung
> over her beauties,—beheld her eyes sparkle, and every feature
> flush with virtuous fondness; when I saw her enchanting bosom
> heave with undissembled rapture, and knew myself the happy
> cause—Heavens! what was my situation![17]

As he says himself, pride is one of "the two chief ingredients in
my disposition".[18] The possibility of being outshone reduces him
to a state of vivid jealousy :

> The ball-night being arrived, I dressed myself in a suit I had
> reserved for some grand occasion; and having drank tea with
> Narcissa and her brother, conducted my angel to the scene, where
> she in a moment eclipsed all her female competitors for beauty,
> and attracted the admiration of the whole assembly. My heart
> dilated with pride on this occasion, and my triumph rejected
> all bounds, when, after we had danced together, a certain noble-
> man, remarkable for his figure and influence in the beau monde,
> came up, and in the hearing of all present, honoured us with a
> very particular compliment upon our accomplishments and
> appearance. But this transport was soon checked, when I per-
> ceived his Lordship attach himself with great assiduity to my
> mistress, and say some warm things, which, I thought, savoured
> too much of passion. It was then I began to feel the pangs of
> jealousy. I dreaded the power and address of my rival. I sick-
> ened at his discourse. When she opened her lips to answer, my
> heart died within me. When she smiled, I felt the pains of the
> damned![19]

His connection with Narcissa does not deter him from other
escapades. On the contrary, by associating her in his mind with
Narcissa he adds zest to his enjoyment of the favours of Nanette :

> In vain did my reason suggest the respect that I owed to my dear
> mistress Narcissa; the idea of that lovely charmer rather increased
> than allayed the ferment of my spirits; and the young paysanne
> had no reason to complain of my remembrance.[20]

He does not let any sentimental regard for Narcissa interfere with the larger issue of how to further his interests by marrying an heiress, although after he has been rejected by Melinda (because his impersonation, financed by Strap, of a rich man does not take in her mother) he does observe:

> This disappointment gave me more uneasiness on Strap's account than my own; for I was in no danger of dying for love of Melinda; on the contrary, the remembrance of my charming Narcissa was a continual check upon my conscience during the whole course of my addresses; and perhaps contributed to the bad success of my scheme, by controlling my raptures and condemning my design.[21]

In this conscience-striken state, he goes on to make attempts on the money of Miss Gripewell and then Miss Sparkle. On hearing the news that Miss Sparkle has a fortune of £12,000:

> I lost all remembrance of gentle Narcissa, and my thoughts were wholly employed in planning triumphs over the malice and contempt of the world.[22]

In his inept enraged cheating, which always ends in his being cheated himself, Random resembles Mrs. Williams. They both pit their furious small wits against the monumental and massively organised depravity of the existing order. Yet even Random's negligible chances are greater than those of a woman. He measured his scope against that of Mrs. Williams:

> I compared her situation with my own, and found it a thousand times more wretched. I had endured hardships, 'tis true; my whole life had been a series of such; and when I looked forward, the prospect was not much bettered; but then they were become habitual to me, and consequently I could bear them with less difficulty. If one scheme of life should not succeed, I could have recourse to another and so to a third, veering about to a thousand different shifts, according to the emergencies of my fate, without forfeiting the dignity of my character beyond a power of retrieving it, or subjecting myself wholly to the caprice and barbarity of the world.[23]

The range of activity accorded to women by eighteenth-century society was, although generally more elegantly expressed, that offered by Tom Pipes to the beggar-girl in *Peregrine Pickle*: "Do but let us bring to a little, and I'll teach you to box the compass my dear. Ah, you strapper, what a jolly bitch you are!"[24]

Addison calls woman "a beautiful romantic animal", to be admired and embellished but never to be taken seriously. An engaging and tongue-wagging trifler, she uses books only to keep patches in, and devotes herself so completely to folly that in a paper on French fopperies Addison devotes one of the eight paragraphs to the French, one to dandies and the remaining six to her alone. Steele writes of ladies "attending their work diligently" at the looking glass, and mentions a girl's "secret satisfaction in herself and scorn of others" because she is wearing a new pair of striped garters. Chesterfield advises his son not to allow women ("children of a larger growth") to meddle in business. Swift grumbles that women "employ more application to be fools than would serve to make them wise and useful". Although this may have been true of women like Lady Vane (whose rabid "true confessions", interpolated in *Peregrine Pickle*, Smollett—he of the caustic long nose and the loose grim mouth—may have encouraged for the sake of laying bare such ladies of quality) the assumption of women's intellectual inconsequence must have thwarted much ability. As Smollett's friend, Lady Mary Montagu, speaking for her sex, said, "Folly is reckoned our proper sphere".

As women started at a disadvantage, the economic distinctions of the time operated against them with a particular intensity. Samuel Richardson, whom Smollett warmly admired, noticed this—indeed, there was little that escaped his small percipient eyes. Whilst Pamela must defer to her would-be ravisher with, "Why then, you are a Justice of the Peace and may send me to gaol if you please, and bring me to trial for my life", Clarissa can tell hers, "I am a person of rank and fortune and I will find friends to pursue you". Like Pamela, Mrs. Williams and Peregrine Pickle's beggar-girl are socially helpless before the power of wealth. Whilst they can be possessed at will, kicked and brutalised as the victims of sexual spleen, Mrs. Gauntlett's high-class daughter remains inviolable:

Sir,—I received the favour of yours, and am glad, for your own sake, that you have attained a due sense and conviction of your unkind and unchristian behaviour to poor Emy. I thank God, none of my children was ever so insulted before. Give me leave to tell you, sir, my daughter was no upstart, without friends or education, but a young lady, as well bred, and better born, than most private gentlewomen in the kingdom; and therefore, though you had no esteem for her person, you ought to have paid some regard to her family, which, no disparagement to you, sir, is more honourable than your own.[25]

Even more closely related to the class-structure than heterosexual relationships are, in Smollett's view, homosexual ones. *Advice* lists, amongst the degrading methods of rising in the world, the practice of becoming a rich man's catamite:

> But, if exempted from the Herculean toil,
> A fairer field awaits him, rich with spoil,
> There shall he shine, with mingling honours bright,
> His master's pathic, pimp and parasite.[26]

He quotes as an example a certain "Brush" Warren, whom he accuses in a footnote of owing "his present affluence to the most infamous qualifications" and of having been kept (like Juvenal's Naevolus) "by both sexes at one time":

> A prostrate sycophant shall rise a Lloyd
> And, won from kennels to the impure embrace,
> Accomplished Warren triumph o'er disgrace.[27]

Smollett's objection is not to Warren's original poverty but to the fact that in such a lamentable state of society, when the single asset of the penniless young is their chastity, only the more worthless and unscrupulous of them can achieve success. Moreover, he sees homosexuality as an aspect of that spread of Luxury to which he was so opposed. He describes how Sir John Chardin of Kempton Park "wore at his own banquet a garland of flowers, in imitation of the ancients" and, also in imitation of the ancients, "kept two rosy boys, arrayed in white, for the entertainment of his guests".[28] He hints at the prevalence of "spurious passion" at Oxford and even in the Church, and darkly mentions a scholar (presumably a statesman or lawyer of great rank, since Smollett calls him Pollio) who has abandoned himself to the pompous if gloomy celebration of his unnatural tastes:

> Pollio! the pride of science and its shame,
> The Muse weeps o'er thee, while she brands thy name!
> Abhorrent views that prostituted groom,
> The indecent grotto, or polluted dome![29]

The reference is obscure and, although it must be of great historical interest, nobody has ever tried to explain it. It is possible that the original of Pollio was the same as the original of Earl Strutwell in *Roderick Random,* in which, as usual, Smollett gives form and colour to the precepts of *Advice*. If this is so, then Smollett was less in sympathy with the original figure by the time he came to write *Roderick Random*.

Earl Strutwell has learnt the ways of the world so well that he is able to wheedle aspiring young men, by promising to use his influence on their behalf, not only out of their chastity but out of their money too. Thus, as an ultimate complication in the structure of eighteenth-century power, they pay him for allowing them to prostitute themselves to him. Lord Straddle, "who lived by borrowing and pimping for his fellow peers" introduces Random to Strutwell, who is "notorious for a passion for his own sex", with a view to Random's obtaining some sinecure. Strutwell invites Random to a private conversation at which he entertains him with promises and frequent squeezes of the hand :

> I could not even help shedding tears at the goodness of this noble lord, who no sooner perceived them, than he caught me in his arms, and hugged and kissed me with a seemingly paternal affection. Confounded at this uncommon instance of fondness for a stranger, I remained a few moments silent and ashamed, then rose and took my leave, after he had assured me that he would speak to the minister in my favour that very day; and desired that I would not for the future give myself the trouble of attending at his levee, but come at the same hour every day when he should be at leisure, that is, three times a week.

An additional irony is that Random has to bribe the porter and the footman in order to be admitted to the earl's presence. On Random's second visit the earl discusses literature with him, asks him his opinion of Petronius and defends Petronius' "taste of love" :

> The best man among the ancients is said to have entertained that passion; one of the wisest of their legislators has permitted the indulgence of it in his commonwealth; the most celebrated poets has not scrupled to avow it. At this day it prevails not only over all the east, but in most parts of Europe; in our own country it gains ground apace, and in all probability will become in a short time a more fashionable vice than simple fornication.

Random in reply quotes Smollett's *Advice* and declares his detestation of "this spurious and sordid desire". Smilingly Strutwell remarks that he is in full agreement with Random and only introduced the subject in order to test the soundness of Random's opinions. During the course of the long interview which follows, Strutwell admires the curious workmanship of Random's watch and Random, thinking that "there could not be a fitter opportunity to manifest in some shape my gratitude", presents him with it, although in fact it belongs to Hugh Strap. Random is never again admitted to a private audience. Random's friend Banter disillusions him, mentioning that as a further refinement Strutwell "allowed his servants no other wages than that part of the spoil which they could glean by their industry":

> I had no room to suspect the veracity of my friend, because, upon recollection, I found every circumstance of Strutwell's behaviour exactly tallying with the character he had described. His hugs, embraces, squeezes, and eager looks, were now no longer a mystery, no more than his defence of Petronius, and the jealous frown of his valet-de-chambre, who, it seems, had been the favourite pathic of his lord.[30]

With the first account of homosexuality in European fiction since that of Petronius himself, Smollett rounds off his study of the mechanics, the motives and the environment of Love. All the time he is working towards a definition of its nature. In that shrewd book, *Launcelot Greaves,* he presents a debate between the romantic and the "realistic" views. Greaves holds forth to Captain Crowe on the conduct of a knight, advocating an impracticable disregard of circumstance. The true knight must, for example, be prepared to "turn his prow full against the fury of the storm and stem the boisterous surge to his destined port". Crowe, who is an experienced seaman, and has no taste for hyperbole, says that to sail into the eye of the wind is impossible. "Nothing is impossible," replies Greaves, "to a true knight-errant, inspired and animated by love." Then, elevated like Socrates at the end of one of Plato's dialogues, he wings into a rhapsodical discourse on a knight's devotion to his mistress:

> "An that be all," replied the sailor, "I told you before as how I've got a sweetheart, as true a hearted girl as ever swung in canvas. What thof she may have started a hoop in rolling, that signifies nothing; I'll warrant her tight as a nutshell."

On these lines the debate continues. Greaves' Aurelia is "altogether supernatural". Crowe's Bess "will sail upon a parallel as well as e'er a frigate that was rigged to the northward of fifty".[31]

In spite of his own fondness for stemming the boisterous surge, Smollett is on Captain Crowe's side in the debate. The raptures and hyperboles of the declarations which Smollett's heroes at times make, are merely examples of his superficial conformity with the novel of his day. Nor are they wholly pre-posterous when one remembers that Random and Pickle are rough country lads trying to become fine gentlemen, and master-ing the forms of courtesy through books. One seldom finds a higher type of love in Smollett than the affable resignation of Hatchway when he supposes that Emilia is not much the worse for wear, and offers to "scud through life with her under an easy sail". *Peregrine Pickle* culminates on the animal transports, so long delayed, of the hero. On his wedding night, Random finds Narcissa "a feast a thousand times more delicious than my most sanguine hope presaged" and at the end of the novel is propriet-orially gratified by the sight of her rounding belly.

Yet it is the image of Narcissa which prevents Random from abandoning himself completely to despair in gaol. Indeed, he

> should have blessed the occasion that secluded me from such a perfidious world, had not the remembrance of the amiable Nar-cissa preserved my attachment to that society of which she con-stituted a part. The picture of that lovely creature was the con-stant companion of my solitude. How often did I contemplate the resemblance of those enchanting features that first captivated my heart![32]

Narcissa, for her part, displays a touching ardour in her attachment to her rogue-lover :

> Our vows being thus reciprocally breathed, a confidence of hope ensued, and our mutual fondness becoming as intimate as inno-cence would allow, I grew insensible of the progress of time, and it was morning before I could tear myself from this darling of my soul! My good angel foresaw what would happen, and per-mitted me to indulge myself on this occasion, in consideration of the fatal absence I was doomed to suffer.[33]

When Random visits her, at some risk to himself, in the garden to which her brother has confined her, her first thought is for Random's safety. He plays the characteristically conceited prank of leaving a miniature of himself on the table of an arbour where she will find it whilst he, in concealment, watches her display of emotion :

No sooner did she cast her eye upon the features, than, startled
at the resemblance, she cried, "Good God!" and the roses
instantly vanished from her cheeks. ... So saying, she kissed it
with surprising ardour, shed a flood of tears, and deposited the lifeless image in her lovely bosom. Transported at these symptoms of
her unaltered affection, I was about to throw myself at her feet,
when Miss Williams, whose reflection was less engaged than that
of her mistress, observed that the picture could not transport
itself hither, and that she could not help thinking I was not
far off. The gentle Narcissa, starting at this conjecture, answered,
"Heaven forbid! for although nothing in the universe could yield
me satisfaction equal to that of his presence for one poor moment,
in a proper place, I would rather forfeit his company almost
for ever, than see him here, where his life would be exposed to
so much danger." I could no longer restrain the impulse of my
passion, but, breaking from my concealment, stood before her,
when she uttered a fearful shriek, and fainted in the arms of her
companion. I flew towards the treasure of my soul, clasped her
in my embrace, and, with the warmth of my kisses, brought her
again to life. Oh, that I were endowed with the expression of a
Raphael, the graces of a Guido, the magic touches of a Titian,
that I might represent the fond concern, the chastened rapture,
and ingenuous blush that mingled on her beauteous face when she
opened her eyes upon me, and pronounced, "O heavens! is it
you?"[34]

There is something equally moving in the affection which
binds together several of Smollett's old married couples. The
Clewlines, debased by their misfortunes, and dram-drinking to
avoid the memory of their grief for their dead son, still have this
affection for each other:

Sometimes the recollection of their former rank comes over them
like a qualm, which they dispel with brandy, and then humorously
rally one another on their mutual degeneracy. She often stops me
in the walk, and, pointing to the captain, says, "My husband,
though he is become a blackguard jail-bird, must be allowed to be
a handsome fellow still." On the other hand, he will frequently
desire me to take notice of his rib, as she chances to pass. "Mind
that draggle-tailed drunken drab", he will say. "What an anti-
dote it is—yet, for all that, Felton, she was a fine woman when I
married her. Poor Bess, I have been the ruin of her, that is certain, and deserve to be damned for bringing her to this pass."
Thus they accommodate themselves to each other's infirmities,
and pass their time not without some taste of plebeian enjoyment

—but, name their child, they never fail to burst into tears, and still feel a return of the most poignant sorrow.[35]

Although abused and deserted by Fathom, Elinor returns to support him in his affliction. The excrescence of chance is at any rate a lasting one. The dying Commodore Trunnion is well aware of his wife's faults, but displays the same loving tolerance as the Clewlines, saying to Pickle :

> There's your aunt sitting whimpering by the fire; I desire you will keep her tight, warm, and easy in her old age; she's an honest heart in her own way, and, thof she goes a little crank and humoursome, by being often overstowed with Nantz and religion, she has been a faithful shipmate to me, and I daresay never turned in with another man since we first embarked in the same bottom.[36]

This is not "the Platonic system of sentimental love"[37] to which Smollett refers incredulously in *Ferdinand, Count Fathom,* but it is not so very unlike it. It is not Dante's Amor, which moves the Sun and the high stars, but it is something which transcends the final accident of Death. When Random's mother died, his father was deprived of his senses for six weeks and his delirium was "succeeded by a profound melancholy and reserve", which indeed never leaves him. In the account of how Random's father first meets Narcissa, his sadness is contrasted with his son's heedless impetuosity :

> He embraced her tenderly, and told her he was proud of having a son who had a spirit to attempt, and qualifications to engage, the affections of such a fine lady. She blushed at this compliment, and with eyes full of the softest languishment turned upon me, said, she should have been unworthy of Mr. Random's attention, had she been blind to his extraordinary merit. I made no other answer than a low bow. My father, sighing, pronounced, "Such once was my Charlotte !" while the tear rushed into his eye, and the tender heart of Narcissa manifested itself in two precious drops of sympathy, which, but for his presence, I would have kissed away.[38]

This quietly transcendant love Smollett depicts in an incident foreshadowing the hand of the man who was to record the death of Colonel Newcome, and to relate how Dobbin gave Amelia her piano—worthy of the endearing and compassionate Thackeray. It would be hard to find another novelist so capable of the unaffectedly pathetic as the sentimental Christian Thackeray and the anti-sentimental free-thinker Smollett. The incident takes place when the axle of Matt. Bramble's coach breaks:

In this dilemma, we discovered a blacksmith's forge on the edge of a small common, about half a mile from the scene of our disaster, and thither the postillions made shift to draw the carriage slowly, while the company walked a-foot; but we found the blacksmith had been dead some days; and his wife, who had been lately delivered, was deprived of her senses, under the care of a nurse hired by the parish. We were exceedingly mortified at this disappointment, which, however, was surmounted by the help of Humphry Clinker, who is a surprising compound of genius and simplicity. Finding the tools of the defunct, together with some coals in the smithy, he unscrewed the damaged iron in a twinkling, and, kindling a fire, united the broken pieces with equal dexterity and despatch. While he was at work upon this operation, the poor woman in the straw, struck with the well-known sound of the hammer and anvil, started up, and not-withstanding all the nurse's efforts, came running into the smithy, where, throwing her arms about Clinker's neck, "Ah, Jacob!" she cried, "how could you leave me in such a condition?"

This incident was too pathetic to occasion mirth—it brought tears into the eyes of all present. The poor widow was put to bed again; and we did not leave the village without doing something for her benefit. Even Tabitha's charity was awakened on this occasion. As for the tender-hearted Humphry Clinker, he hammered the iron and wept at the same time.[39]

Smollet represents love with all its frailties, but does not forget that from the frailties great strength can emerge.

CHAPTER VI

THE TOSSING UP OF A HALFPENNY

"An't you ashamed, fellow," Bramble asks Clinker, "to ride postillion without a shirt to cover your backside from the view of the ladies in the coach?" "Yes, I am, an please your noble honour (answered the man); but necessity has no law, as the saying is. And more than that, it was an accident. My breeches cracked behind, after I got into the saddle." "You're an impudent varlet (cried Mrs. Tabby), for presuming to ride before persons of fashion without a shirt." "I am so, an please your worthy ladyship (said he); but I'm a poor Wiltshire lad. I ha'n't a shirt in the world, that I can call my own, nor a rag of clothes, an please your ladyship, but what you see."[1]

Then Bramble passes judgment:

"Heark ye, Clinker, you are a most notorious offender. You stand convicted of sickness, hunger, wretchedness, and want."[2]

It is with this wry humanity that Smollett introduces the hero of his last novel. Circumstances, often malign, condition all conduct and all character. Everything is the result of chance, and there is nothing which can rectify the insect, accidental sufferings of mankind:

I am old enough (Smollett wrote to Garrick) to have seen and observed that we are all the playthings of Fortune, and that it depends on something as insignificant and precarious as the tossing up of a halfpenny, whether a man rises to affluence and honours, or continues to his dying day struggling with the difficulties and disgraces of life.[3]

Because of Smollett's conviction that we are the playthings of Fortune, the episodic novel was particularly well suited to him. It allowed him to display, in the manner of *Candide* or *Zadig,* a multiplicity of affairs operating on the hero. On these grounds even the creation of the improbable Sir Launcelot Greaves is, because of his ingenuous interventions in a corrupt world, justified. The innocent goodwill of such characters as

Strap, Clinker, and Greaves is trampled upon by the malice of events.

In his *History of England*, sedate though it is, Smollett puts forward the same notion of life as in his novels, giving prominence to the social consequences of each great event, each tossing-up of the political halfpenny. The *History of England* is not of the anecdotal type common in the eighteenth century. It is, to the point of severity, a business history, a history of the State's economy and the effects of that economy upon the community. Smollett pays special attention, for example, to the period of fashionable excess generated by the commercial bustle of the South Sea Bubble. "Intoxicated with their imaginary wealth", the speculators indulged themselves "without taste or discernment" in every luxury and means of ostentation they could procure. They "thought themselves above the normal rules of conduct, and conducted themselves with profligacy and insolence, convinced that they were too rich to be brought to account".[4] Throughout his *Travels* Smollett respects (too much at times) his friend Armstrong's injunction to take into account the effects of "the complexion, the clime, and the habitudes of life". With ludicrous facility he goes as far as to conclude that the Reformation never had a chance with the French, whose education had rendered them "a volatile, giddy, unthinking people, shocked at the mortified appearances of the Calvinists", whereas it did well "among nations of a more melancholy turn of character and complexion".[5]

Smollett's heroes are creatures of their surroundings. How could they be otherwise, Smollett enquires, in a world where all values are relative to material considerations? When Felton, a character in *Sir Launcelot Greaves*, reproaches a Mrs. Clewline with her unladylike behaviour in prison, she replies, "Hark ye, Felton, decorum is founded on a delicacy of sentiment and deportment, which cannot consist with the disgraces of a jail, and the miseries of indigence".[6] Conversely, good fortune improves a man's disposition. At the benevolent end of *Humphry Clinker*, the much-thwarted Lismahago comes in for his share in the general distribution of happiness. For the first time in his life he is treated kindly:

His temper, which had been soured and shrivelled by disappointment and chagrin, is now swelled out and smoothed like a raisin in plum-porridge. From being reserved and punctilious, he is become easy and obliging. He cracks jokes, laughs, and banters, with the most facetious familiarity; and, in a word, enters into all our schemes of merriment and pastime.[7]

Peregrine Pickle, pining in a debtors' prison "with an equal abhorrence of the world and himself", suddenly comes into the possession of £700 :

> The instantaneous effect which this unexpected smile of fortune produced in the appearance of our adventurer is altogther inconceivable; it plumped up his cheeks in a moment, unbended and enlightened every feature of his face; elevated his head, which had begun to sink, as it were, between his shoulders; and from a squeaking dispirited tone, swelled up his voice to a clear, manly accent.[8]

Dr. John Moore, in his recollections of Smollett, wrote that few men could penetrate into character as acutely as Smollett did, and added that nobody was more apt to overlook misconduct when it was accompanied by misfortune.[9] This is particularly true of Smollett's attitude to crime. He remarks, in his account of Nice, that "all the common people are thieves and beggars; and I believe this is always the case with people who are extremely indigent and miserable".[10] The lawlessness of the Boulonnois he attributes in part to their understandable mistrust of how the law is administered: "The interruption which is given, in arbitrary governments, to the administration of justice, by the interpretation of the great, has always a bad effect upon the morals of the common people." Moreover, the peasants are often driven to acts of savage desperation by "the misery they suffer from the oppression and tyranny of their landlords".[11]

Both in France and in England at that period of low wages and casual employment, the criminal was the necessary consequence and victim of the country's social organisation. Miserably housed and fed, with no resources of his own, the labourer or peasant needed only the slightest of economic pushes in order to transgress against the subtleties of a penal code which had a fastidious regard for property, but not much for human life. A child could be hanged for stealing a handkerchief,[12] but a woman who beat her girl apprentice to death could be given a pardon.[13] Every sixth week a cartload of felons was slaughtered at Tyburn. It is horrible to consider to what depraved refinements of cruelty offenders, without any succour beyond the pity of the few (who included Smollett), were submitted. In France they were broken

upon the wheel. In England in 1743 a certain Thomas Rounce
was tortured to death for fighting against his countrymen on a
Spanish privateer, although earlier Lord Bolingbroke, a person of
more consequence than Thomas Rounce, had escaped with something like impunity after siding with the enemy to the extent of
planning on their behalf the sort of war in which Thomas Rounce
suffered. Another slave of the social system, Mother Needham,
an ancient bawd who kept a brothel for men of fashion in St.
James's, and hoped that she might gain enough by her trade to
afford to give it up and repent, was allowed (on grounds of ill
health) to sit in the pillory to be pelted to death, instead of standing. Constantly the heads of those traitors whose acquaintance
was undistinguished hung on Wren's harmonious Temple Bar,
alongside its classical statues.

"A mere sanguinary chaos" is what Lecky calls the eighteenth-
century penal code. Justices of the Peace had autocratic local
power, being charged with most of the functions of the modern
borough council as well as the administration of the law. The
London constabulary made up its own rules, as in the episode of
the Black Hole of St. Martin's Lane in 1742. A party of drunken
constables cleared the streets of twenty-five female strays, including a washerwoman big with child and returning late from work,
and shut them up all night in the tiny round-house, so that four
of them died of suffocation. As the compassionate Horace Walpole, who tells the story, says, "several of them were beggars,
who, having no lodging, were necessarily found in the street".[14]
On the same night the exuberant band of constables raided a
brothel and found Lord Graham and the son of the Duke of
Sutherland there. They intended to put them in the round-house
too, but were bribed out of it.

The supposed humanity of Henry Fielding is hardly demonstrated in his pamphlet of 1751 on the increase of robbers, in
which he advocates the "terror of the example" of the death
penalty, which was beginning to be superseded by transportation,
for theft. He writes with contempt of "ill-judging tenderness and
compassion".[15] To Smollett's great credit his view was here, as
so often, different from that of Fielding. Smollett was in favour
of the death penalty for the survivor of a duel, since, once again
in opposition to Fielding, he regarded duelling as a form of con-
doned murder, but in his *History of England* he joins with
Horace Walpole in deploring the use of capital punishment for
offences against property; the "pompous and tedious procession

of above two hours" to the six-weekly beastliness at Tyburn.[16]
Smollett was always aware of the need behind the offence, and
there is a great deal in his novels about the economic causes of
crime.

Roderick Random, desperate from his losses and unable to
obtain enough money to be acceptable to the family of his
Narcissa, thinks for a moment of turning highwayman :

> While we crossed Bagshot Heath, I was seized with a sort of in-
> clination to retrieve my fortune, by laying passengers under con-
> tribution in some such place. My thoughts were so circumstanced
> at this time, that I should have digested the crime of robbery, so
> righteously had I concerted my plan, and ventured my life in
> the execution, had I not been deterred by reflecting upon the in-
> famy that attends detection.[17]

Martin, the mysterious highwayman of *Humphry Clinker*, has
been thrust into a life of crime :

> Shall I own to you that this portrait, drawn by a ruffian, height-
> ened by what I myself had observed in his deportment, has in-
> terested me warmly in the fate of poor Martin, whom nature
> seems to have intended for a useful and honourable member of
> that community upon which he now preys for a subsistence? It
> seems he lived some time as a clerk to a timber merchant, whose
> daughter Martin having privately married, he was discarded,
> and his wife turned out of doors. She did not long survive her
> marriage; and Martin, turning fortune-hunter, could not supply
> his occasions any other way than by taking to the road, in which
> he has travelled hitherto with uncommon success.[18]

Unlike Random, Martin has no Strap, no obliging uncle, to free
him from his difficulties. As one of the characters remarks, this
man, potentially an asset to society, "is fluttering about justice
like a moth about a candle. There are so many lime-twigs laid
in his way that I'll bet a cool hundred he swings before Christmas". Eagerly Martin snatches at any chance which will give
lawful scope to his abilities, writing in the following terms to
Matt. Bramble :

> Sir,—I could easily perceive from your looks when I had the
> honour to converse with you at Hatfield, that my character is
> not unknown to you; and I dare say you won't think it strange,
> that I should be glad to change my present way of life for any
> other honest occupation, let it be ever so humble, that will afford
> me bread in moderation, and sleep in safety. Perhaps you may

think I flatter, when I say that, from the moment I was witness to your generous concern in the cause of your servant,
I conceived a particular esteem and veneration for your
person; and yet what I say is true. I should think myself happy,
if I could be admitted into your protection and service, as house-
steward, clerk, butler, or bailiff, for either of which places I think
myself tolerably well qualified; and sure I am I should not be
found deficient in gratitude and fidelity.[19]

With pathetic solicitude Martin follows Bramble's entourage
from London to Stockton-on-Tees. Bramble, who has influence
and is disposed to use it well, obtains Martin a commission in the
service of the East Indies Company. Martin, after all, does not
"swing before Christmas", but he owes his life to a haphazard
encounter and a chance benevolence.

It is true that nowadays, when most of the liberalism to which
Smollett contributed has been written into the law of the land,
and there are few of the economic compulsions which there
were in his time, the number of crimes of stealth in proportion
to the population has been reduced. Only rarely is an old-age-
pensioner sent to prison for stealing a few rashers of bacon, and
one can say that in general the right people are rightly punished.
But unfortunately Smollett's main contention—that the greater
welfare of the country as a whole would end crime by removing
its causes—has not been proven. In our own time it is crimes of
disinterested violence, the prerogative of the aristocracy in the
eighteenth century, which are prevalent. The advent of the proletarian Mohock suggests that prosperity, whilst ill-informed and
undisciplined, leads to mischief just as certainly as deprivation
leads to theft. Perhaps Smollett's secondary contention, which
will be dealt with later, and which is that Education largely determines conduct, is more relevant to us today.

Whilst there is little excuse for a woman in modern English
society who chooses to become a prostitute, in the eighteenth
century there were certain women for whom that calling was
inevitable. The sufferings of Mrs. Williams, in *Roderick Random*,
are what the jolly wenchings described in Boswell's journals entailed for the women concerned. Hogarth's *Harlot's Progress* is
not cautionary like his *Rake's Progress*, but a record of social
wrong. Whilst the priest of the first engraving looks the other
way, the girl is tricked into wickedness, poxed, cheated, imprisoned and allowed to perish. An eighteenth-century observer
described the imprisoned prostitutes at Bridewell: "about twenty

young creatures, the eldest not exceeding sixteen, many of them
with angelic faces, divested of every angelic expression, and
featured with impudence, impenitency and profligacy and
clothed in the silken tatters of squalid finery".[20] "The eldest not
exceeding sixteen"—what an unconscious indictment, not of the
unfortunate little girls, but of the state of that society! Armstrong,
in his *Economy of Love*, speculates on the fate of prostitutes
who, with better luck and guidance, might have made good
wives. Smollett too regards the eighteenth-century prostitute as
"unfortunate, not criminal". In his *History* he calls her "the
most forlorn of all human creatures" and blames the savagery
of circumstance for "these unhappy creatures, so wretched in
themselves and so productive of mischief to society". He applauds
the foundation of the Magdalen Hospital for these women.[21]

After a night of debauch Roderick Random accompanies his
acquaintance Bragwell "to Moll King's coffee-house, where, after
he had kicked half a dozen hungry whores, we left him asleep".[22]
In his frequent relationships with prostitutes Boswell, who was
capable of rebuking the mother of his illegitimate son for falling
into such a scrape, showed scarcely more humanity than Bragwell. His *London Journal* has many entries like the following
one, written when he had been in London for six days:

> I had now been some time in town without female sport ... I
> was really unhappy for want of women. I thought it hard to be in
> such a place without them. I picked up a girl in the Strand; went
> into a court with intention to enjoy her.[23]

Later he determined to have nothing more to do with whores, as
his health was of great consequence to him and surgeons' fees
were high in London. As for the health of the whores, that was
of no consequence. When he was afterwards stricken with a
probably recurrent disease of long standing, he sent a letter of
ferocious accusation to the demi-mondaine who had yielded to
his importunities ("a Winter's safe copulation"), demanding the
return of two guineas in order to defray the expenses of his cure.

Roderick Random speaks for Smollett when, pitying Mrs.
Williams for the miseries of her profession, he says:

> Her condition filled me with sympathy and compassion; I re-
> vered her qualifications, looked upon her as unfortunate, not
> criminal.[24]

Although intelligent, well educated and spirited, Mrs. Williams is repeatedly tricked, her passionate and impetuous character making her an easy victim, and is ultimately betrayed into prostitution by the only person she can turn to in her friendlessness and poverty :

> Accordingly, I was almost every night engaged with company, among whom I was exposed to every mortification, danger, and abuse, that flow from drunkeness, brutality, and disease. How miserable is the condition of a courtezan, whose business it is to soothe, suffer and obey the dictates of rage, insolence, and lust! As my spirit was not sufficiently humbled to the will, nor my temper calculated for the conversation of my gallants, it was impossible for me to overcome an aversion I felt for my profession, which manifested itself in a settled gloom on my countenance, and disgusted those sons of mirth and riot so much, that I was frequently used in a shocking manner, and kicked downstairs with disgrace.

She is committed in error to Bridewell :

> Here I saw nothing but rage, anguish, and impiety; and heard nothing but groans, curses, and blasphemy. In the midst of this hellish crew, I was subjected to the tyranny of a barbarian, who imposed upon me tasks that I could not possibly perform, and then punished my incapacity with the utmost rigour and inhumanity. I was often whipped into a swoon, and lashed out of it, during which miserable intervals I was robbed by my fellow-prisoners of everything about me, even to my cap, shoes, and stockings; I was not only destitute of necessaries, but even of food; so that my wretchedness was extreme.

Overwhelmed by so many undeserved misfortunes, she tries to take her own life, and is punished with thirty stripes. When it is discovered that she has been wrongfully imprisoned, she is discharged without apology or compensation, and obliged to accept an offer made to her by the keeper of a brothel :

> The conditions of her offer were, that I should pay three guineas weekly for my board, and a reasonable consideration besides for the use of such clothes and ornaments as she should supply me with, to be deducted from the first profits of my embraces. These were hard terms; but not to be rejected by one who was turned out helpless and naked into the wide world, without a friend to pity or assist her.

A rumour that she suffers from venereal disease reduces the number of her customers, and consequently her ability to pay her way, although she is temporarily relieved by one of Smollett's sea-dogs, as usual replete with kindness, nautical metaphors and ready cash:

> Though the room was crowded with people when the bailiff entered, not one of them had compassion enough to mollify my prosecutrix, far less to pay the debt. They even laughed at my tears; and one of them bade me be of good cheer, for I should not want admirers in Newgate. At that instant, a sea-lieutenant came in, and seeing my plight, began to inquire into the circumstances of my misfortune; when this wit advised him to keep clear of me, for I was a fire-ship. "A fire-ship!" replied the sailor, "more like a poor galley in distress, that has been boarded by such a fire-ship as you; if so be as that is the case, she stands in more need of assistance. Hark'ee, my girl, how far have you over-run the constable?"

She sinks ever lower down the graduations of her profession, becoming at last a street-walker:

> I have often sauntered between Ludgate Hill and Charing Cross a whole winter night, exposed not only to the inclemency of the weather, but likewise to the rage of hunger and thirst, without being so happy as to meet with one cully; then creep up to my garret in a deplorable draggled condition, sneak to bed, and try to bury my appetite and sorrows in sleep. When I lighted on some rake or tradesman reeling home drunk, I frequently suffered the most brutal treatment, in spite of which I was obliged to affect gaiety and good humour, though my soul was stung with resentment and disdain.[25]

Thus she is reduced to the state in which Random finds her, groaning and starving on a truckle-bed in a garret near St. Giles's:

> As I was impatient to know the occasion and nature of her calamity, she gave me to understand, that she was a woman of the town by profession; that, in the course of her adventures, she found herself dangerously infected with a distemper to which all of her class are particularly subject; that her malady gaining ground every day, she became loathsome to herself and offensive to others; when she resolved to retire to some obscure corner, where she might be cured with as little noise and expense as possible; that she had accordingly chosen this place of retreat, and put herself into the hands of an advertising doctor, who, having fleeced her of all the money she had, or could procure,

left her three days ago in a worse condition than that in which he found her.[26]

Having told Random her private story, Mrs. Williams expounds the general miseries of the prostitute's lot:

"I have often seen," said she, "while I strolled about the streets at midnight, a number of naked wretches reduced to rags and filth, huddled together like swine, in the corner of a dark alley; some of whom, but eighteen months before, I had known the favourites of the town, rolling in affluence, and glittering in all the pomp of equipage and dress. And indeed the gradation is easily conceived. The most fashionable woman of the town is as liable to contagion as one in a much humbler sphere. . . . Nobody will afford her lodgings; the symptoms of her distemper are grown outrageous; she sues to be admitted into an hospital, where she is cured at the expense of her nose; she is turned out naked into the streets, depends upon the addresses of the lowest class, is fain to allay the rage of hunger and cold with gin; degenerates into a brutal, insensibility, rots and dies upon a dunghill. Miserable wretch that I am! Perhaps the same horrors are decreed for me."[27]

But the same horrors are not decreed for Mrs. Williams. Cured by Random and befriended by Narcissa, she ends by becoming the irreproachable Mrs. Strap.

As Smollett sees it, economics, which accounts for criminals and prostitutes, accounts in turn for fine gentlemen. When Random, Melinda's suitor, protests his gentility to Melinda's mother, she asks him to "favour her with the perusal of his rent-roll".[28] Smollett describes the trade in titles in Southern France, where a man can become a marquis for three hundred pounds. On the other hand, there are many members of the ancient nobility who are too poor "to maintain their dignity", and have dwindled to the condition of peasants. He tells the story of "one of these rustic nobles, who called to his son in the evening, 'Chevalier, as-tu donné à manger les cochons?' ('Have you fed the hogs, Sir Knight?')"[29] The fashionable English definition of a gentleman is given in *Roderick Random*: "Upon my word, a mighty pretty sort of gentleman—a man of fortune, sir—he has made the grand tour, and seen the best company in Europe, sir."[30]

In our own country the establishment of the Bank of England has signalised the triumph of the commercial interest over the landed one, and it was as an expert on finance and the intimate of financiers that Sir Robert Walpole reached the position from which he was able to impose his own special turn of mind upon a whole century. The ascendant mercantile class was one which Smollett hated. Quite apart from his sincere detestation of its venality and its ignorant presumption he had a particular reason for his hatred. Although by the Act of Union, Scotland, with its nominal and servile representation in Parliament by the land-owners of the ruling party, lost its political independence, it gained the commercial rights of the Empire, a fact which was resented by the English merchants, especially as the trade route from America to Europe now went up the Clyde and down the Forth, through Glasgow instead of London. They took every opportunity to abuse and damn the Scots, and Smollett heartily abused and damned them back, sending them about their business with the observation that they were

> a mob of impudent plebeians, who have neither understanding nor judgement, nor the least idea of propriety and decorum, and seem to enjoy nothing so much as an opportunity of insulting their betters.[31]

The dandified young usurer in *Fathom* excuses himself in these terms :

> I soon observed that without money there was no respect, honour, or convenience to be acquired in life; that wealth amply supplied the want to wit, merit, and pedigree, having influence and plea-sure ever at command; and that the world never failed to worship the flood of affluence, without examining the dirty channels through which it commonly flowed.[32]

The transition from class to class is in fact a matter of money, as Peregrine Pickle finds out in the debtors' prison :

> "If you will take the trouble of going into the cook's kitchen," said he, "you will perceive a beau metamorphosed into a turn-spit; and there are some hewers of wood and drawers of water in this microcosm, who have had forests and fish-ponds of their own."[33]

Roderick Random has been gambling with his fashionable friends, the stakes being provided by Strap. When he comes home, Strap ventures to ask how much he has lost :

> "Why, I suppose, if you had a bad run last night, you would scarce come off for less than ten or twelve shillings." I was morti-fied at this piece of simplicity, which I imagined, at that time, as all affected, by way of reprimand for my folly; and asked with

some heat, if he thought I spent the evening in a cellar with chair-
men and bunters; giving him to know at the same time that my
expenses had amounted to eighteen guineas.[34]

Money, then, however dirtily acquired, is what fits a man for
good society—money and a few easily learnt mannerisms:

> Nay, he moreover observed that the conversation of those who
> are dignified with the appellation of polite company, is neither
> more edifying nor entertaining than that which is met with
> among the lower classes of mankind; and that the only essential
> difference, in point of demeanour, is the form of an education,
> which the meanest capacity can acquire without much study or
> application.[35]

The oyster-wench whom Mr. Hornbeck marries is able to pick
up the correct mannerisms so quickly that on her honeymoon
she already passes for a lady of fashion:

> She returned the compliment with a curtsey, and appeared so
> decent in her dress and manner, that unless he had been pre-
> viously informed of her former life and conversation, he never
> would have dreamt that her education was different from that of
> other ladies of fashion; so easy is it to acquire that external
> deportment on which people of condition value themselves so
> much. Not but that Mr. Pickle pretended to distinguish a certain
> vulgar audacity in her countenance, which in a lady of birth and
> fortune would have passed for an agreeable vivacity that enlivens
> the aspect and gives poignancy to every feature.[36]

That "external deportment" signifies very little is ludicrously
proved by the letter which Mrs. Hornbeck writes to Peregrine
Pickle in Paris:

> "Coind Sur,—Heaving the playsure of meating with you at the
> ofspital of anvilheads, I take this lubbertea of latin you know, that
> I lotch at the Hottail de May cong dangle rouy Doghousten, with
> two postis at the gait, naytheir of um very hole, ware I shall be
> at the windore, if in kais you will be so good as to pass that way
> at sicks a cloak in the heavening, when Mr. Hornbeck goes to the
> Calf hay de contea. Prey for the loaf of Geesus keep this from
> the nolegs of my hussban, ells he will make me leed a hell upon
> urth. Being all from, deer Sur, your most umbel servan wile
> DEBORAH HORNBECK.[37]

Smollett considered the beau monde to be mercenary in origin
and false in its manifestations. With articulate and forceful scorn
he writes of "that goal of perfection":

Yes, refined reader, we are hastening to that goal of perfection, where satire dares not show her face; where nature is castigated, almost even to still life; where humour turns changeling, and slavers in an insipid grin; where wit is volatilised into a mere vapour; where decency, divested of all substance, hovers about like a fantastic shadow; where the salt of genius, escaping, leaves nothing but pure and simple phlegm; and the inoffensive pen for ever drops the mild manna of soul-sweetening praise.[38]

This world of fashion enshrines and upholds distinctions between man and man based on mere accident. At the end of *Humphry Clinker*, Matt. Bramble discovers that the shirtless postillion was his own bastard. At the end of *Launcelot Greaves*, the hero, the patrician-by-circumstance, embraces his kinswoman, the plebeian-by-circumstance, Dolly Cowslip. The distance between Bramble and Clinker, between Greaves and Dolly, is measurable only in terms of money and the sort of education which can easily be acquired, given the money.

Smollett is not even sure whether such an education is a good thing to have. Always contemptuous of Shaftesbury's ideas, he had little patience for the theory that "to philosophise in a just signification is but to carry good breeding a little higher". He finds sounder moral qualities in "low" life. The cook and the dairy maid who both fall in love with Roderick Random, settle their differences by scolding and fisticuffs, not by the poison or the steel which they would have used "if their sentiments had been refined by education". The gipsy whom Pickle trains as a fine lady plays her part well until one day she detects a dowager cheating at cards, and plainly speaks her mind.

Strap is by far a better man than the worthless Roderick Random, that ruffian, spendthrift, deserter and inexpert imposter who is saved from final destitution only by the peripety which provides him with a fixed income. The discussion of what to do with Strap's legacy brings out Roderick Random's complete uselessness :

The business was to make ourselves easy for life by means of his legacy, a task very difficult, and, in the usual methods of laying out money, altogether impracticable; so that after much canvassing, we could come to no resolution that night, but when we parted, recommended the matter to the serious attention of each other. As for my own part, I puzzled my imagination to no purpose. When I thought of turning merchant, the smallness of our stock, and the risk of seas, enemies, and markets, deterred me from that scheme. If I should settle as a surgeon in my own country, I would find the business already overstocked; or, if I pretended to set up in England, must labour under want of friends, and powerful opposition, obstacles insurmountable by the most shining merit. Neither should I succeed in my endeavours to rise in the state, inasmuch as I could neither flatter nor pimp for courtiers, nor prostitute my pen in defence of a wicked and contemptible administration. Before I could form any feasible project, I fell asleep, and my fancy was blessed with the imagine of the dear Narcissa, who seemed to smile upon my passion, and offer her hand as a reward for all my toils.[39]

Strap provides the economic basis for Random's gentility. When he has lost Strap's money at play, Random, instead of trying to come to terms with a practical situation, adopts an inane theatrical posture.

"On my own account," said he, "I am quite unconcerned; for, while God spares me health and these ten fingers, I can earn a comfortable subsistence anywhere; but what must become of you, who have less humility to stoop, and more appetites to gratify?" Here I interrupted him, by saying, with a gloomy aspect, I should never want a resource while I had a loaded pistol in possession.[40]

Random would rather shoot himself than disentangle his own affairs. Base and callow, he is elevated into position of authority by a denouement to which his own efforts have contributed nothing whatever.

In his *Travels* Smollett assembles a great deal of evidence for John Locke's contention that most men are the products of their education. Whilst allowing for the "natural levity" of the French, Smollett suggests that this "is reinforced by the most preposterous education and the example of a giddy people, engaged in the most frivolous pursuits".[41] They are encouraged from infancy to be too voluble. "At the same time they obtain an absolute conquest over all sense of shame, or rather they avoid acquiring this troublesome sensation; for it is certainly no innate idea."[42] He attributes the irrational code of honour of the average French military officer to

a fundamental error in the first principles of his education, which time rather confirms than removes. Early prejudices are for the most part converted into habits of thinking.[43]

Commenting on his own pleasure at seeing the white cliffs of Dover, Smollett generalises:

That seems to be a kind of fanaticism founded on the prejudices of education, which induces a Laplander to place the terrestial paradise among the snows of Norway, and a Swiss to prefer the barren mountains of Solleure to the fruitful plains of Lombardy.[44]

Yet one has only to consider the difference between the kind of Smollett one might expect from his education and the aggressive embodiment of human strength that he actually was, in order to realise that the argument is not quite so pat. The very fact that he gave up medicine and wrote novels instead suggests that there was more to him than can be credited to his early training, and the degree to which he conformed to the sentiments of his time and place was conspicuously slight.

The career of Ferdinand, Count Fathom, amply illustrates Locke's contention. The depravity which he inherits from his parents is nourished by the circumstances in which he finds himself. Born to disadvantages, he soon notices that he is much cleverer than his nominal superior, Renaldo.

This mirror of modern chivalry was none of those who owe their dignity to the circumstances of their birth, and are consecrated from the cradle for the purposes of greatness, merely because they are the accidental children of wealth. He was heir to no visible patrimony, unless we reckon a robust constitution, a tolerable appearance, and an uncommon capacity, as the advantages of inheritance.[45]

He tries to haul himself up to Renaldo's level by an equalising delinquency. Like Ferrett, in *Sir Launcelot Greaves,* he thinks that "every man has a right to avail himself of his talents, even at the expense of his fellow creatures".[46] Thereafter he is more often than not in a position where he must betray or be betrayed. He has been recruited to Hobbes' "war of all men against all men":

He had formerly imagined, but was now fully persuaded, that the sons of men preyed upon one another, and such was the end and condition of their being. Among the principal figures of life he observed few or no characters that did not bear a strong analogy to the savage tyrants of the woods. One resembled a tiger in fury and rapaciousness; a second prowled around like a hungry wolf, seeking whom he might devour; a third acted the part of a jackal in beating the bush for his voracious employer; and a fourth imitated the wily fox, in practising a thousand crafty ambuscades for the ignorant and unwary. This last was the department of life for which he found himself best qualified by nature and inclination.[47]

Smollett stresses the rapacity of Fathom's associates. The episode of the bandits' den shows how completely Fathom has been reduced to a position of *sauve qui peut*. As they are passing through a forest at night, Fathom's guide makes an excuse to drop behind, whilst Fathom rides on, expecting the guide to catch up with him :

> He was, however, disappointed in that hope; the sound of the other horse's feet by degrees grew more and more faint, and at last died altogether away. Alarmed at this circumstance, Fathom halted in the middle of the road, and listened with the most fearful attention; but his sense of hearing was saluted with naught but the dismal sighings of the trees, that seemed to foretell an approaching storm.[48]

Amid the tumult of the storm he leaves the road, where he is afraid of meeting robbers, and makes his way through the boggy undergrowth to a cottage at which an old woman offers him shelter. She leads him up to a loft and leaves him, locking the door on the outside :

> Fathom, whose own principles taught him to be suspicious, and ever upon his guard against the treachery of his fellow-creatures, could have dispensed with this instance of her care, in confining her guest to her chamber, and began to be seized with strange fancies when he observed that there was no bolt to the inside of the door, by which he might secure himself from intrusion. In consequence of these suggestions, he proposed to take an accurate survey of every object in the apartment, and, in the course of his inquiry, had the mortification to find the dead body of a man, still warm, who had been lately stabbed, and concealed beneath several bundles of straw.

Terrified, he rushes into measures for his own preservation. He undresses the corpse and puts it into bed. Later, in concealment, he watches this representation of himself stabbed twice in the chest by the old woman's accomplices. The next morning he comes out of hiding, seizes the old woman and, "the muzzle of his pistol close at her ear", forces her to ride with him to the nearest town.

> He set her upon the saddle without delay, and, mounting behind, invested her with the management of the reins, swearing, in a most peremptory tone, that the only chance she had for her life

was in directing him safely to the next town; and that, so soon as she should give him the least cause to doubt her fidelity in the performance of that task, he would on the instant act the part of her executioner.[49]

He does not hand her over to justice as, if he did so, he would have to give up the articles of which he himself took the opportunity of robbing the corpse. On the contrary, she is the one who, as soon as he dismisses her, goes to the magistrates, to impeach him of the murder. Fathom is like one of the trapped rats of Webster's tragedies.

Fathom's education continues throughout the novel. For this reason there is nothing unlikely in his repentance at the end, and his re-appearance in *Humphry Clinker* as the unaffectedly virtuous apothecary, Grieve. His sickness, and the danger of his death, contribute to his reform, in that they bring to his notice realities larger than a successful career. But what is more important is that he receives the first pause in the rush of his more and more involved affairs. The pause is long enough for him to discover the fallacy of Hobbes' doctrines and to realise that the first principle of human subsistence is not war but mutual aid in its two forms: the imperfect but developing form established by society, and the perfect form derived from those sentiments of benevolence and compassion, the innate existence of which Smollett so strenuously denied and so amply demonstrated in his life and works. The way of life represented by Renaldo's tender heart and Elinor's fidelity is set against the way of life represented by the bandits' den, and it is clear which is the right one:

> All his prospects of gaiety had now vanished, and his heart was softened by his own misfortunes to a feeling of another's woe, as well as to a due sense of his own guilt.[50]

Hitherto Fathom could not draw back from the wash of Hobbesian dogma on which he had embarked. He had exploited the situations in which he had found himself but those situations had not been of his own choosing. The course of his villainy had been determined by inheritance and environment, both of them matters of chance.

CHAPTER VII

A COMPETENT SHARE OF BANKNOTES

THE POLITICAL MORALITY of the Georgians was to make a profit, their fanaticism the rights of property. Most of the two hundred capital offences were crimes against the possessions of others. A woman could not be burnt to death for her religion but she could be hanged for stealing a square yard of cloth. Those who had money were determined to keep it, since it was upon money that the social order was based. There were no restrictions, as in France, upon movement from class to class, no laws to prevent rich traders from acquiring land and the rights which the ownership of land entailed, such as the qualification for Parliamentary candidature. Although one peer claimed fatuously that he looked upon pensions "as a kind of obligation upon the crown for support of ancient noble families whose peerages happen to continue after their estates are worn out",[1] it was wealth, not aristocracy, which now counted. Smollett's Captain Minikin[2] may rail against the *canaille* and the *profanum vulgus*, but he rails as the occupant of a debtors' prison where he has for company a failed king, a mendicant major and a knight whose breeches have been bought for him by the modest gaoler. In the microcosm of the debtors' prison to which Peregrine Pickle is committed there are, as we have seen, "some hewers of wood and drawers of water who have had forests and fishponds of their own".[3]

1688 had been a victory primarily for the commercial class, who (the Roundheads of an earlier generation) admired and copied the busily trading, godly Dutch and brought over a Dutch king to head a state reconstituted on the Dutch model. A conservative like Congreve, writing in a tradition unsympathetic to the age, might grumble about rascally citizens who bought coats of arms at the Heralds' College, but the old animosity between the Court and the City ends of the town lingered only faintly. The merging of the landowners and the merchants, particularly by marriages such as the one portrayed in Hogarth's *Marriage à la Mode*, resulted in the man who gave the century its particular bent. On his father's side Sir Robert Walpole was descended from the squirearchy, the outward characteristics of which he zealously cultivated. On his mother's side he came from a line of City financiers, whose ancestral voices probably spoke to him more quietly but much more to the purpose.

At such pleasure resorts as Vauxhall and Ranelagh, where anyone who could pay was admitted, members of both classes mixed as equals to the extent of their purses. At Bath they accepted a common discipline imposed by Nash, and the marks of social distinction were put on a regular cash basis. As Matthew Bramble complains :

> Every upstart of fortune, harnessed in the trappings of the mode, presents himself at Bath, as in the very focus of observation. Clerks and factors from the East Indies, loaded with the spoil of plundered provinces; planters, negro-drivers, and hucksters, from our American plantations, enriched they know not how; agents, commissaries, and contractors, who have fattened, in two successive wars, on the blood of the nation; userers, brokers and jobbers of every kind; men of low birth and no breeding, have found themselves suddenly translated into a state of affluence unknown to former ages; and no wonder that their brains should be intoxicated with pride, vanity and presumption. Knowing no other criterion of greatness but the ostentation of wealth, they discharge their affluence without taste or conduct, through every channel of the most absurd extravagance; and all of them hurry to Bath, because here, without any farther qualification, they can mingle with the princes and nobles of the land.[4]

In order to see Smollett's criticisms of the misdistribution of wealth in their perspective, we must take into account the fact that in 1688 (according to Gregory King's economic tables drawn up at the time[5]) there were 160 aristocratic families holding a near-monopoly of high offices of state and possessing yearly incomes of over £3,000. Roughly 60 per cent of the population consisted of families with yearly incomes of under £50, and 799,000 families (48 per cent of the population) had yearly incomes of under £15. With such inequality was the nation's wealth distributed that the yearly income of the poorest temporal lord was more than that of 213 labourers or 64 farmers. During the eighteenth century there was a great increase in the total national income, but at the end of the century the state of the labouring poor was the same as it had been at the beginning.[6] There had been no advance whatever in their standard of living. The new wealth remained in the hands of a still severely limited although in one respect enlarged governing class. The weighty dandies of the reign of Queen Anne, a little stupid with port perhaps, but hitherto with nobody in a position to oppose or outwit them, had been joined and sometimes even edged out by financiers like Sir Joshua Vannek, who made a considerable profit out of the Seven Years War, and Sampson Gideon, the friend and adviser of Sir Robert Walpole. In a note to *Reproof* Smollett describes Vannek and Gideon as being two of "a triumvirate of contractors who, scorning the narrow views of private usury, found means to lay a whole state under contribution, and pillage a kingdom of immense sums, under the protection of law".[7]

Such a member of the new elite was the swindler Francis Chartres, about whom Arbuthnot wrote the famous epitaph beginning, "Here continueth to rot". By lending money at compound interest to the landed gentry, and seizing their estates when they were unable to repay him, Chartres garnered a fortune computed by Alexander Pope to be seven thousand pounds a year in land and about one hundred thousand in money.[8] George II himself was known for his dishonesty about money. He destroyed one copy of his father's will and bought the other (which he also destroyed) from the Duke of Wolfenbuttle in exchange for a pension. The will was believed to have contained a large bequest to the Duchess of Kendal. According to Horace Walpole, "the Earl of Chesterfield, who married the Countess of Walsingham, niece and heiress of the Duchess of Kendal, commenced or threatened a suit for the Duchess' legacy, and was supposed to be quitted by a sum of £20,000".[9] Later, having spent two-and-a-half million pounds of his private income on his Hanoverian wars, George II was obliged to borrow £400,000 from international financiers.[10] Even so, thanks to the inflated Civil List which Sir Robert Walpole obtained for him from an acquiescent Parliament, the king was able to leave a large fortune to the Duke of Cumberland upon his death, as payment for Culloden. The least deserved financial success of all, that of Admiral Vernon, must have been particularly repugnant to Smollett. Vernon was in charge of the attack on Carthagena. As a reward he received an ample sum of money, a directorship of the New Herring Fisheries and the freedom of the City of London.

The king and Francis Chartres were not alone in realising the importance of money in the civilisation to which they belonged. When Winifred Jenkins, the maid-servant in *Humphry Clinker*, makes an advantageous marriage, she treats Mrs. Jones, the fellow servant to whom she was formerly an "ever-loving friend", with great mis-spelt condescension :

> Being by God's blessing, removed to a higher spear, you'll excuse my being familiar with the lower sarvents of the family; but as I trust you'll behave respectful, and keep a proper distance, you may always depend upon the good-will and purtection of, yours, W. LOYD.[11]

The reason why Fathom is accepted by London society as "the charming man" and "the non-pareil" is the letter (forged by himself and dexterously made public) describing him as a man of considerable wealth. Lismahago, lacking money, cannot rise above the rank of lieutenant in spite of thirty years' dedication and hardship in the army :

> We were immediately interested in behalf of this veteran. Even Tabby's heart was melted; but our pity was warmed with indignation, when we learned that, in the course of two sanguinary wars, he had been wounded, maimed, mutilated, taken and enslaved, without having ever attained a higher rank than that of lieutenant. My uncle's eyes gleamed, and his nether lip quivered while he exclaimed, "I vow to God, sir, your case is a reproach to the service; the injustice you have met with is so flagrant." "I must crave your pardon, sir," cried the other, interrupting him, "I complain of no injustice. I purchased an ensigncy thirty years ago; and, in the course of service, rose to be a lieutenant, according to my seniority—" "But in such a length of time," resumed the squire, "you must have seen a great many young officers put over your head." "Nevertheless," said he, "I have no cause to murmur. They bought their preferment with their money. I had no money to carry to market—that was my misfortune; but nobody was to blame."[12]

On the other hand, Peregrine Pickle is able to obtain a captaincy for Geoffrey Gauntlett by renouncing a gambling debt of £2,000 owed him by an earl's son.

The traditional awards of attainment could be obtained more directly by making money, and to the making of money was diverted a great deal of talent which could have been used for the betterment of the state. Ingenious projects for making salt water fresh, for extracting silver from lead, for fishing up wrecks on the Irish coast, for transmuting quicksilver into malleable metal, for trading in human hair, for importing jack-asses from Spain, for draining bogs in Ireland, even for "an undertaking which shall in due time be revealed", all found ready investors.[13] Gambling, by which as much as ten thousand pounds could change hands overnight, possessed even such men as Addison and Chesterfield. Chesterfield, when ambassador to Holland, "courted the good opinion of that economical people by losing immense sums at play".[14] He also won such large sums at court that he had to deposit them overnight for safety with Mrs. Howard, who lived there. James Fox (an invalid) sat up all night gambling between a day at Newmarket and a sitting of the House of Commons.[15] Beau Nash bet that a certain footman could run from Bath to London and back in a stipulated time. The footman did so, collapsed, and died. Beau Nash got up a collection for his widow. For a bet of a guinea Lord Cobham spat in the hat of one of his guests.[16] Sir Robert Walpole had a bet with Pulteney during a debate in the House of Commons, calling upon the speaker to adjudicate and throwing down his stake on the floor of the House. Such was the whirl of speculation and gambling that one weak-minded nobleman wrote, shortly before losing his whole fortune in the South Sea Bubble: "I grow rich so fast that I like stock-jobbing best of all things." It will be remembered that Roderick Random, Peregrine Pickle and Count Fathom all lose in such pursuits much of the money which they so improperly came by.

The supreme achievement for the frantic eighteenth-century money-maker would have been to ascend into one of the four families (the Churchills, the Pelhams, the Stanhopes and the Granvilles) which, with their connections by marriage, largely managed the country. The vast spread of these families took in six First Lords of the Treasury (Prime Ministers) and fifteen Secretaries of State (Foreign Secretaries) in the space of the hundred years between 1710 and 1810. In 1710 there were fifty-one members of one family in Parliament. Walpole was linked, by his sister's marriage, with the Pelhams, who in turn were connected by marriage with the Churchills, into which family had married the son of Godolphin. Chatham's uncle by marriage was a Stanhope. As solidly flank-to-flank as a row of pigs delectating in the same trough, they left no gap for the deserving outsider to push through. To have his tragedy acted Smollett first was obliged to obtain the unzealous approbation of Philip Stanhope, Fourth Earl of Chesterfield. To obtain a consulship in Southern Europe when his health and life depended on it, Smollett applied in vain to Lord Shelbourne, husband of a Granville. Towards the end of Smollett's life he was coldly taken up as a ministerial propagandist, and as coldly dismissed, by the Earl of Bute, another connection by marriage of the Granvilles. It is not surprising that, beating away on the shields of this unheeding phalanx, Smollett became more and more exasperated. His life was spent learning the truth of his early lines :

> Too coy to flatter, and too proud to serve,
> Thine be the joyless dignity to starve.[17]

Emphatically at the top during most of Smollett's life was George II, self-willed but kept within the bounds of the rational and the feasible by his wife Caroline. His decisions were subject only to common law, and could be obstructed but not opposed by the body of self-interested property owners who composed Parliament. The political philosophy of the time was expressed by a Tory member : "Pray, what is the nation to us, provided our friends get into power, and are in a condition to make us thrive?" The king exerted his power most forcefully as a leader of upper-class society, arbiter of the great families. The government was at St. James', not Westminster. Opposition from outside the royal family was regarded as treason. Such permitted opposition as there was gathered at Leicester House, round the heir to the throne, still within the Hanoverian context. Sir Robert Walpole, for his own motives, kept the country prone to the monarchy. The chief distributor of crown patronage in each county was the Lord Lieutenant, almost always a member of the government. Newcastle (the "Germanised Minister" of *Sir Launcelot Greaves*) kept three such lieutenancies in his own hands when he was First Lord.[18] With no secret ballot, the control of electoral votes enabled the local landowner to secure posts and pensions for his friends. There were no examinations, no interviews. Governmental appointments were made through contacts.[19]

Thus James Boswell had the entree into London society from the first because his father, an influential landowner, had interest with Lord Eglington, a hanger-on of Lord Bute. Dr. Johnson regarded Boswell as a future landowner, concerned himself with the economy of the parental estate, and told Boswell to learn only as much law as is necessary for a man of property.[20] One of the most amusing passages in the *London Journal* is that which describes how Lady Northumberland (Horace Walpole's "fat and vulgar countess"), perhaps doubtful about the chatterbox connection which she has made, interrupts Boswell to ask him about the extent of his father's estate at Auchinleck. Boswell observes that, as society is constituted, a man is paid a great deal of respect for being a possessor of property: "In civilised society external advantages make us more respected by individuals." A twist of Smollett's irony in *Launcelot Greaves* is the fact that his reforming hero is only effective (so far as he is effective at all) because of his stately connections. Time after time Greaves uses his rank as a talisman to extricate himself from situations which would have been the ruin of a less conspicuous man. His reprimand to Justice Gobble is full of the pride of class. The accident of Greaves' being shut up in the private madhouse brings justice to it. The law existed, but only a man of means could have it applied. At the worst, Greaves knows during his illegal imprisonment that he, a baronet, cannot be murdered with impunity.

During the bad years of his life, from 1753 to 1760, Smollett was trying all sorts of possibilities for earning an independent living as a writer without resorting to aristocratic patrons or jobbing book-sellers: a review, a magazine, serialisation, sixpenny numbers. His struggle for success outside the contact system was a furious one. As he points out in *Peregrine Pickle,* any tolerable performance by a person of fortune will be considered "an instance of astonishing capacity", whilst the same production published "under the name of an author in less affluent circumstances" would be disregarded, "so much is the opinion of most people influenced and overawed by ridiculous considerations".[21] There is justified pride in his description of himself in *Humphry Clinker* as "one of those few writers of the age that stand upon their own foundation, without patronage and above dependence".[22] With his forearm rubbed sore from constant writing, he could claim that he had avoided the sycophancy and sharp practice which he had denounced in *Advice,* and still not gone under even though he had shortened his life.

Addison had professed that his aim was reform, but in fact Addison was much in favour of keeping society as it was, and contented himself with resisting innovations. He gave his blessing to current opinion. Chesterfield had singled out as the only ambition, to which morality, wit and learning are to be sacrificed, acceptance by the existing social order. In this respect they were representative of their time. Smollett was far from sharing their view. *Roderick Random* is an account of how a young man of fair possibilities becomes utterly worthless by conforming to contemporary society and thus helping to perpetuate it. This

society was one in which in 1757, whilst the poor were rioting for
food and being hanged as a result, the Fourth Duke of Bedford
paid £64 to have a suit embroidered in gold, a sum which would
have provided 5,120 families with a pound of beef.[23] In the
absence of a national policy for the succour of the needy, men
like Coram, Oglethorpe and Hanway were digging away unaided
in such a wilderness of suffering that even a thousand men like
them would not have made a perceptible difference. Their work
was the sort of thing which the ruling class disowningly and dis-
dainfully referred to, in Lady Mary Montagu's phrase, as "raking
in the lowest sinks of vice and misery".

Social conditions from 1730 to 1750 at the height of the
fashionable extravagance were so bad that there appears to have
been an actual decline in the population of England.[24] Even the
conservative Dr. Johnson spoke bitterly of "a world which is
bursting with sin and sorrow", and asked, "If every man who
wears a laced coat was extirpated, who would miss them?"[25]
Johnson's acknowledgment of the unfair distribution of wealth
at this time is contained in two notable rebukes to Mrs. Thrale:

> "But you, madam," replies the Doctor, "have been at all times
> a fortunate woman, having always had your hunger so fore-
> stalled by indulgence, that you never experienced the delight of
> smelling your dinner beforehand." "Which pleasure," answered
> I pertly, "is to be enjoyed in perfection by such as have the
> happiness to pass through Porridge Island of a morning." "Come,
> come," says he, gravely, "let's have no sneering at what is serious
> to so many. Hundreds of your fellow-creatures, dear lady, turn
> another way, that they may not be tempted by the luxuries of
> Porridge Island to wish for gratifications they are not able to
> obtain. You are certainly not better than all of them; give
> God thanks that you are happier."
>
> I received on another occasion as just a rebuke from Mr. John-
> son, for an offence of the same nature, and hope I took care never
> to provoke a third; for after a very long summer, particularly hot
> and dry, I was wishing naturally but thoughtlessly for some rain
> to lay the dust as we drove along the Surrey roads. "I cannot
> bear," replied he, with much asperity and an altered look, "when
> I know how many poor families will perish next winter for want
> of that bread which the present drought will deny them, to hear
> ladies sighing for rain, only that their complexions may not suffer
> from the heat, or their clothes be incommoded by the dust. For
> shame! leave off such foppish lamentations, and study to relieve
> those whose distresses are real.[26]

Another effect of the misuse of riches was an increasingly dis-
organised economy. At the end of the eighteenth century there
were seldom fewer than ten thousand unemployed domestic
servants in London out of season, yet, whilst most of the working
population of London was dancing attendance on the rich, or
waiting for them to re-appear, the unattended roads were so bad
that in 1757 it was considered an achievement that a coach
could travel from Liverpool to London in three days.[27] Whenever
there was a shortage of food and raw materials, prices and
unemployment went up together, so that the labouring poor had
less money and had to pay more. In an epidemic or an emergency
the employers just threw up their hands and closed down.[28]

Smollett emerges as a critic of society most openly in the early
verse-satires and in *Sir Launcelot Greaves*. In *Reproof* he
expresses a very decided opinion about the value of the ruling
class :

> Corruption, roll'd in a triumphant car,
> Displays his burnish'd front and glitt'ring star;
> Nor heeds the public scorn, or transient curse,
> Unknown alike to honour and remorse.
> Behold the leering belle, caress'd by all,
> Adorn each private feast and public ball;
> Where peers attentive listen and adore,
> And not one matron shuns the titled whore.[29]

In *Launcelot Greaves*, although he scatters his condemnations
over both the political parties and most of the institutions of his
age, he appeals as much to compassion as to anger in such
episodes as that of the two hungry little boys who go picking
berries for food.

Launcelot Greaves contains one of Smollett's most ambiguous
characters, the persecuted misanthrope, Ferret, whose characteristics, including "a perverse spirit of contradiction", have so
much in common with Smollett's. Discontented and persecuted
by the authorities for his discontent, he looks "as if he wanted
to shrink within himself from the impertinence of society".
Although Smollett, for safety's sake, disassociates himself from the
opinions of Ferret, he also lends them all the strength of his
dialectic, and shows how Greaves' attempts to prove Ferret wrong
end in Quixotic mishaps, from which only a display of his imposing connections can extricate him. Thus Ferret is one of that
line of odd spokesmen for the author which includes Crabtree
and Lismahago. Greaves in his helmet and Ferret in a whimsical

series of disguises are both attacking the wicked. They are com-
plementary figures. The novel opens with Ferret complaining in
the inn kitchen that the nation is bankrupt and beggared and
"steering into the gulf of inevitable destruction". There is a
crash on the door and Sir Launcelot Greaves enters, in full
armour, a preposterous godsend to the nation. After Greaves has
married and given up reform, the novel ends with Ferret depart-
ing for London, "where there would always be food sufficient
for the ravenous appetite of his spleen".

The whole point of *Launcelot Greaves* is that a radical
change, far greater in scope than the hit-or-miss goodness of Sir
Everhard Greaves or the fortuitous relief provided by Sir Launcelot on his chance visit to the debtors' prison, is needed in a
system under which, for example the Clewlines' son dies of the
smallpox because they cannot afford to pay a doctor to cure him.
(This was a situation with which Smollett was professionally
familiar. One of the few documents relating to his medical career
is a letter he wrote requesting free treatment at a hospital for
a young child.) That haphazard distributions of largesse are useless to what he calls "modest want that pines in silence"[30] is a
strong principle with Smollett. Noted for his own generosity, and
obviously fond though he is of his character, Matt. Bramble, who
sheds tears of approbation on hearing of a charitable action,
Smollett thinks that charity is an inadequate shift for social evils.
Dr. Johnson once remarked to Boswell that a decent provision
for the poor is the true test of civilisation. It is a test in which
the eighteenth century did badly, as the need for Johnson's own
exertions proves. He appears to have spent his weekdays with
the Thrales partly to save money for his numerous dependents in
Fleet Street, whom he kept on a settled allowance. "He nursed
whole nests of people in his house, where the lame, the blind,
the sick and the sorrowful found a sure retreat from all the evils
whence his little income could secure them."[31] Even at its most
humane, as in the rules for admission to Foundlings' Hospital, the
eighteenth century was often grim by our standards.

The only effect of the poor rate was to make the richer citizens
pay their inadequate contribution (a small enough price for the
privileges which they possessed), grumble over it, and think that
they had done enough. The publican in *Humphry Clinker* dismisses his sick postillion because

> having sold or pawned everything he had in the world for his
> cure and subsistence, he became so miserable and shabby that

he disgraced the stable, and was dismissed; but that he never heard anything to the prejudice of his character in other respects. "So that the fellow being sick and destitute," said my uncle, "you turned him out to die in the streets?" "I pay the poor's rate," replied the other, "and I have no right to maintain idle vagrants, either in sickness or in health; besides, such a miserable object would have brought a discredit upon my house."[32]

Whilst the peasantry could not afford to eat the eggs which their hens laid, nor the fruit which grew on their trees (except that which was not saleable), whilst they were counted affluent if they ate fresh meat more than once a month, and subsisted mainly on skim-milk and whey-curds, the people who squandered their produce wasted their time in degenerate amusements and neglected the responsibilities of their rank:

> Let ev'ry polish'd dame, and genial lord,
> Employ the social chair and venal board;
> Debauch'd from sense, let doubtful meanings run,
> The vague conundrum, and the prurient pun;
> While the vain fop with apish grin, regards
> The giggling minx half-chok'd behind her cards;
> These and a thousand idle pranks I deem
> The motley spawn of ignorance and whim.
> Let pride conceive and folly propagate,
> The fashion still adopts the spurious brat.[33]

The "venal board" was well loaded. In eighteenth-century cookery books one comes across recipes for a soup requiring six chickens and eight eggs and a pie-crust in the making of which six pounds of butter were to be used.[34] The bill for a seven-man feast at a tavern in 1752 contained fifty-four items (including ten different wines) and came to over £81.[35] The second course of a Guildhall banquet given to George III in 1761 consisted of forty-eight dishes, including quails, ortolans, woodcocks, pheasants, teal, snipe and partridges.[36] It was not considered extraordinary that the meat-bill for the Younger Pitt was £96 for one month.[37] As Smollett complains, even manual workers, if they could, ate and drank extravagantly, so making their labour dear and increasing the chances of a period of unemployment which they had no resources for.[38] The onslaught in *Reproof* is not merely the product of Smollett's spleen. Horace Walpole, a man of fashion himself (although curiously sympathetic to the working class), wrote concerning the increase of robbers: "How should the morals of the people be purified when such frantic dissipation reigns above them? Contagion does not mount, but descend."[39] Walpole digresses on a bishop's wife who takes three hours to undress, compares London to Jerusalem when Titus was at the gates, and prophesies that some ages later, when New York is the city which gives its laws to Europe, "this little island will be ridiculously proud of its former brave days".

In *Peregrine Pickle* Smollett illustrates the ease with which the accomplishments of fashionable life can be acquired by a person having the necessary material advantages. Pickle adopts a beggar-girl of sixteen who exhibits "a set of agreeable features, enlivened with the complexion of health and cheerfulness". He has her "cleaned and clothed in a decent manner":

> Tom having provided himself with swabs and brushes, divested the fair stranger of her variegated drapery, which was immediately committed to the flames, and performed upon her soft and sleek person the ceremony of scrubbing, as it is practised on board of the king's ships of war. Yet the nymph herself did not submit to this purification without repining. She cursed the director who was upon the spot, with many abusive allusions to his wooden leg; and as for Pipes, the operator, she employed her talons so effectually upon his face that the blood ran over his nose in sundry streams; and next morning, when those rivulets were dry, his countenance resembled the rough bark of a plum-tree, plastered with gum. Nevertheless he did his duty with great perseverance, cut off her hair close to the scalp, handled his brushes with dexterity, applied his swabs of different magnitude and texture, as the case required; and, lastly, rinsed the whole body with a dozen pails of cold water, discharged upon her head.

Pickle has already decided that

> the conversation on those who are dignified with the appellation of polite company, is neither more edifying nor entertaining than that which is met with among the lower classes of mankind; and that the only essential difference, in point of demeanour, is the form of an education, which the meanest capacity can acquire, without much study or application. Possessed of this notion, he determined to take the young mendicant under his own tutorage and instruction; in consequence of which, he hoped he should, in a few weeks, be able to produce her in company as an accomplished young lady of uncommon wit, and an excellent understanding.

Before long she is able to attract the applause and admiration of the local squirearchy. Pickle is encouraged to introduce her into London society. The negligible scraps of education which she needs to hold her own in these surroundings are soon acquired. Pickle makes her memorise some well-known quotations from Shakespeare and Pope, instructs her how to mention the names of theatrical celebrities "with an air of careless familiarity", and teaches her how to play cards. From Pickle's valet she learns how to dance and drop a few phrases in French. As a result of all this cultivation she passes for "a sprightly young lady of uncommon learning and taste". Unfortunately, like Eliza Doolittle, whose story this episode (Chapter 87 of *Peregrine Pickle*) anticipates, she spoils her effect by injudicious swearing:

> But one evening being at cards with a certain lady, whom she detected in the very fact of unfair conveyance, she taxed her roundly with the fraud, and brought upon herself such a torrent of sarcastic reproof, as overbore all her maxims of caution, and burst open the floodgates of her own natural repartee, twanged off with the appellation of . . . and . . . , which she repeated with great vehemence, in an attitude of manual defiance, to the terror of her antagonist, and the astonishment of all present; nay, to such an ungarded pitch was she provoked, that, starting up, she snapt her fingers in testimony of disdain, and as she quitted the room, applied her hand to that part which was the last of her that disappeared, inviting the company to kiss it, by one of its coarsest denominations.

It is in the same fashionable world of affected values that the charlatan Fathom has so great a success until his credit gives out.

Because of the extravagance of the beau monde money was passing rapidly from the hands of the aristocracy to those of the merchants. They were growing richer than their masters on their masters' candle-ends, on the gala suits which Swift told Stella "the great folks never wear above once or twice". This was one thing which led to the supremacy of the middle class when the stake-money was laid down for the industrial revolution. In the meantime, the countryside was being depopulated because of the departure of agricultural workers to non-productive work in the big towns, where they provided adornments for the rich or became their domestic servants.[40] Having become instruments of waste, they soon acquired the insolence and guile of their superiors. Winifred Jenkins writes from Bath:

> O Molly! the sarvants at Bath are devils in garnet. They lite

the candle at both ends. Here's nothing but ginketting, and wasting, and thieving, and tricking, and trigging; and then they are never content. They won't suffer the squire and mistress to stay any longer, because they have been already above three weeks in the house and they look for a couple of ginneys a piece at our going away; and this is a parquisite they expect every month in the season, being as how no family has a right to stay longer than four weeks in the same lodgings; and so the cuck swears she will pin the dish-clout to mistress's tail, and the house-maid vows she'll put cow-itch in master's bed, if so he don't discamp without furder ado.[41]

It is at Bath that Matt. Bramble begins his tirade against luxury : "All these absurdities arise from the general tide of luxury, which hath overspread the nation, and swept away all, even the very dregs of the people."[42]

Humphry Clinker is not only Bramble's but Smollett's own denunciation of Luxury, which he sees as a sign of the misdistribution of wealth. He surveys the wasteful diversions of London and the wasted land in Scotland, the scarlet waistcoat with its gold binding on the valet and the split breeches on the starving postilion, Tabitha Bramble in a rose-coloured négligé and Morgan's orphans naked. The callousness of the situation is summed up by Tabitha's protests that the £20 which her brother has given to the mother of a dying child would have bought Tabitha a suit of flowered silk. Baynard's garden, formerly stocked with the best fruit which England can produce, has been turned by his modish wife into "a naked circus of loose sand, with a dry basin and a leaden Triton in the middle".[43] She has converted Baynard's hitherto productive estate into a ruinous piece of landscape gardening :

It now appeared that her travels had produced no effect upon her but of making her more expensive and fantastic than ever. She affected to lead the fashion, not only in point of female dress, but in every article of taste and connoisseurship. She made a drawing of the new facade to the house in the country; she pulled up the trees, and pulled down the walls of the garden, so as to let in the easterly wind, which Mr. Baynard's ancestors had been at great pains to exclude. To show her taste in laying out ground she seized into her own hand a farm of two hundred acres, about a mile from the house, which she parcelled out into walks and shrubberies, having a great bason in the middle, into which she poured a whole stream that turned two mills and afforded the best trout in the country. The bottom of the bason, however, was so ill secured that it would not hold the water, which strained through the earth, and made a bog of the whole plantation. In a word, the ground which formerly paid him one hundred and fifty pounds a year, now cost him two hundred pounds a year to keep it in tolerable order, over and above the first expense of trees, shrubs, flowers, turf and gravel. There was not an inch of garden ground left about the house, nor a tree that produced fruit of any kind; nor did he raise a truss of hay or a bushel of oats for his horses, nor had he a single cow to afford milk for his tea, far less did he ever dream of feeding his own mutton, pigs, and poultry. Every article of housekeeping, even the most inconsiderable, was brought from the next market-town, at the distance of five miles, and thither they sent a courier every morning to fetch hot rolls for breakfast.[44]

In antithesis to the story of Baynard, Smollett tells the story of Dennison, for whose constructive and unostentatious life Smollett has nothing but praise. Dennison inherits a wilderness and makes it fertile:

I drained bogs, burned heath, grubbed up furze and fern; I planted copse and willows where nothing else would grow; I gradually enclosed all my farms, and made such improvements, that my estate now yields me clear twelve hundred pounds a year. All this time my wife and I have enjoyed uninterrupted health and a regular flow of spirits, except on a very few occasions when our cheerfulness was invaded by such accidents as are inseparable from the condition of life.[45]

As part of the good-natured conclusion of *Humphry Clinker* even Baynard's troubles are put right. Matt. Bramble takes his estate in hand:

With Baynard's good leave, I ordered the gardener to turn the rivulet into its own channel, to refresh the fainting Naïads, who had so long languished among mouldering roots, withered leaves and dry pebbles. The shrubbery is condemned to extirpation; and the pleasure-ground will be restored to its original use of corn-field and pasture.[46]

It is clear from these passages that Smollett is not so great a pessimist as to suggest that human happiness is impossible. What he does say is that, by creating a social organisation which is not only unfair but also bad sense, the few have imposed unhappiness upon the many, and to some extent upon themselves too. Smollett's final position is summed up in the posthumously published *Ode to Independence*:

In fortune's car behold that minion ride,
  With either India's glittering spoils oppress'd,
So moves the sumpter-mule, in harness'd pride,
  That bears the treasure which he cannot taste.
For him let venal bards disgrace the bay,
  And hireling minstrels wake the tinkling string;
Her sensual snares let faithless Pleasure lay;
  And jingling bells fantastic Folly ring;
Disquiet, Doubt, and Dread shall intervene;
  And Nature, still to all her feelings just,
In vengeance hang a damp on every scene,
  Shook from the baleful pinions of Disgust.
Nature I'll court in her sequester'd haunts,
  By mountain, meadow, streamlet, grove, or cell,
Where the pois'd lark his evening ditty chants,
  And Health, and Peace, and Contemplation dwell.
There Study shall with Solitude recline;
  And Friendship pledge me to his fellow swains;
And Toil and Temperance sedately twine
  The slender cord that fluttering life sustains;
And fearless Poverty shall guard the door;
  And taste unspoil'd the frugal table spread;
And Industry supply the humble store;
  And sleep unbrib'd his dews refreshing shed;
White-mantled Innocence, ethereal sprite,
  Shall chase far off the goblins of the night;
And Independence o'er the day preside,
  Propitious power! my patron and my pride.[47]

The happy life, as Smollett sees it, is one close to Nature, the life
of useful simplicity which, reminiscing in his *Ode to Leven
Water*, he associates with his own boyhood:

Still on thy bank so gayly green,
May num'rous herds and flocks be seen
And lasses chanting o'er the pall
And shepherds piping in the dale
And ancient faith that knows no guile
And industry embrown'd with toil
And hearts resolved, and hands prepared
The blessings they enjoy to guard.[48]

To those unfamiliar with the bizarre affiliations of eighteenth-
century politics it may seem strange that a writer of such radical
tendencies should have been a Tory. But although Smollett disliked both parties (as the election-scene in *Launcelot Greaves*
shows), he disliked the Whigs most. Apart from the fact that for

the greater part of Smollett's life the Whigs had been answerable for the state of England, Smollett vividly resented the
"Germanised ministers" who had brought about the attack on
Carthagena and the slaughter of 1745. Above all, the Whigs
were corrupt. Sir Robert Walpole, in Smollett's opinion, was "the
father of corruption" whose "venal drudge" was the Duke of Newcastle.[49] The Whig party, which they headed, practised "national
usury, receiving wholesale the rewards of venality and distributing
the wages of corruption by retail".[50] So whilst the Tory candidate
at the election in *Launcelot Greaves* is no worse than an illiterate
and self-assertive fox-hunter, dependent on his interest with the
local gentry, the Whig is a stock-jobber working by bribery and
the use of ministerial influence, "a sordid knave, without honour
or principle ... who worships no God but Mammon".[51] Although Smollett claimed that he had kept himself free of any
party connections which might have affected the truth of his
Continuation of the History of England, and although his father
was a prominent Whig, Smollett's accounts of the massacre of
Glencoe and the various administrations of Sir Robert Walpole
are decidedly antagonistic to the Whigs.

Dealing with the accession of George II, Smollett remarks
that the Whigs had been wasting the wealth of the nation on
foreign subsidies, and had made dangerous encroachments on
civil liberties. Their mismanagement they protected by corruption. "The means were in the hands of the Ministry; the public
treasure was at their devotion : they multiplied places and pensions to increase the number of their followers."[52] The Duke of
Newcastle owed his high place to "his uncommon zeal for the
illustrious house of Hanover, and to the strength of his interest
in Parliament, rather than to his judgment, precision or any other
intellectual merit".[53] Walpole himself, whose importance was
enhanced by the extensive connections which he had with the
money-corporations, "perceived that the bulk of mankind were
actuated by a sordid thirst of lucre; he had sagacity enough to
convert the degeneracy of the times to his own advantage; and on
this, and this alone, he founded the whole superstructure of his
subsequent administration.... He knew the maxims he had
adopted would subject him to the hatred, ridicule and reproach
of some individuals who had not yet resigned all sentiments of
patriotism . . . but the number of these was inconsiderable."[54]

That these were not Whigs in a fine Macaulay-like flush,
ardently carrying Reform Bills, is clear from the evidence of

Walpole's own son, Horace, who records that Sir Robert "dipped up to the elbow" in corruption.[55] Horace Walpole comments that by the time of Newcastle's Ministry of 1754 the auction of votes had become "an established commerce".[56] He reports elsewhere a dialogue between Lord Grenville, then Prime Minister, and the Lord Chief Justice. In reply to the latter's request that a particular friend of his should be made a King's Counsel, Grenville grandly replied that it was of no importance to him who became a judge or who a bishop, since it was Lord Grenville's business to make kings and emperors and to maintain the balance of power in Europe. To this the Lord Chief Justice made a significant answer: "Then they that want to be bishops and judges will apply to those who will submit to make it their business."[57] And it is true that Lord Grenville did not remain in power for long. Even the largest and most general Whig measures had some trace of private bribery in them. Thus Sir Robert Walpole introduced the Excise Bill, which would have reduced the tax on land and made up the deficit from the pockets of the population as a whole, in order to gain for his government the support of the country gentlemen who had so many constituencies at their disposal. Before bringing the Bill before Parliament, he won the King over by promising him one-sixth of the revenue on wine and tobacco. The profit of every political development was measured and distributed.

The initiating piece of political corruption, which qualified a man for larger operations, was to contrive an election to Parliament. Smollett examines this exercise in *Peregrine Pickle*. Pickle, hoping to "establish his reputation and interest with the Minister", decides to stand for Parliament, "and lined his pockets with a competent share of banknotes for the occasion". But the contest proves to be so costly (his opponent is prepared to spend ten thousand pounds) that Pickle is obliged to borrow twelve hundred pounds from public funds, which the Prime Minister places at his disposal. Because of this loan, for which he has given a promissory note, Pickle is obliged to relinquish his seat when there is a sudden change in the Prime Minister's policy. Pickle is dragged from the field, cursing "the whole chain of his court connections" and "the rascally scheme of politics" to which (because of his incapacity as a rogue) he has been sacrificed.[58]

Even the idealist Sir Launcelot Greaves is obliged to admit that with the scurrility of his remarks on contemporary politics Ferrett "had mixed some melancholy truths". Ferrett appears at the election in *Sir Launcelot Greaves* disguised as a mountebank selling an elixir of life, and compares himself (favourably) with the candidates. He is not, he says, like the High German quacks who have "blistered, sweated, bled and purged the nation into an atrophy". He will not puzzle his audience with medical jargon, "just as a Germanised minister throws dust in your eyes . . . acting like the juggler, whilst he picks your pockets". For his part, if the populace has a mind to betray its country, he has no objection: "In selling yourselves and your fellow-citizens, you only dispose of a pack of rascals who deserve to be sold."[59] Certainly the behaviour of the electorate justifies Ferrett's severity. When Greaves addresses the crowd, calling for moderation, and observing that "to you belongs the inestimable privilege of choosing a delegate properly qualified to represent you in the High Court of Parliament", these inestimably privileged people reply by pelting him with dirt and stones. Greaves' opinion of the candidates is Smollett-like in its belligerence. The Tory is an "illiterate savage . . . who holds his estate by factious tenure". The Whig is a "sordid knave, without honour or principle", who "sues to be the hireling and prostitute of a weak and worthless minister".[60]

The minister referred to is presumably the Duke of Newcastle. Horace Walpole says of Newcastle that "he succeeded young to an estate of about £30,000 per annum, and to great influence and interest in several counties. This account in reality contains his whole character as minister; for to the weight of his fortune he owed his in every other way unwarrantable elevation."[61] In spite of his lack of ability, from 1724 to 1760 he wholly controlled crown patronage. He saw to it that even the obscurest post in the government service was filled by somebody who voted for the ministerial candidate at elections. Every Admiralty clerk, every Customs officer, had to use his vote as Newcastle decreed. Out of the Secret Service Fund Newcastle paid local landowners £1,500 a seat for boroughs in their control.[62] From 1736 Newcastle managed Church patronage as well. Deaneries and bishoprics went to the families with political influence. (During the eighteenth century twenty bishops emerged from the family of the Duke of Rutland.) Once in the House of Lords, a bishop's preferment depended on how he used his vote.[63] In the House of Commons members who were also military officers were kept well in hand. Colonels lost their regiments for injudicious votes.[64]

In *Humphry Clinker* Smollett describes the arrival at the king's levee of the Duke of Newcastle, by this time ousted from power :

> who, squeezing into the circle with a busy face of importance, thrust his head into every countenance, as if he had been in search of somebody, to whom he wanted to impart something of great consequence. My uncle, who had been formerly known to him, bowed as he passed, and the Duke, seeing himself saluted so respectfully by a well-dressed person, was not slow in returning the courtesy.
>
> "Odso!" cried the Duke; "I remember you perfectly well, my dear Mr. Bramble. You was always a good and loyal subject—a staunch friend to administration—I made your brother an Irish bishop—"[65]

In fact Matt. Bramble's brother had not been made a bishop, and far from being a staunch supporter of the ministry, Bramble had voted for it only three times during the period he sat in Parliament. These were the three occasions when his conscience told him that the ministry was in the right. Bramble discourses on the character of Newcastle with a rounded severity :

> Of his grace I shall say nothing at present, but that for thirty years he was the constant and common butt of ridicule and execration. He was generally laughed at as an ape in politics, whose office and influence served only to render his folly the more notorious; and the opposition cursed him as the indefatigable drudge of a first mover, who was justly styled and stigmatized as the father of corruption. But this ridiculous ape, this venal drudge, no sooner lost the places he was so ill qualified to fill, and unfurled the banners of faction, than he was metamorphosed into a pattern of public virtue; the very people who reviled him before, now extolled him to the skies, as a wise, experienced statesman, chief pillar of the Protestant succession, and corner-stone of English liberty.[66]

Smollett does not let the unlucky duke, on whom he concentrated the full blast of his detestation of political corruption, go even with that. Later in the novel Smollett describes a visit paid to Newcastle by a Turkish ambassador who thinks that Newcastle is still Prime Minister :

> Certain it is, the Duke seemed eager to acknowledge the compliment. A door opening, he suddenly bolted out, with a shaving-cloth under his chin, his face frothed up to the eyes with soap lather; and, running up to the ambassador, grinned hideous in

his face "My dear Mahomet" said he, "God love your long beard;
I hope the Dey will make you a horse-tail at the next promo-
tion—ha, ha, ha? Have but a moment's patience, and I'll send
to you in a twinkling." So saying, he retreated into his den, leaving the Turk in some confusion. After a short pause, however, he
said something to his interpreter, the meaning of which I had
great curiosity to know, as he turned up his eyes while he spoke,
expressing astonishment mixed with devotion. We were gratified
by means of the communicative Captain C—who conversed with
the dragoman as an old acquaintance. Ibrahim, the ambassador,
who had mistaken his grace for the minister's fool, was no sooner
undeceived by the interpreter than he exclaimed to this effect:
"Holy prophet! I don't wonder that this nation prospers, seeing
it is governed by the counsel of idiots; a species of men whom
all good Mussulmen revere as the organs of immediate inspiration!"[67]

Particularly important to Smollett must have been the fact that
Newcastle was the chief sponsor of the attack on Carthagena.
"It is your war," Sir Robert Walpole had said to Newcastle,
"and I wish you joy of it." Smollett had been a front-line observer
of Newcastle's war, and had witnessed the effects of his management of it, the bitter payment made by the ordinary sailors and
soldiers for a divided cabinet, a reluctant Prime Minister and
a Secretary of State who wanted to send all available forces to
the West Indies but not sure what they should do when they
arrived there.[68]

Carthagena was one of the two shaping events of Smollett's
early life, the Revolt of 1745 the other. Smollett was aware that
Lord Chesterfield had recommended the executions of the High-
land peasantry which followed the Revolt. It is likely that he
also knew that this same Lord Chesterfield had been negotiating
with the Pretender in 1740 to bring about the Revolt.[69] The
difference was that in 1745 he was in the government, whilst in
1740 he was outside it and wanted, for that reason, to bring it
down. In these terms one can understand Smollett's reference, in
Advice to the "polished ruffians of the state". What was to them
a game of power was, to many of the common people, death.

CHAPTER VIII

REASON IS THE PACE

It is the ominous Crabtree who encourages Peregrine Pickle's taste for "practical satire", that is to say, practical jokes which expose human weakness. One of Smollett's regular techniques is to place a character in a moderately distressing situation, and then to see what happens to his self-esteem. When fire breaks out at the Society of Authors which Pickle attends, a satirist almost bites off the ear of a lyric bard, and the literary gentlemen rip up each other's clothes and periwigs. With the sour gratification of a man who finds himself to be correct in a disheartening notion, Smollett surveys the sad rent periwigs on the floor, the struggle on the landing, the whole spectacle of human indignity. He is at one with Sancho Panza, at one with Launcelot Greaves' squire, who claimed that all the confused bother of their errantry took place because his master had "run mad for a wench".

The indignity can be tragic, as when Commodore Trunnion, making his death-bed speech, is interrupted by a violent hiccough. That is the tragedy of human necessity. There is also the tragedy of human folly. In *Roderick Random* Smollett describes the Battle of Carthagena with a damning Swift-like near-relish for the idiocy of it all, especially when a sequence of needless and unjustifiable miseries ends in Thomson's suicide.

Smollett, who is doggedly rational, has no time for the old heroic conventions. Impatient with the pretentious ritual of the duel, he insists upon its purpose. When Roderick Random risks, in a duel with the fine Lord Quiverwit, a life distinguished mainly by brutality and defection, realism breaks into the polite arrangements, and the combatants end on the ground, struggling like apes. Random even knocks out three of Quiverwit's teeth with the hilt of a sword. It is all decidedly ungentlemanly. Smollett employs this contemptuous but regretful burlesque in order to ridicule the irrational code of honour to which duelling conformed.

> Ridebat curas, nec non et gaudia vulgi
> Interum et lachrymas fundebat.[1]

In the *Travels* Smollett laments the cruel tradition of "a worthy man's being obliged to devote himself to death because it is his misfortune to be insulted by a brute, a bully, a drunkard of a madman".[2] Smollett's perfect knight, Sir Launcelot Greaves, did not favour deciding issues "by homicide", and "never adopted those maxims of knight-errantry which related to challenges". The duel, in Greaves' opinion, violates "every suggestion of reason and every precept of humanity".[3]

When Peregrine Pickle resolves to fight a duel with Mr. Hornbeck, whom he has already cuckolded, Smollett comments that nothing could be more

> insolent and unjust than this determination, which induced him to punish a person for his want of courage to redress the injury which he himself had done to his reputation and peace; and yet this barbarity of decision is authorised by the opinion and practice of mankind.[4]

Even the humane Dr. Johnson shared the opinion which Smollett mentions. Feeling a sudden complaisance at hearing his moral protégé, that young property-owning rake, Boswell, speak with spirit on the subject, Johnson assured him that "as men have agreed to banish from their society one who puts up with an affront without fighting", it is lawful to take part in a duel. Fielding, who can always be relied upon to interpret faithfully the conventions of his age, also approved of duelling. Exclaiming, "Shall I incur the Divine displeasure rather than be called—ha—coward—scoundrel?—I'll think no more; I am resolved, and must fight him", Tom Jones, noble fellow, rises from his sick-bed to engage in a duel.[5] In this way Tom Jones settles the conflict between Religion and Honour, and sets out to exercise what Smollett calls "the privilege of gentlemen to kill one another". Whether such an heroic conflict took place in the mind of the 5th Lord Byron in 1765, when he killed another nobleman who claimed that his methods of game-keeping were better than Lord Byron's,[6] or whether they were just "cutting each other's throats pour passer le temps" (as Lady Mary Montagu puts it), we must decide for ourselves.

Smollett the glum rationalist refused to admire the Romans, the stories of *Virtus* and martial splendour. "What beastly fellows these Romans were!" exclaims Pallett, on hearing that they ate pies of dormice and syrup of poppies. Smollett agrees with this assessment. He has no doubt that they were a barbarous people, who delighted in horrible spectacles. They viewed with pleasure the dead bodies of criminals dragged through the streets, or thrown down the Scalæ Gemoniæ and Tarpeian rock, for their contemplation. Their rostra were generally adorned with the heads of some remarkable citizens, like Temple-Bar at London.[7]

The tart comparison in the last sentence should be noticed. Smollett's "natural horror of cruelty", to which he alludes in a letter of 1758, is conspicuous in this passage.

Even the mind of Edward Gibbon, not given to enthusiasm, was agitated when he first "approached and entered the Eternal City". He lost several days in a classical intoxication before he could "descend to a cool and minute examination".[8] A less temperate traveller, James Boswell (who knew forty odes of Horace by heart), on arrival in Rome tried to identify himself completely with the Ancients whom he had been taught to admire so much. He and his companions spoke Latin as they went about the city, discussing the antiquities in "the language of the Romans themselves".[9] He looked back on the age of Virgil, "when man had organs framed for manly enjoyment and a mind unbroken by dreary speculation—when he lived happy and died in hope".[10] When he went whoring he congratulated himself on emulating, in their own city, "the rakish deeds of Horace and other amorous Roman poets".[11] Smollett was a good deal less penetrated with emotion when he surveyed these happily living and hopefully dying people. To his mind they were "a very frowzy generation" :

> If we consider that the city and suburbs of Rome in the reign of Claudius, contained about seven millions of inhabitants, a number equal at least to the sum total of all the souls in England; that great part of ancient Rome was allotted to temples, porticos, basilicæ, theatres, thermæ, circi, public and private walks and gardens, where very few, if any, of this great number lodged; that by far the greater part of those inhabitants were slaves and poor people, who did not enjoy the conveniencies of life; and that the use of linen was scarce known; we must naturally conclude they were strangely crouded together, and that in general they were a very frowzy generation.[12]

The Ancient Romans were on another count dirty creatures, and for good measure nasty and gluttonous :

> and when Heliogabalus ordered all the cobwebs of the city and suburbs to be collected, they were found to weigh ten thousand

pounds. This was intended as a demonstration of the great number of inhabitants; but it was a proof of their dirt, rather than of their populosity. I might likewise add, the delicate custom of taking vomits at each other's houses, when they were invited to dinner, or supper, that they might prepare their stomachs for gormandizing; a beastly proof of their nastiness as well as gluttony.[13]

A regular antithesis could be struck up between Boswell in Rome and Smollett in Rome. Boswell bestowed some of his copious zeal on the other great Roman institution. Whilst disagreeing with the Pope on various points of doctrine, Boswell was not willing to lose an opportunity for the display of feeling. Watching the Pope celebrate Mass in St. Peter's, he struck his breast and prostrated himself on the floor. "Let cold beings sneer", Boswell wrote to Rousseau about this demonstration, "I was never more nobly happy than on that day".[14] There is no doubt whatever that Smollett would have qualified as a cold being, had he been informed of this act of religious awe. Smollett might indeed have chosen the incident to illustrate his own maxim that ignorance is the mother of devotion.

The maxim is Smollett's comment, in one of his notes to Voltaire,[15] on the medieval Church and how it retarded rather than advanced civilisation. It is in these notes, in the posthumously published *Ode To Independence* and in the asides of his novels and *Travels*, that one must search out Smollett's attitude to religion. Outwardly he conformed, which is one of the few instances of his showing discretion. A statute of 1698 imposed loss of civil rights and three years' imprisonment on anyone who denied the truth of the Holy Scriptures.[16] No doubt if Smollett had not been engaged in so many quarrels with authority already he would have taken on this one too, but he had to conserve his time. As it was, he wrote in a letter of 1758 that he regarded the Church "not as a religious but as a political establishment".[17] On such terms, and cynical about hoodwinking a tyranny of opinion to which he did not subscribe, Smollett went through the forms of occasionally attending Church of England services, and even (since the governing body of a parish church had considerable secular powers, especially over the local poor) went along mirthfully to vestry meetings. Perhaps, like many an outlaw before him, he found it useful to have some friends amongst the powers-that-be.

Smollett's good-humoured relationship with the blasphemous

Wilkes is significant. Excusing himself from a Spring visit to Wilkes' country house, Smollett wrote that nevertheless "I love the country, especially at this season, and I long to see your house at Aylesbury as much as ever Akenside or Gilbert Cooper or any other wrong-headed Platonist longed to visit the groves of Academus".[18] The practices at Wilkes' country house, and the company to be found there, are sufficiently well known. Probably if Smollett had gone, he would have taken a long spoon with him.

The eighteenth century was indeed a period when the Church was particularly worldly. The natural vivacity of the French was greatly increased by the presence of quantities of dissolute abbés, some of them hereditary. In England a mercenary society had made the higher clergy its creatures. The bishops were an oligarchy, corresponding to the political one, at a great social remove from the parish priests, most of whom earned less than £50 each a year. Walpole methodically appointed bishops who could be relied upon to support him in the House of Lords, and was in fact twice saved from defeat by their grateful votes. As Richard Watson, Bishop of Llandaff, explained, "I happened to please a party and they made me a bishop". Preferment in the Church of England was largely a matter of connection with the ruling families. The opportunities for royal chaplains and the ex-tutors of Prime Ministers were excellent. One of the Grevilles divided bishoprics into two classes: "bishoprics of business for men of abilities, and bishoprics of ease for men of family and fashion". The secularist Hoadley never visited Bangor during the six years he was bishop of it.[19] Where the loyalty of the bishops lay is tartly pointed out in Swift's epigram, *On Seeing A Worthy Prelate Go Out Of Church In The Time Of Divine Service, To Wait Upon His Grace The Duke Of Dorset*:

> His station despising, unawed by the place,
> He flies from his God, to attend on his grace :
> To the court it was fitter to pay his devotion,
> Since God had no hand in His Lordship's promotion.[20]

The bishops expected the same obsequiousness from their subordinates as they had shown themselves, so engrossing the abilities of the more ambitious. In Hogarth's *Harlot's Progress* a clergyman, too busy studying a letter of introduction to a bishop, does not observe a bawd snapping up the girl who just arrived from the country. Whilst Smollett's priests are mostly safely

foreign, when he does represent an English priest, that priest is
always busied about worldly concerns, like the chaplain on
Roderick Random's ship, who leaves the apparently dying surgeon's mate without the consolations of religion in order to con-
sort with the gentry on board, and drink their wine and
grog.[21]

Here Smollett is very fair, and does not blame the Church
merely because its representatives partook of the corruption of
the age. He directs his covert assault against the Church's reason for existing at all. In the angry opening of his *Ode To Independence* he describes how "frantic Superstition" made
Charlemagne baptise four thousand Saxon prisoners before he
had their throats cut:

> The Saxon prince in horror fled
> From altars stain'd with human gore;
> And Liberty his routed legions led
> In safety to the bleak Norwegian shore.
> There in a cave asleep she lay,
> Lull'd by the hoarse resounding main;
> When a bold savage pass'd that way,
> Impell'd by destiny, his name Disdain.[22]

After having taken exception to York Minster, which he considered ill-proportioned and barbarous, in *Humphry Clinker*,
Smollett goes on to consider the suitability of the Assembly Room
as a place of worship:

> There is nothing of this Arabic architecture in the assembly-
> room, which seems to me to have been built upon a design of
> Palladio, and might be converted into an elegant place of wor-
> ship; but it is indifferently contrived for that sort of idolatry
> which is performed in it at present.[23]

One sort of idolatry implies another.

It is in the important notes to Voltaire that Smollett comes
nearest to making a direct statement about religion. His tone is
one of thorough-going approval. Admittedly he comments once
on Voltaire's inadequate knowledge of the symptoms of venereal
disease, but otherwise he is full of admiration for the master's
"usual precision" of ideas. "M. de Voltaire cannot be too much
commended for the spirit of independence, candour and moderation, so sensibly and elegantly displayed in this chapter", he
records in one footnote,[24] a handsome overflow of enthusiasm.
The notes are drawn up in a spirit of outright proselytism:

All the mischiefs of religious zeal are, we apprehend, deducible from the single doctrine of faith, implying that our eternal happiness or misery depends on our believing or disbelieving certain tenets, concerning which the faculty of reason cannot be exercised.[25]

This is a severe satire on those cruel bigots who persecute all such as presume to differ from established opinions, however speculative.[26]

The book of Don Calmet, *Sur Les Vampires Et Sur Les Apparitions*, has been looked upon as the work of a disordered brain but it plainly shows how much the mind of man is addicted to superstition.[27]

Commenting on an obscure religious sect, Smollett remarks that its doctrines were "composed of a great number of absurdities, borrowed from the religion of the Jews, Persians, and other pagans".[28] To suggest that the religion of the Jews contains absurdities is of course to imply that absurdities are embodied, with the Old Testament, in the Christian religion.

Because of the severity with which open disbelief in Christianity was punished, and because even the most vocal of freethinkers would be ineffective in prison, those eighteenth-century writers who wished to contest the authority of the Bible generally chose irony as their method. Addisonian restraint and purity of language were used for savage purposes. Pierre Bayle, whose *Dictionnaire Historique et Critique* had appeared at the end of the seventeenth century, set the style. Whilst claiming to have orthodox opinions, Bayle naughtily assembled, with much clucking of his tongue and in great detail, all the arguments against Christianity, then observed that Faith is always preferable to mere Reason. Following his example, the English free-thinkers issued little pamphlets, with wickedly concessive titles such as *Christianity As Old As Creation* and *Christianity Not Founded On Argument*, in which they permitted their sarcasms to spark round the combustible doctrines of the Church. Tindal draws from the stories of Elisha and the bears, Elijah and the three years' drought, the conclusion that the holier men are, the more addicted they are to execrating their fellows. He advocates the following method for interpreting the Bible: "In order to maintain its infallibility without doing violence to reason, you have, when you find irrational statements, to torture them and depart

from the literal sense".[29] Woolston notices that the miracles of
the pool of Bethesda and the woman with the bloody flux were
oddly haphazard ways of conveying Divine Mercy. Dodwell lays
down that, as reasoning is fatal to belief, the results of reasoning
must be disregarded.[30]

Gibbon, in his famous account of the early development of
Christianity, perfects this ironical treatment of religion. He
accuses Seneca and the elder Pliny of a "supine inattention" to
the miracles which were taking place in Galilee during their life-
time. He regrets that the Church, having forgotten "the style of
the divine artist", lost its power to perform miracles before the
age when reliable historians were able to testify to them. He reflects that perhaps nowadays "men's reason is not sufficiently prepared to sustain the visible action of the deity".[31]

The account of the Roman Catholic missionaries in America
which Smollett places in the mouth of Lieutenant Lismahago
towards the end of *Humphry Clinker* has all the guile and deadly
surface innocence of Voltaire. A ridiculous character relates what
some savages thought of Christian doctrine, but the savages' case
is stated so that the whole weight of Reason evidently is on their
side :

> The lieutenant told her that, while he resided among them, two
> French missionaries arrived, in order to convert them to the
> Catholic religion; but when they talked of mysteries and revela-
> tions, which they could neither explain nor authenticate, and
> called in the evidence of miracles which they believed upon hear-
> say; when they taught that the Supreme Creator of heaven and
> earth had allowed his only Son, his own equal in power and glory,
> to enter the bowels of a woman, to be born as a human creature,
> to be insulted, flagellated, and even executed as a malefactor;
> when they pretended to create God himself, to swallow, digest,
> revive, and multiply him ad infinitum, by the help of a little
> flour and water, the Indians were shocked at the impiety of their
> presumption. . . .
>
> They persisted in saying mass, in preaching, baptizing, and
> squabbling with the conjurers or priests of the country, till they
> had thrown the whole community into confusion. Then the
> assembly proceeded to try them as impious impostors, who re-
> presented the Almighty as a trifling, weak, capricious being, and
> pretended to make, unmake, and reproduce him at pleasure.
> They were therefore convicted of blasphemy and sedition, and
> condemned to the stake, where they died singing Salve regina,

in a rapture of joy, for the crown of martyrdom which they had thus obtained.[32]

Lismahago's account is in the same manner as Gibbon's list of the objections which the Gnostics had to the Old Testament. No refutation is attempted, no pious propitiation is offered to orthodox opinion, although the beliefs which Lismahago cites are. not restricted to the Roman Catholic Church but common to all Christendom. As Smollett himself says in a note to Voltaire, "The reader will perceive that these are satiric hints thrown out against certain articles of faith common to all the professors of Christianity".[33] Also common to all Christendom is what Smollett in his own person calls "the nauseous repetition of the figure of the cross, which in itself is a very mean and disagreeable object".[34] Lismahago is clearly speaking for the author. It is typical of Smollett, always impatient of the heroic conventions, that he chooses such a grotesque and cantankerous spokesman.

With inner merriment Smollet finds protection in the very intolerance of his time, by directing his censures against the Roman Catholic Church alone. In the *Travels* he deplores "the implements of Popish superstition, such as relics of pretended saints".[35] His accounts of Roman Catholic rituals and ceremonies are contemptuously sharp-sighted. He describes a procession in Florence, during the course of which a statue of the Virgin Mary was carried by "dressed in a gold stuff, with a large hoop, a great quantity of false jewels, her face painted and patched, and her hair frizzled and curled in the very extremity of the fashion".[36] He explains the retail and wholesale trade in masses for the dead, with the price-cutting which takes place on All Souls' Day, and with whimsical sympathy records the problem of a gentleman of Nice. This gentleman's estate was engrossed in paying for a perpetual mass which his great-grandmother had ordered for her release from Purgatory fifty years previously, and the gentleman was of the opinion that she must surely have got out of Purgatory in fifty years. Smollett suggested to him that he should ask his great-grandmother's ghost to appear before a magistrate to give an affidavit of her being at peace. "He mused a little, and shrugging up his shoulders, replied, that where the interest of the Church was at stake, he did not believe a spirit's declaration would be held legal evidence."[37]

Except for his delight in natural scenery, there is little lyrical feeling in Smollett, and certainly no sense of the beauty, sureness and huge compassionate concepts of the established Church. "My notions are not quite so sublime", he wrote of Lord Shaftesbury's Platonism. His notions of most things were not quite so sublime. The peculiar quality of Smollett's mind may be brought out by a comparison between him and another writer who also had a great deal to bear in the way of worldly affliction, George Herbert.

Like Smollett consumptive, like Smollett checked in all his hopes, blown along by the furious wind of human suffering, Herbert could well appreciate the massive, sanctioned solidity of the sheltering Church, so firm even in mere institutional stability, so four-square against any gale:

> Mark you the floor? That square and speckled stone
> Which looks so firm and strong. . . .

Although Herbert always stressed its enduring usefulness, the loveliness of Church ritual had mounted in his heart like the faint mist in the vaulting of a cathedral. The spasmodic pleading of the bell as the organ plays before a service; the hypnotic slow swing of censers, flaming out in clouds of scent, like fragrant suns; the descant in the choir and the suspended second after the benediction has been given; above all, "church musick": such things as these might well hale forth a soul already shivering to depart. In those moments of obliterated agony, what were earthly crowns, what were obsequious promising secretaryships?

> Now I in you without a body move,
> Rising and falling with your wings:
> We both together sweetly live and love,
> Yet say sometimes, "God help poor kings".

On the other hand, Smollett considers that the look of an old cathedral

> cannot be but displeasing to the eye of every man who has any idea of propriety or proportion, even though he may be ignorant of architecture as a science; and the long slender spire puts one in mind of a criminal impaled, with a sharp stake rising up through his shoulder.[38]

Inside these "magazines of rheums", the air is so moist and stagnant, so "surcharged with damps from vaults, tombs and charnel houses", that the buildings might well have been erected for the benefit of the medical profession.[39] As for the liturgy and the singing in the choir, they are just part of the theatrical performance, whether it is the Roman Catholic comedy or the Calvinist tragedy.[40] What occupy his thoughts are the magazines of rheums and the dead polluting the air of the living. He would be glad to know

> what offence it would give to tender consciences if the house of God was made more comfortable, or less dangerous to the health of valetudinarians; and whether it would not be an encouragement to piety, as well as the salvation of many lives, if the place of worship was well floored, wainscoted, warmed, and ventilated, and its area kept sacred from the pollution of the dead.[41]

After all, the practice of burying in churches was instituted by knavish priests for their own profit.[42]

The busy and well-meaning materialist is at work. This is the constructive side of Smollett, his desire for the betterment of humanity's physical condition. The issue of human welfare was simpler for him as he had never encountered (as we have) the malaise of a prosperous modern society, the melancholia of the New Towns. He was content to value things according to their utility. There is little evidence in his work of, for example, an aesthetic sense. Although he has a fellow feeling for the arrogant verve of Salvator Rosa and the voluble truthfulness of the Italian Mannerists, his appreciation of works of art does not go much further than a taste for verisimilitude (well-carved marble feathers and accurate dorsal muscles) and agreeable subjects. He discerns in Michelangelo's *Last Judgement* a lack of repose. He objects to paintings of saints and martyrs, "which can only serve to fill the mind with gloomy ideas and encourage a spirit of religious fanaticism, which has always been attended with mischievous consequences to the community where it reigned".[43] In a charming aside he disavows any claim to be a judge of art. It is just that he has always been used to speak his mind freely on whatever is brought to his notice, "though I must as freely own, there is something more than common sense required to discover and distinguish the more delicate beauties of painting".[44] That protagonist of common sense, Smollett's Matt. Bramble, is very rueful about the inconvenience of inhabiting Palladian architecture, particularly when, in an English September, he has to dine in a hall paved with marble. About the new buildings at Bath, nowadays reckoned its chief distinction, Matt. Bramble becomes whimsical:

The same artist who planned the Circus has likewise projected a crescent; when that is finished we shall probably have a star; and those who are living thirty years hence may perhaps see all the signs of the zodiac exhibited in the architecture at Bath.[45]

Bramble is as convinced as any New Town architect that a house should be a unit of habitation, and from this point of view considers the Circus at Bath a failure:

The figure of each separate dwelling-house, being the segment of a circle, must spoil the symmetry of the rooms, by contracting them towards the street windows, and leaving a larger sweep in the space behind.[46]

Smollett's programme is that laid down by Thomas Hobbes: "Reason is the pace: increase of Science the way: and the benefit of mankind the end." Nobody can deny that the compiler of a Universal History in sixty volumes contributed towards the increase of Science. Smollett's concern for the benefit of mankind is no less apparent. One of the greatest social evils of his time was the unhygienic state of the towns. In 1741 Dr. Johnson wrote that London was "a city famous for wealth, commerce and plenty, and every other kind of civility and politeness, but which abounds in such heaps of filth as a savage would look on with amazement".[47] In his early treatise on the external use of water, in the letters from abroad, in the Bath and London sections of *Humphry Clinker*, and in many of his usually justified quarrels, he insists that cleanliness is important. He had as little patience with dirt as he had with quacks or cheats. His personal fastidiousness was far in advance of his time. Nothing but extreme necessity can induce him to lie in a bed which is not perfectly clean.[48] He has the same kind of antipathy to bugs "that some persons have to a cat or a breast of veal". He is disgusted by the English habit of drinking from a tankard "in which, perhaps, a dozen of filthy mouths have slobbered".[49] He alone protests when the drinking water at Bath is collected in an open basin liable to be defiled by "dead dogs, cats, rats, and every species of nastiness".[50] He alone is worried that the water in the Pump Room is drawn from the baths themselves.[51] In an unclean age it is necessary to be outspoken about uncleanliness. Much which has been found offensive in Smollett is part of a remedial scheme.

An Englishman of the eighteenth century would not just have shrugged his shoulders at modern concepts of personal cleanliness. He would have been bewildered. Dr. Johnson himself was no lover of baths and clean linen. Conspicuous private dirtiness, in rank overcrowded cities, had resulted in frequent epidemics of fever and contributed to an infant mortality in London which in some years was over fifty per cent. It was Smollett's friend, John Hunter, who first rightly attributed the epidemics to poverty, congestion and bad sanitation. Squalor made the streets hideous. The houses, airless because of the window-tax which had caused windows to be walled up, were rat-holed with occupants, the plentiful and waiting creatures of a hovering Death. Fielding wrote of the poor in a pamphlet of 1753, "They starve and freeze and rot among themselves but they beg and steal and rob among their betters".[52]

It was a time for a great deal more indignation than Fielding, commonly supposed to be particularly humanitarian, felt like displaying. Smollett does not make such blood-chilling utterances, or, confronted with such evil, look the other way and say nothing. Nor does he spray the corrupt air with scent when he encounters an inn bed, still in use, on which someone has recently died of the plague, or sees a scrofulous child bathing in the same water as consumptives. He protests volubly. He grasps the odious situation, and the odious complacency about that situation, firmly in order to wring their necks. The message of the treatise on the external use of water is simple : people should wash more often. Proceeding by examples, he presents this message more powerfully to the imagination of readers of his novels. The stench of the persons of fashion at Bath is so overwhelming that when they gather for the country dances at the assembly room Matt. Bramble, unwillingly present, swoons away :

> It was indeed a compound of villainous smells, in which the most violent stinks and the most powerful perfumes contended for the mastery. Imagine to yourself a high exalted essence of mingled odours arising from putrid gums, imposthumated lungs, sour flatulencies, rank arm-pits, sweating feet, running sores and issues; plasters, ointments and embrocations, Hungary water, spirit of lavender, assafoetida, drops, musk, hartshorn, and sal volatile; besides a thousand frowzy steams which I could not analyse. Such, O Dick! is the fragrant ether we breathe in the polite assemblies of Bath; such is the atmosphere I have exchanged for the pure, elastic, animating air of the Welsh mountains.[53]

Bramble's account of the uncleanliness of London, even more disagreeable in its detail, is, to use Bramble's own words, fit "to facilitate the operation of a vomit".

These descriptions exemplify Smollett's method. He was no theorist and formulated no system or policy. His own medium, the novel, was at hand. Brusquely, surely, like a surgeon cutting away at something he does not like but must understand, Smollett contests vicious unreason. He did not have time, he packed his arguments in where he could find room for them in the rococo elaborations of his plot. He chose, most often, to demonstrate by illustration. To generalise, to assemble his ideas, he left to them who enjoyed greater ease.

Smollett the propagandist, with his beneficent anger, wrote the following passage, which describes the treatment of the sick aboard ship:

> Here I saw about fifty miserable distempered wretches, suspended in rows, so huddled one upon another, that not more than four-teen inches space was allotted for each with his bed and bedding; and deprived of the light of day, as well as of fresh air; breathing nothing but a noisome atmosphere of the morbid steams exhaling from their own excrements and diseased bodies, devoured with vermin hatched in the filth that surrounded them, and destitute of every convenience necessary for people in that helpless condition.[54]

There is a similar passage in the *Compendium of Voyages*, where Smollett relates how the British sailors were forced to work in the tropics without water, "sweating under the sun, which was vertical, and fed with putrid beef, rusty pork and bread swarming with maggots".[55] One understands why it was the tradition for British sailors, visiting Leghorn, to plant a laurel at Smollett's grave. He had made the desperate protest of the man of goodwill faced with the cruel and wasteful results of in-competence in office. Whenever he questions the intentions of authority, he knows what a foolish answer he will receive:

> I asked why their cardinals and princes did not invite and en-courage industrious people to settle and cultivate the Campania of Rome, which is a desert? Why they did not raise a subscription to drain the marshes in the neighbourhood of the city, and thus meliorate the air, which is rendered extremely unwholesome in the summer, by putrid exhalations from those morasses?[56]

In England the condition of the poor provided pressing ubiquitous evidence of how incapably and how wickedly society was constituted. The poor were kept down, not by law, as in France, but by economic circumstance. In eighteenth-century legal theory all Englishmen were equal and had the same right to follow their own inclinations. But legal freedom is not the same as economic freedom. A farm worker driven by the enclosure system to non-productive work or besotted starvation in a large town cannot properly be called free, nor can the paupers depicted by Rowlandson in one of his cartoons as selling their teeth to be transplanted into the mouths of the rich. In 1688, three English people in every 550 were vagrants[57] and there is no evidence that the proportion of the totally destitute declined during the earlier part of the eighteenth century. Where society made any arrangements at all for them, the arrangements were heartless ones. In 1765 only seven out of every hundred parish foundlings survived their second year, and those who survived were settled as unpaid so-called apprentices until the age of 24.[58] There was a trade in them amongst the authorities. A kindred system of slavery by devolution took place in the parish workhouses, which were leased to local contractors who ran them for private profit. Most often society did not make even heartless arrangements. The Poor Rate, which the rich regarded as their more than sufficient contribution towards the happiness of their fellows, was generally misapplied and often misappropriated. Such was the state of society in the years 1740-2 (during which the lifework of Sir Robert Walpole culminated) that twice as many people in London were dying as being born. Sir Gilbert Heathcote, a director of the Bank of England, deposed to a committee investigating the Charitable Corporation (which had been set up to lend money to the poor on pledge and enrich the projectors) that "every man in want is knave or fool".[59] In this opinion all those who had never been in want evidently concurred, but certainly not such men as Johnson and Smollett.

Dr. Johnson treated his impoverished dependents with "perhaps more ceremonious civility than he would have done by so many people of fashion".[60] In answer to somebody's objection that beggars would only spend money which they received upon gin or tobacco, Dr. Johnson observed: "And why should they be denied such sweeteners of their existence? It is surely very savage to refuse them every avenue to pleasure reckoned too coarse for our own acceptance. Life is a pill which none of us can bear to swallow without gilding, yet for the poor we delight in stripping it still barer, and are not ashamed to show even visible displeasure if the bitter taste is taken from their mouths."[61]

Like Dr. Johnson, Smollett's character Matt. Bramble is fastidiously courteous towards the poor whom he relieves:

> My uncle, though a little lame, rose up when she came in, and, setting a chair for her, desired she would sit down; then he asked if she would take a dish of chocolate, which she declined with much acknowledgement. After a short pause he said, in a croaking tone of voice, which confounded me not a little, "Madam, I am truly concerned for your misfortunes, and if this trifle can be of any service to you, I beg you will accept it without ceremony." So saying, he put a bit of paper into her hand, which she opening with great trepidation, exclaimed in an ecstasy, "Twenty pounds! Oh, sir!" and, sinking down on a settee, fainted away.[62]

Jerry Melford, who describes the incident, adds that he feels a strong inclination to follow his uncle's example in helping the unfortunate woman, whose daughter is dying of consumption, but is afraid "of being detected in a weakness that might entail the ridicule of the company" upon himself. Jerry Melford's humorous implication—that the standards of conduct observed by people of fashion actually inhibit the exercise of charity—is borne out in the episode of *Peregrine Pickle* which leads up to the "Memoirs of a Lady of Quality". An assembly of fine ladies, which includes a duchess, is solicited for contributions towards the upkeep of "a poor gentlewoman, who was reduced to the most abject misery by the death of her husband, and just delivered of a couple of fine boys":

> My lady duchess concluded that she must be a creature void of all feeling and reflection who could survive such aggravated misery, therefore did not deserve to be relieved, except in the character of a common beggar; and was generous enough to offer a recommendation, by which she would be admitted into an infirmary to which her grace was a subscriber; at the same time advising the solicitor to send the twins to the Foundling Hospital, where they would be carefully nursed and brought up, so as to become useful members to the commonwealth . . .
> The duchess to her immortal honour, began the contribution with a crown; so that the rest of the company were obliged to restrict their liberality to half the sum, that her grace might not be affronted.[63]

The way in which Pickle and his friend Cadwallader Crabtree do obtain money for the poor is by setting up as consultant fortune-tellers and charging ladies of fashion half-a-guinea a time to reveal their own follies. The considerable profits are "distributed to poor families in distress".[64]

From the miseries of working-class life in the eighteenth-century ale and porter, filling empty stomachs, provided a temporary easement, and the brewing of these drinks supported all the elegances of the Thrales' little circle at Streatham. A more dangerous relief (sought by the Clewlines in *Sir Launcelot Greaves*) was gin, which it was deemed patriotic to drink, and which carried a low duty, because it was a home product. In the distilling of gin corn was consumed more profitably than in the making of bread. As this was good for the landed interest, especially the great grain-lords of Hampshire and Norfolk, Parliament encouraged the retail of gin until about 1736, when it recognised that gin-drinking was having a deplorable effect on the health of "people of lower and inferior rank . . . rendering them unfit for useful labours".[65] In 1733 there were over 6,000 gin shops in London. By 1743 the larger part of the urban proletariat might be said to have been crazy and uncontrollable with gin.[66] Henry Fielding remarked that gin "is the principal sustenance of more than 100,000 people in this metropolis".[67] Unheeded sufferings and cheap gin led inevitably to viciously punished crime.

The prisons in which the oppressed were further oppressed were all the more hateful by the disorder and neglect which characterises the social institutions of the eighteenth century. So pestilent were they that in 1750 four judges and forty officials at the Old Bailey died from the gaol-fever, which they caught from the prisoners standing trial. Thereafter the prisoners were disinfected with vinegar before they were brought into the dock.[66] Five years later a prisoner discharged from Exeter gaol brought the small-pox with him and depopulated Axminster.[67] But the authorities did not stop short at negligence. They were active in their spite and cruelty. One hears, for example, of George II's rejection of an appeal against a capital sentence because he did not like the judge who recommended the criminal (a petty forger) to mercy.[68] Well did Smollett call prisons "the mansions of the damned"! In four of his five novels Smollett takes the reader an angry tour of eighteenth-century prisons, particularly eighteenth-century debtors' prisons, against which he campaigns in his *History of England*. In the fifth, *Humphry Clinker*, he praises York Prison as being well ventilated and spacious:

The first, which was heretofore a fortress, is now converted into a prison, and is the best in all respects I ever saw at home or abroad. It stands in a high situation, extremely well ventilated, and has a spacious area within the walls for the health and convenience of all the prisoners, except those whom it is necessary to secure in close confinement. Even these last have all the comforts that the nature of their situation can admit of.[69]

York Prison comes off much better than York Minster, and is dealt with first.

It is in *Launcelot Greaves*, the most openly purposeful of Smollett's novels, that he makes his final indictment of the penal system. One long episode depicts the frustration of ability, the pent-up and spiritless dissipation, which took place in the debtors' prisons. Another gives an account of the "living monuments of inhumanity" consigned by a "modern magistrate", Justice Gobble, to his small borough gaol. Gobble "tyrannised over the poor and connived at the vices of the rich".[70] He made havoc among "the poorer sort of people, who were unable to call him to account", industriously contriving, with all the expertise of a retired city merchant, to ruin any defenceless person who crossed him in the least particular. Greaves, brought by accident into the gaol, asks the "naked wretches" there to tell him their stories. They crowd around him "and, like a congregation of rooks, opened their throats all at once, in accusation of Justice Gobble". There is the shop-keeper who did not vote for the candidate favoured by Gobble in a vestry election, the publican who refused to sell Gobble a horse which had been bred for his own use, the farmer's widow who affronted Mrs. Gobble's social pretensions, the poacher whom Gobble made use of till he was unsuccessful in carrying out one of Mrs. Gobble's commissions. All have been vindictively and carefully hunted down. "Where," exclaims Greaves, "is our admired constitution?" He is able to bring about the downfall of Gobble by sponsoring "divers prosecutions for corrupt practices, which had lain dormant until some person of courage and influence should take the lead against Justice Gobble".[71] The laws existed, but the chance appearance of a "person of courage and influence" was needed before they could be applied.

It makes a fine chiaroscuro piece, worthy of those seventeenth-century Italian painters, with their turbulent flicker-lit fervour, whom Smollett so much admired: the open throats of accusation, Gobble sitting in judgment in a crimson velvet night-cap, Mrs.

Gobble "puffed up with the pride and insolence of her husband's office, fat, frowsy and not over-clean", Greaves in his armour and Smollett tilting at installed cruelty on a rushing mount of words.

Yet Smollett's position, when not in the exhilerating saddle, is that of all materialists, one of ultimate gloom and misgiving. The best which can be done, he suggests, is to improve the physical conditions of existence. To him the highest conceivable aim is the salvation of many lives. But how much, in his estimate, are those lives worth when saved?

> My uncle and he are perfectly agreed in their estimate of life; which Quin, says, would stink in his nostrils, if he did not steep it in claret.[72]

Smollett himself was a very sober man.

"Et genus et virtus, nisi cum re, vilior alga est."[73] Life, at its best a spasm of glory between dust and dust, was more often unjust, slavish, nasty, an obscure contest with "the sordid and vicious disposition of the world".[74] Timothy Crabshaw goes to the conjuror and asks what his fate is. "The conjuror gravely replied that he would steal a dappled gelding on a Wednesday, be cast at the Old Bailey on a Thursday and suffer on a Friday".[75]

So much for Tim Crabshaw and his small mishaps on different days of the week. To a materialist, nobody's future is much brighter. Cast at the Old Bailey, marked out by a consumption, delivered up to the cruelties of chance, what is the difference? When Man is chained in the flesh and circling under the blows of a malign Nature, what use are the eight chirurgical treatises of Wiseman, or Cleland's strictures on the water at Bath? One can only shore up the rotten edifice, one can only shift the dung-hill miseries of disease and indigence a little out of the way, so that at least some measure of human dignity is possible. And one can register a protest. It will do no good whatever, it is a hopeless protest, like the black flag under which the Greeks sailed to Crete, not wanting to be misunderstood, not wishing those on land to think, even for one moment when they first sighted the ship, that their mission was a joyful one.

CHAPTER IX

SOME STATED MODE

WITH THE WATCHFUL belligerence of a Grand Master, Smollett played an implacable game of chess with his age. Hardly a move passed without a counter-move from Smollett, hardly a piece was brought into position without his slipping a dexterous pawn in its path. The concept of Authority, so important in eighteenth-century thought, upon which the certainty and order of orthodox opinion was founded, he opposed at every turn.

What assurance there is behind Dr. Johnson's claim that his principles of criticism are established on unalterable and evident Truth! He is wholly satisfied that he knows what Truth is. Criticism, he says, is useful "when it rectifies error and improves judgment". He has no doubt about what is correct and what is corrective.

Addison's trunkmaker regulates the behaviour of audiences at the theatre, so that there shall be nothing wild or irregular about the applause. Addison considers it to be of great use to the audience that a man of sound judgment should preside over it, awakening its attention at the right moment, and conducting its applause. Addison's standard of literary excellence, apart from the modern works which had the sanction of "the politer part" of his contemporaries, is the celebrated works of antiquity which have stood the test of time, and which the modern works should follow as closely as possible. Where he has no classical precedent to quote, Addison's reasoning is often odd, as when he cites the Cock Lane ghost as evidence for Christianity.

The laws of literature were almost as fixed as the laws of the land, and according to Blackstone in his *Commentaries on the Laws of 1770*, the English constitution could not be altered for the better. One feature of the perfect constitution which Blackstone pointed out was that the horrid penalty for treason was applicable, for example, "when a person is reconciled to the See of Rome, or procures another to be reconciled".[1] Johnson gave his emphatic assent to Blackstone's pronouncement. The Law he considered to be "the last result of human wisdom acting upon human experience for the benefit of the public".[2]

Smollett makes a brisk survey of the Law in *Advice*, with the couplet:

> Nor this, nor that, is standard right or wrong
> Till minted by the mercenary tongue.[3]

Justice, then, is a marketable commodity. As Ferrett says in *Launcelot Greaves*, in a little well-rounded speech with which Smollett is obviously in sympathy:

> That which is acknowledged to be truth in fact, is construed falsehood in law; and great reason we have to boast of a constitution founded on the basis of absurdity.[4]

In the same novel the hero, reckoning up the different ways in which the magistrate Gobble has abused his authority, exclaims:

> Oh! if such a despicable reptile shall annoy mankind with impunity, if such a contemptible miscreant shall have it in his power to do such deeds of inhumanity and oppression, what avails the law? Where is our admired constitution, the freedom, the security of the subject, the boasted humanity of the British nation![5]

Few other writers of Smollett's time were prepared to dispute that all was well with the constitution either of the State or of Letters, since both in jurisprudence and in literature the same complacent dogmatism prevailed. Many an attempt was made to codify the rules according to which books were to be written, ranging from Pope's one-man effort in the *Essay of Criticism* to Swift's argument, in his *Proposal for Correcting the English Tongue* of 1712, in favour of appointing a body of authorities on the mode of the French Academy for the purpose of "ascertaining and fixing our language for ever". In the period of consolidation which followed the experimenting exuberance of the early seventeenth-century stylists, what Johnson called "some stated mode" was always being sought. Johnson describes versification as "a science aspiring to constancy", and wishes that to make poetry more exact there were rules to govern the admission of such irregularities as Alexandrines. This is the literary equivalent of the influential philosopher Hobbes' insistence on the need for a curb to passion. Authority was the curb. There were three kinds of authority to which the eighteenth-century critic could appeal: Classical Antiquity, Good Sense and Revelation.

A knowledge of the classics was considered so important that Lord Chesterfield defined an illiterate man as one who was ignorant of Latin and Greek. The Latin or Greek quotation under which each number of the *Tatler* and the *Spectator* flies is a flag of convenience to show that the vessel is registered in a classical port. With a certain amount of grumbling about French servility, the English critics adopted the maxims of Boileau's *Art Poetique*, which begins with the rules for eclogues, and ends with a panegyric in which Louis XIV is praised with the same extravagant sycophancy that Boileau has previously bestowed on the classical poets. Whilst the *Art Poetique* embodies a number of sound practical precepts (such as those about the avoidance of prolixity and the importance of hard revision), it also contains the remarkable statement that an aspiring poet must copy Theocritus and Virgil, since Theocritus and Virgil were inspired by the gods. Such is Boileau's classical fixation, that he forgets that those particular gods are no longer believed in. He is like the fifth-century bishop, Sidonius Apollinaris, who invokes the pagan deities in his Latin hymns of praise. The incongruous mythologies of the eighteenth-century monuments in Westminster Abbey, the bare-bellied admirals in smutted long wigs and petal-nippled Roman armour, the pagan allegories in a Christian burying-place, are the result of the same lapse of memory. Apollo and Athene in the ambulatory, Hercules, Neptune and figures of Navigation in the great certain nave, amoretti frisking with a looking-glass in the transept, conspire to people with classical nudities the dusty but trim necropolis in which Death, presided over by arch-nosed heroes in marble lace, becomes quaint.

"Follow Homer," Horace had said. "Follow Horace," said Boileau. The writers of the time had Horace beaten into them at school, and as fledged wits they recollected with the rueful awe of those eight years of conformity that Horace had written a book on how to compose poems. So with the stunned conscientiousness of their schooldays, they obeyed Horace's rules. Pope, whose nightmares consisted of dreams about long journeys through unknown ways, seldom diverges from what is safe, established and familiar. As that neglected critic, John Dennis, observes, the dictatorial air of the *Essay on Criticism* is coupled with an exaggerated respect for authority and accepted opinion.

Edward Gibbon, dealing with the Revival of Learning, says of a knowledge of the classics that:

Such an intercourse must tend to refine the taste, and to elevate the genius, of the moderns : and yet, from the first experiment, it might appear that the study of the ancients had given fetters, rather than wings, to the human mind. However laudable, the spirit of imitation is of a servile cast; and the first disciples of the Greeks and Romans were a colony of strangers in the midst of their age and country. The minute and laborious diligence which explored the antiquities of remote times, might have improved or adorned the present state of society : the critic and metaphysician were the slaves of Aristotle; the poets, historians, and orators were proud to repeat the thoughts and words of the Augustan age; the works of nature were observed with the eyes of Pliny and Theophrastus; and some Pagan votaries professed a secret devotion to the gods of Homer and Plato.[6]

Gibbon's account of the curriculum at his own preparatory school suggests that in Education there had been little change since the Revival of Learning, and reveals why the educated classes were so ridden by the classics. The curriculum consisted exclusively of Latin syntax, Phaedrus' fables and Cornelius Nepos' *Lives of the Illustrious Romans*.[7] Oxford University did not take him much further than his preparatory school had. He condemns absolutely the stagnation of University life in his time, and remarks that the fourteen months which he spent at Magdalen College were "the fourteen months the most idle and unprofitable of my whole life".[8]

In the public schools repetition fixed grammar and metrical quantity in the boys' minds. The writing of Latin verses was obligatory and false quantity resulted in a flogging. For this reason the boys avoided the risks of originality and merely combined trite units from the Latin poets. The habit, once formed, was carried over into English verse, so that the bulk of Johnson's Poets wrote like Homer in Pope's version. Rills purl, locks are ambrosial, ill-omened hour is succeeded by dire debate and heroes lie bleeding on the conscious plain. So strong was the inclination to use ready-made phrases derived from the classics that Pope describes the Thames at Twickenham as reflecting "hanging mountains". Lady Mary Montagu, striving to educate herself as if she was a man, exhausted herself in a painful study of the military historian, Quintus Curtius. Her respect for Latinity is evident in her copying and transmitting to England any Roman inscriptions, no matter how trivial, which she encountered on her travels.

Johnson, in a conversation with the Scottish poet Allan Ramsay, compared modern literature to the moon, shining with a light borrowed from the sun of ancient literature, of Greece the source of knowledge and Rome the source of elegance. Addison made out a case for dressing the figures in portrait statues in "everlasting" Roman drapery. According to Reynolds, the painter should correct the defects of Nature, creating an ideal beauty which conforms to the rules of art as established by such masters as Raphael and the Caracci. It is an advantage to dress the figures in a painting in classical garments, since classical antiquity, being familiar to all Europe, has a universal significance. The artistic situation is best represented by Zoffany's painting of the Royal Academy in session. The little gentlemen in long waistcoats, a fuss of lace at throats and wrists, square toes turned out, twitter around a naked coal-heaver amid a muddle of casts from the antique. The eighteenth-century patron of the arts in England agreed with Winckelman's estimate that the shortest way to perfection was the imitation of the ancients. At home English artists had to earn a living by making such sad copies of the Old Masters as are to be found at Ham House, or else by painting portraits in the manner of Van Dyck. Otherwise they went to Rome like Nollekens and fabricated antique statuary to sell to English visitors.

Approximation to the classics was the aim of literature too, at least in the earlier part of the century. Swift advises the young poet "to improve upon them and make their sentiments your own". The imitation of the classics by way of topical paraphrase was a flourishing genre, the whole art of which lay in dexterous substitutions and lucky parallels. Sometimes a poem which could have stood in its own right is given an extra sanction by being called an imitation of a classical piece. Johnson's *Vanity of Human Wishes*, for example, does not follow Juvenal at all closely. Affiliations to the classics were attempted everywhere. Addison compared *Chevy Chase* with the *Aeneid* and Pope projected an epic poem on Brutus the Trojan and his settlement of Britain.

Rounding off his account of the Roman Empire, Gibbon concludes:

The map, the description, the monuments of ancient Rome, have been elucidated by the diligence of the antiquarian and the student : and the footsteps of heroes, the relics, not of superstitions, but of empire, are devoutly visited by a new race of pilgrims from the remote, and once savage, countries of the North.[9]

The very marble columns with which the patricians and Trimalchios of second-century Rome had made their houses palatial were fished out of the Tiber and re-erected here, so that the milords of sixteen hundred years later might recall the Ancient World not only in the literature which they favoured but in the setting of their everyday life. Whilst a Captain in the Hampshire militia, Gibbon studied Quintus Icilius on the art of war, and repeated the complaints of Cicero about the privations of a military command. On the analogy of Quintilian's preference for a Roman boy's beginning his education with Greek (since he would soon pick up Latin anyway, "while the fact that Latin learning is derived from Greek is a further reason"[10]) the English boy of the eighteenth century started with Latin, in spite of a much wider remove of period and situation than that between Aristotle and Quintilian. Dreams of consular grandeur were lived out in the temple-like Great Halls, curly-wigged senators paced the eloquent colonnades, upon the dramatic Corinthian staircases the silken-stockinged emissaries of power passed and re-passed. Imperial Rome and imperial England were in every detail equated.

For his part, an unruly figure amid such perspectived solemnity, Smollett lays about the Ancient Romans with the same zeal that Shaftesbury and Voltaire assaulted the Ancient Hebrews, and does so from the same motive, in order to discredit their authority. Smollett concentrated the whole force of his brisk contempt for such slavery to the classics on the unfortunate figure of the physician in *Peregrine Pickle*. This physician converses in Latin and Greek quotations. He enters the novel quoting Horace in a picture gallery, and directly afterwards adds forty to fifty lines from Homer. He cites a number of Greek paintings which were destroyed before the beginning of the Christian era and which are known only through classical allusions to them, and says that nothing by Titian and Rubens can equal them. He gives a dinner at which only Ancient Roman delicacies, such as porridge made of honey, oil, pickles and flour, are served. Five cooks resign because they cannot prevail upon their own consciences to follow such recipes. In his *Travels* Smollett carries out a programme of purposeful abuse of the classical world, especially against the inhabitants of Imperial Rome, who, he says, were undoubtedly barbarous. For the Roman navy he has the utmost scorn, and considers that half a dozen English frigates could have taken on both sides at the Battle of Actium.[11] "As for the Tyber," he volunteers, "it is, in comparison with the Thames, no more than an inconsiderable stream, foul, deep and rapid."[12] Classical mythology he asserts to be "no other than a collection of extravagant romances",[13] and his only classical allusions are by way of burlesque, as in the opening chapters of *Ferdinand, Count Fathom*.

For the Gothic, a term the meaning of which they enlarged to take in almost everything which happened in Europe between the founding of Constantinople and the restoration of Charles II, the classicists of the eighteenth century entertained a reproving disdain. Addison alludes to Chaucer and Spenser as the unpolished poets of a barbarous age:

> An age that yet uncultivate and rude
> Where'er the poet's fancy led, pursued
> Through pathless fields and unfrequented floods
> To dens of dragons and enchanted woods.[14]

Nor was Addison better pleased with the "ill-judged wit of metaphysical poetry" which exemplified "the extravagance of an irregular fancy".[15] Of the Gothick writers Shakespeare alone was allowed some measure of qualified approval. Even so, Addison takes up Dryden's complaint that Shakespeare's style is "pestered with figurative expressions" and "as affected as it is obscure", and deplores for his own part the way in which the heroes of Shakespeare's tragedies "weep and quibble for a dozen lines together".[16] Shakespeare was often made more tolerable to eighteenth-century taste in regularised versions of his plays, such as the adaptation of *King Lear* by Nahum Tate, in which Cordelia has an intrigue with Edgar ("giving occasion to a new scene or two") and Edmund and Goneril are discovered "amorously seated in a grotto". In his preface Tate describes how he found the play as a heap of jewels, unstrung and unpolished and threaded the jewels together by such devices. Even when the text was not altered, the presentation of Shakespeare on the stage was generally more decorous than Shakespeare, in all his extravagance, proposed it should be. Quin declaimed the part of Coriolanus in a flared frock-coat. Garrick, as Macbeth, was expressive in knee-breeches.

Just as he rejected the classicism of his age, so Smollett valued the poets whom the classicists despised. In his *Account of the Greatest English Poets*, Addison, after having smartly dismissed Chaucer and Spenser, lists Cowley, Milton, Waller, Roscommon, Denham, Dryden, Congreve (whom Pope called "the last of the Romans"), Dorset and Montague. In *Humphry Clinker* Smollett gives Chaucer, Spenser and Shakespeare pre-eminence as "our best poets", and in a subsequent speech of Lismahago's demonstrates his own appreciation of the need for historical understanding in dealing with authors of a past age :

> "For instance," said he, "how have your commentators been puzzled by the following expression in the *Tempest*—He's gentle, and not fearful; as if it was a paralogism to say, that, being gentle, he must of course be courageous; but the truth is, one of the original meanings, if not the sole meaning of that word was, noble, high-minded; and to this day a Scotswoman, in the situation of the young lady in the *Tempest*, would express herself nearly in the same terms—Don't provoke him for being gentle, that is high-spirited, he won't tamely bear an insult. Spenser in the very first stanza of his Faery Queene, says—
> 'A gentle knight was pricking on the plain'; which knight, far from being tame and fearful was so stout, that 'Nothing did he dread, but ever was ydrad'."[17]

Although far from given to the awed repetition of other men's words, Smollett quotes Shakespeare eleven times in *Ferdinand, Count Fathom*, and devotedly took the complete set of Shakespeare's plays with him on his travels in France and Italy at the end of his life.

In his respect for the old English authors Smollett anticipated Charles Lamb and the writers of the Romantic Movement, as he also did in his feeling for landscape-painting and for landscape itself. The following passage could have come from Dorothy Wordsworth's journal :

> Though in the morning there was a frost upon the ground, the sun was as warm as it is in May in England. The sea was quite smooth, and the beach formed of white polished pebbles; on the left-hand side the country was covered with green olives, and the side of the road planted with large trees of sweet myrtle growing wild like the hawthorns in England.[18]

Johnson, though he was very good at defining words, seldom troubled to define his terms. His appeal is first to classical author-

ity and secondly to what he calls "the general sense or experience
of mankind". Nothing seems to have prompted him to enquire
where this general sense was recorded or where its characteristics
were laid down. Thus, when he praises Gray's *Elegy* for its reflection of every mind, we can only conclude that he means the
mind of a thoughtful European conditioned by a particular educa-
cation, or even just the mind of Samuel Johnson. There is little
room for the passionate individualism of a Smollett here. Literature is viewed as the collective effort of a polite group of people.
Addison asserted that men of genius seldom rise up singly, but in
bodies, as in the reigns of Augustus or Louis XIV. To cultivate
taste one must be conversant with the politest authors and used
to polite society. Corneille would not have written so well had
he not been the friend of Racine. Smollett was aware that one
had only to cross the channel to find that Johnson's "prompt
and intuitive perception of consonance and propriety" was not
the same in all countries. Pointing out the differences between
the English attitude and the French one, Smollett goes on to
observe that "a Parisian likes mortified flesh : a native of Legiboli
will not taste his fish until it is quite putrified ... the Green-
landers eat in the same dish as their dogs : the Caffres, at the
Cape of Good Hope, p ... upon those whom they delight to
honour".[19]

The eighteenth century is often mistakenly called the Age of
Reason. What reason was shown was often very limited and
took the form of an appeal to an indefinite Good Sense or to
Revelation. No Spinoza attempted to account for the nature
of the Universe in terms of his naked, unaided logic. Dr. Johnson called the Bible the source of all external truth, regarded
the Universities as ancillaries to the Church of England, and for
this reason approved of the exclusion of Methodists from Oxford.
It was, however, an age which aspired to Reason. Boileau, in his
Art Poetique, pronounced that, before writing, the poet must
learn to think. Thought had been defined by Hobbes as mental
activity steadily directed to some approved end, and it was
Hobbes who had persuaded a large number of poets to write only
what is factually correct about the conduct of men in everyday
situations, so that, after all the passionate complexity of seventeenth-century speculation, simple ideas, showily elaborated, now
passed for cleverness.

Presumably because it was not steadily directed towards some
approved end, writers such as Addison and Johnson had little

respect for music. Addison writes slightingly of "Mynheer
Handel" and makes Ironsides (the hero of *The Guardian*) prefer
the singing of the birds to that at the Opera. Pope, although
he once wrote an *Ode to St. Cecilia,* asked his friend Arbuthnot
if it was really possible for anyone to take an unaffected pleasure
in Handel's music. On one occasion Lord Chesterfield left
George II's presence at an oratorio by Handel, saying that he
did not wish to disturb the privacy of the monarch. Johnson was
always-contemptuous in his remarks on music and musicians.
Mrs. Thrale records that he delighted no more in music than in
painting, for which he entertained "an utter scorn". Smollett
was almost alone amongst the great writers of his time in loving
music. The Prince of Wales, piqued with Handel (mainly because the king admired him), did his best to impoverish him by
leading the world of fashion elsewhere, and helping to set up a
puppet show as a rival attraction to the Opera. Smollett came
to Handel's defence in *Advice*:

> Again shall Handel raise his laurelled brow,
> Again shall harmony with rapture glow;
> The spell dissolves, the combination breaks,
> And Punch no longer Frasi's rival squeaks.[20]

In *Sir Launcelot Greaves* Smollett warmly sets about Boileau for
having made "the celebrated Lulli" the object of a lampoon "for
which reason every man of a liberal turn must, in spite of all his
poetical merit, despise him as a rancorous knave".[21]

As well as writing three songs on other occasions, in 1748
Smollett was at work on a masque called *Alceste,* for which
Handel was to supply the music. Of all frustrated projects, this
ranks with Dr. Johnson's history of the British Parliament and
Coleridge's grand polytechnical poem in potential curiosity.

The bearings of the eighteenth century and its relation to the
preceding age are often forgotten. Steele's Major Matchlock
remembers the Battle of Marston Moor in 1644. Jenny Distaff's
wedding reception is held in the Apollo Room of the Old Devil,
with Ben Jonson's rules for the conduct of a club of poets still
written on the wall. Milton had been dead for less than 30 years
when Addison returned from the Grand Tour to start his literary
career. Milton was as close to Addison as Lytton Strachey is to
us. Vanbrugh lived to erect a monument to the Battle of Blenheim. The old rift between cavaliers and roundheads was not far
away, except that the roundheads were winning the economic

battle as surely as they had lost the political one. England's commercial dominance was leading to the supremacy within the country of the trading classes. In a plutocratic society money means position and position demands a knowledge of polite forms. The aim of the previously upright and stiff merchants was absorption into the ruling class, hitherto the corrupt and easy-going ex-Cavaliers whose chosen writers were colloquial, free and essentially aristocratic writers who indeed kept up in their comedies the propaganda war of the court against the city which had been started by Middleton in the reign of James I.

Addison reconciles the two classes, and Richardson seals the bond between them. Of the two knights in the Spectator Club, one is a landowner and the other a dignitary of the City. Between them they arrive at sound sense. The arbiters of the new elegance, Addison, Pope, Swift, Johnson, Nash, Reynolds, Adams and Brummel, were all in fact of indubitably middle-class origins. They set out on one hand to civilise the farouche old aristocracy and on the other to help the middle class in its aspirations towards gentility. The era of epic heroes and royal tragedies was over. The mercantile culture represented by Dyer's *Fleece* and Lillo's *London Merchant* had begun. Chesterfield did indeed attempt a counter-movement towards the court-manners suitable to an absolute monarchy, towards the standards of his youth, when he and the Baron Tronck had rioted like stallions when Dryden had spoken of "the debaucheries and repartees of gentlemen", and Queen Anne complained that her Lord Treasurer often came to her drunk, behaving towards her with indecency and disrespect. Sir Roger de Coverley himself had been a wild young man. But whilst the middle class were still genuinely respectful to the landed gentry, they preferred an Addisonian notion of refinement. By the end of the century they were the main producers and consumers of the fine arts. Two of the most considerable artists of the century, Hogarth and Bewick, were to start life engraving tradesmen's bill-heads. Especially after Walpole's establishment of a stable régime which needed no support from political pamphleteers, the patronage of literature lay in the hands of men of business. The stranded writers were employed on hack work, on compilations to enlighten them and their wives about the big world.

They found a willing public. The middle class desired acceptance and approval, and since their objective was not self-improvement but the consummation of social pretence, they were uncritical of the ideas which had been current in the previous ruling class. Thus authority was given a new intensity. To share the views of polite society was a step towards assimilation into it. The acceptance of authority accompanied an anxious striving to be genteel. *Evelina*, a novel about a pretty modest middle-class girl's endeavours to escape her bourgeois connections and marry a lord, is very largely concerned with what constitutes good manners. It was the *Spectator*, with its clear easy fluency and confidence, which acted as chief instructor to the rising bourgeoisie.

Whilst the work of such writers as Addison is obviously of more lasting merit than the manuals of learning and politeness which were produced for the avid middle class at this time, its purpose was often the same, Isaac Bickerstaff, the chief character of the *Tatler*, plays the role of an arbiter elegantiarum and adopts the title of Censor of Great Britain. He instigates a Court of Honour "to correct enormities in dress and behaviour". The taste for exhortation was strong in the eighteenth century. Seldom has such a copious literature of advice been produced. Swift advised young clergymen and Stella. Steele advised his fellow soldiers on Christian conduct. Chesterfield advised a large legitimate and illegitimate family, proceeding from son to grandsons and ultimately to the last available godson. Johnson superintended the spiritual operations of Boswell, Mrs. Thrale and Fanny Burney. Pope's verse is for the most part either admonitory or hortatory. The *Spectator* and the *Rambler* are full of hints on courtship, marriage and the proper use of time. Fielding is for ever breaking off his narrative in order to wag an understanding forefinger. Gibbon's attitude to the bad Emperors is definitely reproachful.

The spate of advice was never interrupted by any blunders made by the givers of it in their own private lives. Chesterfield attached himself to and was discarded by two successive crown princes of England, staking everything on worldly success to the extent of relinquishing his mistress, Mrs. Howard, to George II (on the understanding that she would be more useful to Chesterfield as the king's mistress than as his own) and even bringing himself to marry the unengaging, poverty-stricken and arrogant illegitimate daughter of George I. Yet he went on his way, looking agreeable, from indignity to indignity, from failure to signal failure. His brief tenure of a vestige of power brought him the ignominy of having recommended the ferocious measures taken against the Scotch rebels in 1745. His attempts at literary patronage elicited the vigorous and deserved contempt of Johnson and

Smollett. Swift's career was one of sycophancy to his patrons and severity to everyone else, inexpert apostasy, miscalculated chances and deserting the wrong people. Addison, after having issued so many warnings about marrying scolds, married the Countess of Warwick and was driven to redouble his attentions to the bottle. Johnson, who also gave so much matrimonial advice, was married to a tippling old lady and made a fool of himself over Mrs. Thrale.

The mingling of the classes by the process of giving and accepting advice created a greater number of people with an informed respect for the types of authority which have been described. The merchants were enfranchised only in order to vote for the right party, and the old Addisonian standards were observed in the new middle-class salons. Such a salon was that of Mrs. Thrale, an eighteenth-century Mme. Verdurin whose husband engrossed so much money that he paid £20,000 a year in tax. Supported by the profitable spurt and bubble of Mr. Thrale's brewery, the salon spread and enfolded like the yeast in his vats, taking in Johnson, Reynolds, Burke and the Burneys. There at Streatham Mrs. Thrale rallied and consolidated middle-class opinion, promulgating the Augustan gospel in a revised version, and living on to read and dislike *Frankenstein*. Johnson himself accepted the mercantile standards of the little circle at Streatham. He once placed Literature and brewing on the same footing. Explaining how he hated to write for nothing or for a low payment, he added, "One hates, besides, ever to give away that which one has been accustomed to sell", and, turning to Mr. Thrale, asked, "Would you not, sir, rather give away money than porter?"[22] When he was given a pension by George III, he jokingly told Boswell that, although his political principles were unchanged, it would not be decent for him to drink King James's health in wine paid for by King George. Nevertheless, he considered that the pleasure of cursing the House of Hanover, and drinking King James's health, was amply over-balanced by three hundred pounds a year.

The extent of the Thrale Salon's revision may be judged by the prim dislike entertained by all members of it except Johnson himself for Boswell, who, raffish and upper class, represented the older tradition. The panache and enthusiasm of Boswell, sensitive to immediate impressions but lacking in any burgher-like staying power, puzzled and vexed them. Boswell presented himself to the world as the man who had read Gray's *Odes* till he

was almost mad, who always wished to rush into the fray when
he heard military music, who had called on Voltaire and argued
him to a standstill with his rush of words, who periodically was
obliged to take mercury and who was recording on the spot in
a big notebook Johnson's every utterance. The resemblance to
Vanbrugh's Lord Foppington in *The Relapse* before their friend
Sheridan had cleaned up that reprehensible old play was too
strong for the little circle at Streatham.

Entrenched as the new plutocracy was in a stable Hanoverian
society, it was unlikely that the social criticism of its chosen
mentors would be severe. Life, at least for the articulate classes,
was sedate. At Blenheim and Glencoe it was the peasantry which
was sacrificed and the peasantry had neither the ability nor the
chance to express an opinion or to perpetuate its sentiments. For
the enfranchised it was a period of level general events. Men
risked little and gained little. The last opportunity for a grand
personal action, with life at stake, was on the death of Queen
Anne, when Bolingbroke attempted to bring over the Pretender.
Here the well-calculated tolerance of the Whigs flattened out
the dramatic possibilities of the incident.

Addison imagines the indignation of Juvenal were Juvenal
to see a lady wearing a riding jacket. He thinks that Juvenal
would have called her a monster and a token of the degeneration
of Roman womanhood. But Juvenal was used to worse pranks
than that. Between the first *Spectator* and the last *Rambler* lie
forty years. In Rome during forty years of the first century, the
earlier part of Juvenal's long lifetime, the rites of the Bona Dea
flourished, the head of state performed in the theatre, there were
two great fires at Rome, an Emperor was murdered, Christians
were burnt to death in the public gardens, a Vestal Virgin was
buried alive and Saint John had occasion to write the Apocalypse.
One doubts if Juvenal would have noticed the lady's riding habit.
There were grim and real evils in Addison's time, of which
Smollett is angrily aware, but the small polite society which
Addison chose as his world cut him off from these. He records
instead the small outrages of head-dresses, pin-money, and similar
objects of fashionable interest. Side-stepping "the bellowings and
distortions of enthusiasm", he clears up the shop-signs, disposes
of party patches and regulates street cries. Steering, as Boileau
had recommended, gracefully from grave to light, he avoids the
crude misery which was to be found on all sides of him. The unheeded sufferings of the inelegant classes led, with the assistance

of the only alleviation, cheap gin, to acts of desperate crime. There is a drawing at the British Museum of women prisoners at the Old Bailey, chained together, meek and feverish, led by a bully with a cudgel, victims of those with physical power over them. Addison, to place his achievement at his own assessment, "brought philosophy out of closets and libraries, to dwell in clubs and assemblies, at tea-tables and in coffee houses".

Smollett was quick to see what was going on, and as quick to bring the heaped lightning of his contempt to bear upon it. He examines the mingling of the traders with the nobles at Bath, one of the great centres of fashionable indoctrination :

> Every upstart of fortune, harnessed in the trappings of the mode, presents himself at Bath, as in the very focus of observation. Clerks and factors from the East Indies, loaded with the spoil of plundered provinces; planters, negro drivers and hucksters, from our American plantations, enriched they know not how; agents, commissaries, and contractors, who have fattened, in two successive wars, on the blood of the nations; usurers, brokers and jobbers of every kind; men of low birth and no breeding, have found themselves suddenly translated into a state of affluence, unknown to former ages; and no wonder that their brains should be intoxicated with pride, vanity and presumption.[23]

As if to show his impartiality, Smollett points out that the class which these newly rich aspire to is quite as bad. He does so in one of those scenes of observant and apparently objective description which he can charge with so much satire. Jack Holder, an eccentric figure in *Humphry Clinker*, gives a tea-party at Bath. The guests are not to touch the delicacies until a bell rings, but after that they may help themselves without restriction. This is what happens :

> The tea-drinking passed as usual; and the company having risen from the tables, were sauntering in groups in expectation of the signal for attack, when, the bell beginning to ring, they flew with eagerness to the dessert, and the whole place was instantly in commotion. There was nothing but justling, scrambling, pulling, snatching, struggling, scolding, and screaming. The nosegays were torn from one another's hands and bosoms; the glasses and china went to wreck; the tables and floor were strewed with comfits. Some cried, some swore, and the tropes and figures of Billingsgate were used without reserve in all their native zest and flavour; nor were those flowers of rhetoric unattended with significant gesticulation. Some snapped their fingers, some forked them out,

some clapped their hands, and some their backsides; at length they fairly proceeded to pulling caps, and everything seemed to presage a general battle; when Holder ordered his horns to sound a charge, with a view to animate the combatants and inflame the contest; but this manoeuvre produced an effect quite contrary to what he expected. It was a note of reproach that roused them to an immediate sense of their disgraceful situation. They were ashamed of their absurd deportment, and suddenly desisted. They gathered up their caps, ruffles, and handkerchiefs, and great part of them retired in silent mortification.

Quin laughed at this adventure; but my uncle's delicacy was hurt. He hung his head in manifest chagrin, and seemed to repine at the triumph of his judgment. Indeed his victory was more complete than he imagined; for, as we afterwards learned, the two amazons who signalized themselves most in the action did not come from the purlieus of Puddledock, but from the courtly neighbourhood of St. James's Palace. One was a baroness, and the other a wealthy knight's dowager.[24]

This, then, was the strength of the good manners which Addison and a dozen other officious helpers had imposed. The good manners, and the Authority which had initiated and informed them, collapsed, not merely under the urgency of human need, not merely under the stress of a desperate time, but at the ringing of a tea-bell.

As might be expected of the son of a general and descendant of an earl, who ran through a fortune in social ostentation and spent five years holding down the proletariat of London, Fielding was an exponent of the conformity we have been dealing with throughout this chapter. As such he differs from Smollett in four main aspects : style, respect for the classics, philosophy and view of society.

Except in his facetious epic similes, Fielding employs an un-ambitious Addisonian style, far less figurative than that of Smollett. Parson Adams was "a man of good sense, good parts and good nature; but at the same time was as entirely ignorant of the ways of the world as an infant just entered into it could be".[25] A good man "is a standing lesson to all his acquaintance, and of far greater use in that narrow circle than a good book".[26] But it is not merely a calm, explanatory, axiomatic manner which Fielding shares with Addison. He has the same taste for moral reflection, which he indulges, not only in the introductory chapter to each book of *Tom Jones* ("A Comparison between the World and the Stage" and the like), but in sly insertions into the dia-

logue of *Joseph Andrews* and *Amelia*. These conversational ex-
cursions are in fact short essays in the manner of the *Spectator*
on such topics as mortality and the coquetry of women. "Then
Joseph made a speech on charity which the reader, if he is so
disposed, may see in the next chapter",[27] is a typical opening.
The connection with Addison is sometimes direct. In *Tom Jones*
Fielding compares his hero's conscience to the trunk-maker in
Addison's famous paper about the theatre. Parson Adams, in
Joseph Andrews, quotes Addison's *Cato* with approval, adding
that it is the only English tragedy which he, as a scholar and a
priest, has ever troubled to read.

Fielding's use of classical allusion is not confined to the pseudo-
Virgilian apparatus of *Tom Jones*. Everywhere there is a pro-
fusion of classical citation and reference. Describing Fanny, in
Joseph Andrews, Fielding quotes Latin twice and refers to Pyg-
malion and Narcissus. In the shuffling moralising exordium to
Amelia he quotes six lines of Claudian, and then later makes Dr.
Harrison direct a distressed couple (Booth and Amelia) to Cicero's
Tusculan Disputations for the answer to their problems. Nor is
Dr. Harrison a figure of fun. There is every indication that Field-
ing regards him as an authoritative and beneficent personage.
Parson Adams, holding forth on the subject of cowardice, men-
tions Homer, Paris, Hector, Pompey, Julius Caesar, Cicero and
Paterculus. On the subject of travel he brings in the Pillars of
Hercules, Carthage, Archimedes, the Cyclades, Helle, Apollonius
Rhodius, Daedalus, Colchis and the Golden Fleece. This is nothing to the eight hundred words of casual chat which he later
devotes to an exposition of Homer's *Iliad*. Parson Adams *is* a
comic character, but his whimsicality always consists of a naïve
exaggeration of views with which Fielding demonstrably had
every sympathy. Fielding's parade of classical learning did not
come from an education superior to that of Smollett. It was a
matter of preference. Smollett probably worked quite as hard at
his Scotch grammar school as Fielding did at Eton, and certainly
before leaving school he would have been expected to have
mastered large parts of Claudian, Ovid, Phaedrus, Cornelius
Nepos, Cicero, Sulpicius, Virgil, Horace, Juvenal, Livy and
Sallust.[28] That Smollett continued to read Latin all his life we
know from the antiquarian sections of the *Travels* and the fact
that amongst the books which he took abroad with him on his
tour through France and Italy was a copy of the poems of
Tibullus.

Fielding's philosophy of life is not notable for its originality. Apart from a belief in Providence, and in spite of the frequency of his moral discourses, it does not go far beyond admiring a courageous young dog when he sees one. Not that he is unwilling or slow to point out an undeniable truth about the nature of mankind. When by a highly managed piece of dramatic irony, Captain Blifil falls down dead of an apoplexy whilst calculating how much money he will inherit from Mr. Allworthy, Fielding remarks: "He took, therefore, measure of that proportion of soil which was now adequate to all his future purposes."[29] He then quotes Horace to the effect that Blifil needed only six feet by two. Providence, which is the stated theme of *Amelia*, is also conspicuous in *Joseph Andrews*. One chapter is given to "the grave and truly solemn discourse of Mr. Adams" in the course of which he states:

> You are to consider you are a Christian, that no accident happens to us without the Divine permission, and that it is the duty of a man, and a Christian, to submit. We did not make ourselves; but the same power which made us rules over us, and we are absolutely at his disposal; he may do with us what he pleases, nor have we right to complain.[30]

Providence eventually takes the form of Squire Booby's arriving with a big bag of money.

For his part, Joseph Andrews is "perfectly content with the state to which he was called" and does not "repine at his own lot, nor envy those of his betters".[31] Parson Adams, who heartily approves of these sentiments, replies:

> Well said, my lad, and I wish some who have read many more good books, nay, and some who have written good books themselves, had profited as much by them.

Fielding was only in a minor way a social reformer. Perhaps the tenderness of his conscience, which made him so kind towards animals, was nullified by his belief in the justness of Providence. Certainly he approved of capital punishment for felons and coercion for the poor. In his *Proposal for making effective Provision for the Poor,* he treats poverty as if it was a retribution for some crime, suggesting that the unemployed should be held under duress in County Houses if diligent, and, if vagrants, be placed in Houses of Correction with dungeons and fasting rooms.

This being conformity, one can understand why Smollett was so pugnaciously non-conformist. A lifeless acquiescence, dull to the cruelty which it perpetuated, in the ways of a so-called Providence, was what irritated Smollett most in the England of his time. In a letter to Alexander Carlyle he writes of "this land of indifference and phlegm, where the finer sensations of the soul are not felt, and felicity is held to consist in stupefying port and overgrown buttocks of beef, where genius is lost, learning undervalued, taste altogether extinguished".[32] Himself he displayed untiring vitality as a reformer and social critic.

His first principles concerning the social order are most concisely stated during the course of an episode in *Roderick Random*. A broken-down French soldier tells Random, who is already very irked by the fatigues of a long march, how happy he is to have had the honour of helping to establish the glory of Louis XIV :

> When I looked upon the contemptible object that pronounced these words, I was amazed at the infatuation that possessed him; and could not help expressing my astonishment at the absurdity of a rational being, who thinks himself highly honoured in being permitted to encounter abject poverty, oppression, famine, disease, mutilation, and evident death, merely to gratify the vicious ambition of a prince, by whom his sufferings were disregarded, and his name utterly unknown. I observed that, if his situation was the consequence of compulsion, I would praise his patience and fortitude in bearing his lot; if he had taken up arms in defence of his injured country, he was to be applauded for his patriotism; or, if he had fled to this way of life as a refuge from a greater evil, he was justifiable in his own conscience, though I could have no notion of misery more extreme that that he suffered; but to put his condition on the footing of conducing to the glory of his prince, was no more than professing himself a desperate slave, who voluntarily underwent the utmost wretchedness and peril, and committed the most flagrant crimes, to soothe the barbarous pride of a fellow-creature, his superior in nothing but the power he derived from the submission of such wretches as him.[33]

The French soldier, not unnaturally offended, comments on the rebellious insolence with which the English treat their kings :

> In vindication of my countrymen, I repeated all the arguments commonly used to prove that every man has a natural right to liberty; that allegiance and protection are reciprocal; that, when the mutual tie is broken by the tyranny of the king, he is accountable to the people for his breach of contract, and subject to the penalty of the law.

As a corollary to this, Smollett states in *Ferdinand, Count Fathom* that the King of Corsica has "the best possible title" to his throne—that of the unanimous election of his subjects.[34] Smollett does not venerate the social order as being divinely ordained. He regards it as a practical arrangement which must be put right in a workmanlike manner where and when it goes wrong. Above all he sees the sovereign as answerable to his subjects, whose personal liberty and well being must be safeguarded.

Smollett dismisses Authority as a device by which the few make the many submit to their will. The submission, once obtained, results in a despotism prolonged by the use of physical force as an ultimate measure. Smollett gives two examples in *Roderick Random* of the base supremacy of physical force. As a boy, Random, guilty only of being poor and defenceless, is repeatedly flogged by his schoolmaster :

> The contempt which my appearance naturally produced in all who saw me, the continual wants to which I was exposed, and my own haughty disposition, impatient of affronts, involved me in a thousand troublesome adventures, by which I was at length inured to adversity, and emboldened· to undertakings far above my years. I was often inhumanely scourged for crimes I did not commit; because having the character of a vagabond in the village, every piece of mischief whose author lay unknown was charged upon me.[35]

Later as a man, Random once more falls a victim to the spite of those set in power over him :

> About a week after this exploit, as I was going my rounds among the sick, I was taken prisoner, and carried to the poop by the master-at-arms, where I was loaded with irons, and stapled to the deck, on pretence that I was a spy on board, and had conspired against the captain's life. How ridiculous soever this imputation was, I did not fail to suffer by it all the rigour that could be shown to the worst of criminals, being exposed in this miserable condition to the scorching heat of the sun by day, and the unwholesome damps by night, during the space of twelve days, in which I was neither brought to trial, nor examined touching the probability of the charge.

The boy, by raising a rebellion amongst his class-mates, is able to revenge himself on the schoolmaster, who is himself birched. The man, in a much more serious situation, can do nothing but give way, although with what bitterness Smollett well knew.

CHAPTER X

THE SNAKES OF ICELAND

In 1746 Smollett's first publication, *Advice*, appeared under the mast-head of two mottoes from Juvenal. *Advice*, a little-known and underestimated verse-satire, is in the form of a dialogue between a poet and his worldly friend. The poet has been disappointed in his quest for fame and, fooled by false promises, is dwindling into indigence. (Smollett's tragedy, *The Regicide*, had just been rejected by the management of Drury Lane Theatre in spite of Lord Chesterfield's assurances that he would exert his influence in its favour.) The satire opens expletively, with the poet's acknowledgement that, in the civilisation he belongs to, poverty is thought shameful:

> Enough, enough; all this we knew before;
> 'Tis infamous, I grant it, to be poor.

Yet the poet cannot escape poverty unless he catches the attention of the ruling class, which has dedicated itself to worthless amusements, prefers puppet-shows to Handel's operas, and has no interest in the fine arts:

> But one thing more,—how loud must I repeat,
> To rouse the engag'd attention of the great;
> Amus'd, perhaps, with C-'s prolific bum,
> Or rapt amidst the transports of a drum;
> While the grim porter watches ev'ry door,
> Stern foe to tradesmen, poets, and the poor.[1]

He is weary of bribing "base mongrel" footmen to admit him, so that he can fix his "mute imploring" gaze upon "some proud lord who smiles a gracious lie". He reflects upon the irresponsible national stewardship provided by the aristocracy:

> Is there, ye varnish'd ruffians of the State!
> Not one, among the millions whom ye cheat,
> Who, while he totters on the brink of woe,
> Dares, ere he falls, attempt th'avenging blow!

A steady blow! his languid soul to feast;
And rid his country of one curse at least?[2]

(It should be remembered that this same obliging Chesterfield
had recommended the brutalities with which the Scots were
punished for the rebellion of 1745.)

Aghast at such revolutionary sentiments, the poet's friend
recommends a more prudent way of thinking, which is summed
up in the line:

The lower still you crawl, you'll climb the higher.

The poet is to rise by prostration and sycophancy. He is to
flatter and to draw up panegyrics. He must profit by the follies of
others or else starve. He is to pimp, act as a parasite, hunt a fortune in marriage; if necessary, sacrifice his chastity to "some insati-
ate dame" or to a homosexual master. In this fashion he will please
the people who already have money and so get money for himself.

The poet says that he will do no such thing. Calling on his
Muse to "fix the brand of infamy on vice", he denounces the
distribution of wealth which has placed all power in the hands
of the corrupt few, who indulge in ostentatious waste at the
expense of the suffering many:

What if, arous'd at his imperious call,
An hundred footsteps echo through his hall;
And, on high columns rear'd, his lofty dome
Proclaims th'united art of Greece and Rome:
What though whole hecatombs his crew regale,
And each dependant slumbers o'er his ale;
While the remains, through months unnumber'd past,
Indulge the beggar and the dogs at last:
Say, friend, is it benevolence of soul,
Or pompous vanity, that prompts the whole?
These sons of sloth, who by profusion thrive,
His pride inveigled from the public hive;
And numbers pine in solitary woe,
Who furnish'd out this fantasy of show.[3]

The poet goes on to lament the fact that the livelihood of the
cheated millions depends on the private whim or fortuitous
charity of the rich man:

When silent misery assails his eyes,
Did e'er his throbbing bosom sympathize?
Or his extensive charity pervade
To those who languish in the barren shade,

Where oft by want and modesty suppress'd,
The bootless talent warms the lonely breast?
No! petrify'd by dulness and disdain,
Beyond the feeling of another pain,
The tear of pity ne'er bedew'd his eye,
Nor his lewd bosom felt the social sigh![4]

Advice contains a number of the leading·themes of the novels which Smollett was later to write: the corruption of the individual by a society which puts a premium on base conduct; the worthlessness of the ruling class; the unfair distribution of the nation's wealth; the inadequacy of private charity and other such patchings-up of an irreparable system.

Roderick Random, the hero of Smollett's first novel, puts into practice the precepts of the poet's friend in *Advice*. Although he is naturally of an intractable and impetuous disposition (in the words of one of his employers, possessing "more veracity than prudence") the successive calamities of his career teach him to play the hypocrite, so that, uniting the characteristics of the bully and the time-server, he becomes a complete although inexpert rogue. Smollett presents this as an ironical triumph for Reason, making Random say in his ultimate depravity, "The impetuous transports of my passion are now settled and mellowed". Having been "debauched by a commerce with mankind", Random is able to protect better men, such as Strap and Bowling, against the way of the world—the implication being that only the debauchees survive. He learns through destitution to study men's humours with a view to gaining an ascendancy over them, to conceal resentment for prudential motives, to lie, cheat and extort. "I every day improved in my knowledge of the town", he remarks. This is the ascendancy of reason over "a disposition which was touchy and impatient of control". Yet even whilst playing the world's own dirty game, Random slithers from calamity to calamity. It is only chance which extricates him each time, and here Smollett uses the old trick of surprise with a new satirical intention. Everything depends on the "tossing up of a halfpenny". That is the lesson of *Roderick Random*. Crime does not pay unless it is given the right backing, and then it pays astonishingly well and is called expediency. Although Random claims to be a gentleman "by birth, education and character", it is his father's money, conveniently falling into his hands, which eventually makes the world accept him as one. By that time he has long forfeited his character.

Roderick Random, then, is an extension, in approximately Picaresque form, of the verse-satire, *Advice.* So marked is the continuity from one to the other that even the topic of homosexuality, which takes up a large part of *Advice,* is preserved in *Roderick Random.* In fact, just as the characters in one of Molière's plays whimsically discuss Molière's plays, so Roderick Random quotes from *Advice* when he is asked for his opinion on the subject of sodomy by the interested Earl Strutwell.

Since *Roderick Random* is a development of *Advice,* it is not surprising that Smollett introduces himself in the first few lines of the Introduction to *Roderick Random* as a satirist:

> Of all kinds of satire, there is none so entertaining and universally improving as that which is introduced as it were, occasionally, in the course of an interesting story, which brings every incident home to life.

In other words, the story is there to carry the satire. He has chosen to write prose fiction because it makes easy reading, gives scope for social rapportage and allows "the vicissitudes of life" to appear "in their peculiar circumstances". Smollett's concern is avowedly with the truth about human experience. He distinguishes between "Romance" and the kind of fiction which he wants to write. Romance is the product of superstition:

> But when the minds of men were debauched, by the imposition of priestcraft, to the most absurd pitch of credulity, the authors of romance arose, and losing sight of probability, filled their performances with the most monstrous hyperboles. If they could not equal the ancient poets in point of genius, they were resolved to excel them in fiction, and apply to the wonder rather than the judgment of their readers.

He comments on the false values of Romance, the heroes of which are conspicuous, not for their "dignity of sentiment and practice", but for their "bodily strength, activity, and extravagance of behaviour".

As Smollett sees it, the function of the novelist is not merely to make up a story and tell highly circumstantial lies at great length. He would certainly not agree with the modern novelist who has declared that fiction is "a kind of magic and sorcery—a confidence trick, trying to make people believe something is true which is not". If fiction was no more than artful verisimilitude, then one could understand why Plato charged the poets (that is to say, the only writers of fiction in Periclean Athens) with mendacity, and wanted to exclude them from his Republic. Smollett proposes to use the novel, with its "peculiar circumstances", to exemplify certain general truths about the nature of society and, ultimately, about the nature of Man, who has made society what it is. He does not leave at that. He is also a reformer, and hopes to inspire "that generous indignation which ought to animate the reader against the sordid and vicious disposition of the world". Smollett was a novelist with a social purpose, and accordingly in *Roderick Random* the word of *Advice* is made flesh.

What was it which made the young Tobias Smollett, a failed tragic poet with a savage social conscience, decide upon prose fiction as his medium? Clearly much was due to the influence of Le Sage, with whose work Smollett must have been familiar from an early period. *Le Diable Boiteux,* a translation of which Smollett corrected in 1759, had appeared in 1707. Since Smollett published both *Roderick Random* and his translation of *Gil Blas* in the same year (1748) it seems likely that he was working on them concurrently. What is more, Smollett states plainly in the Introduction to *Roderick Random* that he has modelled his own work on the plan of *Gil Blas,* although whilst praising the "infinite humour and sagacity" of Le Sage, he makes certain reservations:

> The following sheets I have modelled on his plan, taking the liberty, however, to differ from him in the execution, where I thought his particular situations were uncommon, extravagant, or peculiar to the country in which the scene is laid. The disgraces of Gil Blas are, for the most part, such as rather excite mirth than compassion; he himself laughs at them; and his transitions from distress to happiness, or at least ease, are so sudden that neither the reader has time to pity him, nor himself to be acquainted with affliction.

Le Sage was the first writer to use the novel purposefully for social satire. He had already depicted, in his comedy *Turcaret,* the extravagances of a financier who has risen to the highest rank of society by cheating other people. A corrupt society, recognising the criticism, had banned the performance of *Turcaret* for several years. In his novels he was more careful, setting the action nominally in Spain, a foreign country, the social structure of which it was permissible to criticise. Le Sage also adopted the conventions of the Spanish Picaresque novel, with its juggling intrigue so suggestive of the big world; with its rogue-hero who preys on society and (though staking more on shorter odds) reproduces in little the stratagems of the men of affairs; and with its rapid transitions from place to place and from class to class. The misbehaviour of the socially inconspicuous was a permissible topic. Gil Blas is a proletarian Turcaret, and Asmodeus, the hero of *Le Diable Boiteux,* is one of the minor and less well-connected devils. In spite of these disguises it was fairly clear what Le Sage had in mind. We know that Boileau, the laureate of Louis XIV, threatened to dismiss a valet whom he found reading *Le Diable Boiteux.*

The device of *Le Diable Boiteux* is a brilliant one for Le Sage's purpose. All walls are transparent, all societies are open, to the soundless invisible devil, Asmodeus, and his friend Don Cleophas, to whom Asmodeus says: "You shall survey the labours which wretched man takes upon himself in obtaining what happiness he can to fill the little space which is given to him between the cradle and the grave." Unobserved, they observe. A party of robbers raiding a bank discover that the banker has anticipated them by absconding with the deposits. A notary's clerk finds by chance a hoard of diamonds and purchases an exalted position in society. A duenna, bribed to sacrifice the virtue of her charge, regrets having filled the girl's mind with notions of propriety which are now difficult to overcome. A count considers it dishonourable for him to marry the girl whom he has seduced, as she is not of noble birth. A printer subversively issues a book in which Religion is given pre-eminence over Honour. A prosperous beggar refused his daughter in marriage to a one-armed soldier, saying: "You are not half lame enough. My son-in-law must be a sad-looking sight capable of drawing blood from a stone."

Whilst *Gil Blas* lacks the knowing sarcasm of *Le Diable Boiteux,* its story is less fantastic and provided exactly the satirical apparatus which Smollett was looking for. Like the rogue-hero of the *Satyricon,* a work with which Smollett was also well acquainted, Gil Blas is a scholar who has no hope of succeeding by honest means in a world which esteems only external advantages, such as rank and money. Tricked at the outset and thrown defensively back on his own wits, Gil Blas attempts to make some slight although not very reputable adjustments in the existing order so that it will be more favourable to Gil Blas. The fluctuations of his fortunes provide many chances for incidental satire on all classes of society, from the aristocracy to the common people themselves. This is what Smollett derived from Le Sage —the story of the hero, at odds with mankind, who moves rapidly through the whole range of contemporary society. The story was a plausible one in the century of Casanova and Cagliostro.

In a note to Voltaire, Smollett calls *Zadig* "a diverting picture of human life, in which the author has ingeniously contrived to ridicule and stigmatise the follies and vices which abound in every station". Such a picture Smollett himself painted over the canvas provided by *Gil Blas*. The vast scope of his novels was equal to almost everything the eighteenth century could provide. The highway which Roderick Random sets out upon leads south to inns, brothels, sea-fights, the squirearchy, the French army, the beau monde, prisons, peripeties and a tidy estate. Peregrine Pickle hurries after him, filling in the gaps in Random's preliminary investigation. No sooner does Pickle arrive in Paris than he finds out what the inside of the Bastille is like. He cannot visit Holland without one of his companions falling in the Mouth of the Rhine. In Pickle's wake the lynx Fathom lopes up from Central Europe, heading for Great Britain, where a mad knight crashes through the county boroughs and a cantankerous coach-load waits at Abergavenny for the round-trip to Loch Lomond.

At this point, since it has seemed important to some critics to determine how far Smollett falls within the Picaresque tradition, we may as well consider the momentous question. The Picaresque novel, a Spanish form although derived ultimately from late Latin fiction, is the comic biography of a wandering rogue-hero, who is an occasional criminal but most of the time a none-too-honest manservant. Usually, like Roderick Random he serves a succession of masters. The form was necessarily a loose and episodic one, and, since it depended a great deal on the author's observation of life, it always contained opportunities for social criticism. In the first Picaresque novel, the hero, Lazarillo de Tormes, learns to cheat other people because he is starved and that is the only way in which he can obtain food. He finally makes his fortune by marrying a whore in order to provide cover for the archdeacon who frequents her. The novel is about hunger; the debasing pang which makes Lazarillo kiss and mumble over the loaves which his master, the priest, keeps locked in a chest; the degrading clamour of the beggars who are whipped out of town because there is a scarcity of corn. *Lazarillo de Tormes* was published anonymously in 1554 and shortly afterwards translated into English. Smollett may well have known the book. Certainly the relationship between the all-providing plebian, Strap, and the penniless but arrogant Roderick Random strongly resembles that between Lazarillo and the Squire of Castilla, although neither Strap nor Random is more than partially a Picaresque hero. As might be expected, *Lazarillo de Tormes* was not well received by the Church, and, except for the purpose of helping various far-fetched chivalrous ideas on their way out, social criticism was avoided in its Spanish successors. Sorel, in his *Histoire Comique,* introduced the Picaresque form into France, although his hero is not a rascally flunkey but a gallant and adventurous amorist. Sixteen years later, in 1657, Scarron developed the knockabout qualities of the Picaresque novel in his so-called *Roman Comique,* which deals with the pranks and vicissitudes of a band of strolling players. The first chapter opens with a classical simile and, like many others in the book, ends with the din of blows and curses. The burlesque tone is set by the hero, a travelling actor who wears tragic buskins spattered with the mud of the march. In improvised theatres the actors make do with whatever they can lay their hands on, so that Herod postures with a strawberry plummet for a crown. Stroking his sleek belly, Scarron disowns any connection with the more romantic Spaniards, and introduces "an episode in the Spanish taste" with the words : "He was the greatest fool that ever ran madding about since the time of Orlando Furioso." Scarron disclaims even any serious interest in his own novel. "If the reader doubts how the story will continue, perhaps I am in the same situation as he is."

So far as Smollett is Picaresque at all, it is in the French tradition, as refined by Le Sage from the crudities of Scarron, that he is Picaresque. The healthy irreverence and realism of the French Picaresque must certainly have attracted Smollett when he was casting about for a medium for his satire. So must the fact that the hero is a creature of circumstance frequently changing the scene of his activities. After all, Smollett regarded the novel as "a large diffused picture of life". But apart from his particular debt to Le Sage, he owed little to the Picaresque form. As F. W. Chandler shrewdly remarks in his definitive work on the Picaresque novel, the value of Smollett's work "consists less in his form than in his matter . . . Smollett had outgrown the Picaresque form, although he could not forget Picaresque episodes". Even at its most conventional, the Picaresque novel was more an escape from the severities of form than an imposition of them. Fielding's novels, for example, are largely pastures for Fielding to gambol in, to tell stories, to display a classical education, to insert pamphlets and preach sermons—the expression of a heedless vitality. So far as Smollett was concerned, the Picaresque novel was no more than a form which took in a wide range of characters from eighteenth-century society and proceeded by the rapid accumulation of moving or entertaining accidents. These were due either to the "sordid and vicious disposition of the world" or else to the exploitation of human weakness by a trickster-hero. Smollett was a reporter more than a contriver, and like the films of Jacques Tati, his novels proceed by a succession of telling but not closely related incidents. To write a chapter on the structure of Smollett's novels is rather like writing the chapter on the snakes of Iceland which Dr. Johnson boasted of knowing by heart: "There are no snakes to be met with throughout the whole island."

This is not to say that Smollett lacks unity of theme—far from it. One of his main themes is the deplorable state of society, and he is ingenious in finding ways to make his novels serve this theme. We have already seen how, in *Roderick Random,* Smollett exposes the follies and wickedness of the world by relating how it first debauches and then victimises a young beginner. In *Peregrine Pickle* Smollett hits on another device His hero shows from childhood an aptitude for practical jokes. After some haphazard experiments on the Continent whilst making the Grand Tour, Pickle uses the practical joke systematically as a direct attack on English society of the time, enlisting as his ally the misanthrope Crabtree. But in spite of these peripherally successful jokes, it is society which outwits Pickle in important matters. More competent tricksters than he is swindle him out of his fortune. In retaliation Pickle writes satires on the world and in counter-retaliation the world puts him in prison. During his imprisonment he is irritated into "a rancorous resentment against mankind in general" and does not care how soon he quits "his miserable existence". Then, as in *Roderick Random,* chance intervenes and he inherits a second fortune. With money in his pocket and all his rancour gone, he solidly takes up his important position in society.

In *Ferdinand, Count Fathom* Smollett varies his line of

attack. The state of society is defined by Fathom's understanding manipulation of it. For ever plotting "crafty ambuscades for the ignorant and unwary", Fathom becomes what Random would have become if Random had been more intelligent. Smollett observes that "had he been admitted as a pupil to any political academy, he would have certainly become one of the ablest statesmen in Europe", but as he did not have that advantage he is forced to exercise his talents for deception upon a smaller scale and in a private capacity. However, the wavering iniquity of the individual is no match for the sustained iniquity of society. Fathom softens for a moment, lets up, and immediately goes down before the unresting encroachments of his adversary. Society, the arch-cheat, packs off the lesser cheat to perish in a hovel. Except in the whimsically proper preface and in the pat triumph of the jerky Ruritanian marionette, Renaldo, little effort is made to conceal the fact that this novel, in many ways Smollett's most accomplished piece of work, is a careful indictment of the social order of the time.

Unlike Richardson and Fielding, he seldom interrupts the course of his narrative in order to draw morals, and yet he is more polemic than either. The fusion between Smollett's subject-matter and his intellectual purpose is complete, and if this can be called form, then he is a master of form. The consciously moral tale is usually worthless as art and unconvincing as argument because the reader can find in it no approximation to any life which he might conceivably lead himself. In this respect one might say that Richardson succeeded in spite of himself. What he considered most important in his novels, the moral interpolations, are what we would most readily discard. It is unlikely that these fine, long Addisonian exercises ever made anyone think about the rights and wrongs of conduct. But it is another matter when Richardson fixes his understanding eyes on Lovelace after the death of Clarissa. Lovelace never survives the wrong which he has done her. He has had his way, she is gone, and he "creeps into holes and corners like an old hedgehog". Here Richardson is dealing with the stuff of the human sympathies, as in his account of Pamela's little outburst to Mr. B. : "Have I robbed you? Why then, you are a Justice of the Peace and may send me to gaol if you please, and bring me to trial for my life!" This pretty statement of her social helplessness cannot fail to move the reader to pity. The homely tale of Lovelace's wasting his life to accomplish wickedness is much more effective than any exhortation to righteousness would be. It lends a warm immediacy to the truth that there is little joy in having a hard heart.

It is the incidental morality that tells most in a novel. Thackeray's *The Newcomes* does make one feel in a particular way about loveless marriages, Trollope's *Doctor Thorne* does make one aware of the horrors of alcoholism. But the morality of these works is a practical morality, and depends for its effect largely on the artistic tact with which it is suggested. Thackeray records the graded miseries of Clara Newcome, and makes it clear how easily Ethel Newcome could have sunk down the same scale. Trollope, with a deceptive detachment, brings the known consequences of alcoholic poisoning before the reader's eyes, so that the reader can see for himself. Thackeray and Trollope are not so simple as to contend merely that vice is inexpedient. They do refer to expediency but they also refer to something else. The conduct of Colonel Newcome is far from expedient, but there is that in it which makes one wish that one was more like him. It is this quality which has to be assessed. Whilst the novelist may indicate an architecture of conduct, founded on his own experience and observation, which will not come apart under the stresses of real life, he is more concerned with quickening and refining the reader's response to events than with illustrating an abstract code of behaviour. He is prepared to let morality take its chance in the larger awareness which he seeks to promote. He deals not in ethical pronouncements but in an uncovenanted sense of what is decent, and makes his appeal not to reason but to human sympathy. To him the passions and the virtues have the same root. Beneath the outward play and dazzle of the plot's interacting circumstances, the novelist's purpose, whether he is tracing the twists and turns of a motive or defining the exact slant of a shaft of morning light, is to explore actualities. Inevitably life is put on trial, and with it morality. For this reason the novelist cannot detach himself, even if he wants to do so, from a notion of conduct.

When George Moore, piping up in the heavy aftermath of Theophile Gautier, writes, "I learned that correction of form is the highest ideal . . . I would have held down my thumbs in the Colosseum that a hundred gladiators might die and wash me free of our Christian soul with their blood", one thinks it nonsense. But when George Moore describes his delight in the extreme and helpless sufferings of a harmless creature (a guinea pig which he tied up so that it might be approached and swallowed by his pet python), one's feelings militate against him in a turbulence of vivid disgust. Compared with vileness of this sort (an offence against decency) the adulteries of Restoration Drama (offences against a moral code) seem light things. In fact, the Restoration dramatists are not concerned with the encouragement of adultery as such, and if they had been so concerned, they would have been unsuccessful. The spectacle of two people abusing a trusting third party who does not deserve such treatment is not an attractive one, and can inspire only distaste. The point of Restoration Comedy is that everyone receives his deserts except for the hero and heroine, who receive more than they deserve. To protest against the tricking of Fondlewife or Sir John Brute is as absurd as to say that Lady Wishfort is badly treated. The truth is that Fondlewife and the others, like Chaucer's January and the husbands of the Decameron, did not marry for the reasons which made marriage an institution so valued by Lord Macaulay.

Smollett's only openly moral novel is the relatively unsuccessful *Launcelot Greaves,* yet even here the plan is given subtlety by Smollett's satirical exposition of how futile it is to intervene privately in a social system which needs a more radical change. With his usual wry originality Smollett makes his reforming hero a comic figure. In the character of Sir Launcelot Greaves the "bodily strength, activity and extravagance of behaviour", which Smollett had described as being the attributes of Romance heroes, are laughably well developed. When falsely imprisoned, he rolls his eyes around and snatches up an oaken bench, "which three ordinary men could scarce have lifted from the ground" and attempts to shatter the door. His situation is as pathetic as that of Don Quixote, with whose lunatic endeavours Greaves' attempt to change a corrupt society single-handed are equated. By using the Romance convention Smollett implies that a tale about a man who devotes himself disinterestedly to bettering the conditions of his fellows is a "monstrous hyperbole" better suited to the age when men's minds were "debauched to the utmost pitch of credulity". The novel rings, not only with Greaves' Gothic armour, but with a hacking ironical cough-laugh. There is a further twist. Greaves only starts to put the world to rights when he has been frustrated in love, and once he obtains Aurelia Darnel he gives up, leaving the occupants of the debtors' prisons, country gaols and private madhouses of England to fend for themselves once more.

Although Smollett does not take much trouble to camouflage the moralising turn of *Launcelot Greaves,* the most effective passages are those in which he proceeds by his familiar method, which is illustration rather than exposition. Such a passage is one about the two hungry small boys whose only relief is to be found in the hit-or-miss goodness of Sir Everhard. Down the centuries come the crude but damning words: "Yesterday the squire seized the keawes for rent, God rot'un! Mammy's gone to bed sick and sulky, my two sisters be crying at hoam vor good, and Dick and I be come hither to pick haws and bullies." There is in this little speech all the humbling patience of the poor.

Directly or indirectly, whether it is Virgil's account of Dido's agony or Walter Pater's appreciation of the paintings of Botticelli, literature is a consideration and assessment of real life. It is unavoidably so, since imagination is inseparable from experience. Experience accounts for the difference between the vigorous actuality of Rubens and the standardised nudes of Boucher, between the men and women of Shakespeare and the ethic impersonations of Corneille. It is to the literature of exactly observed and significantly recorded experience that the novels of Smollett belong.

CHAPTER XI

GRINNING MOST FORMIDABLY

Bishop Hurd, in his *Letters on Chivalry and Romance* of 1762, divides Literature into three periods: the Classical, the Gothic and the Modern. The term "Gothic" he uses widely enough to take in Ariosto, Spenser and Shakespeare. As we have already seen, the writers of the early eighteenth century were very deferentially aware of their classical predecessors, but for the so-called Gothic ones they had little but disdain. Swift, in a paper on the corruptions of style, published in the *Tatler* of 1710, deplored the barbarity of the "Gothic strain", which, directly contrary to the example of the Greeks and Romans, delights in monosyllables ("the disgrace of our language") and abbreviated words in which "consonants of the most obdurate sound are joined together, without one softening vowel to intervene". In a later work, the *Proposal for Correcting the English Tongue,* he regretted that, since Latin was never rooted in this country, English is less refined than Italian, Spanish or French. He objected in particular to the affected phrases, newly coined words, French borrowings and abbreviations of Restoration style. Fearing a relapse into Northern barbarity, he proposed an Academy for the purpose of "ascertaining and fixing the language for ever". In the *Essay on Conversation* he grumbled that in England "the little decorum and politeness which we have are purely forced by art". Addison was in full agreement, and mourning the fact that so many monosyllables prevent our tongue from becoming truly elegant, wrote sadly that "the multitude of syllables, which make other languages more tuneable and sonorous" is lacking in English.[1]

Such a view of language was appropriate to the early eighteenth century, with its ponderous and showy houses, with the swishing amplitude of its costume, the stiff-skirted, panniered coat massive with thick embroidery, the convoluted knee-length waistcoat, the large dangled handkerchief moist with jasmin or *eau de mille fleurs*. With the reaction in favour of plainer and more conventional prose came the solid, level opulence of

Georgian architecture and a fashion for loose coats, plain shirt-fronts, buckskin breeches and terse uncommunicative waist-coats. Later, the Gothic Revival in literature and architecture was, still appropriately, accompanied by the eclectic flamboyance, ribboned, buckled and fobbed at every salient point, of the Macaroni Club.

Boileau had said that the associations of a word are for ever changing, so that a word which is sublime in the classics may be low or unduly familiar in modern times. Pope considered that words are removed from vulgarity by being out of use, a view shared by Addison, endorsed by Johnson, and finally asserted by Gray in his famous dictum that "the language of the age is never the language of poetry". In this connection a conversation recorded in Boswell's *London Journal* is of particular interest. Boswell rhapsodises over Gray whom, he says, he admires prodigiously, and whose *Odes* he has read till he was almost mad. Goldsmith objects that they are terribly obscure. Davies, the publisher of Johnson and Goldsmith, intervenes with the question, "And why not? He is not writing for porters and carmen".

Thus the steadfast avoidance of familiar terms, such as porters and carmen could understand, and of monosyllables, which were contrary to the example of the Ancients, created a mandarin style of writing. A modern philologist could have pointed out to Swift that in true Gothic there were more and lengthier poly-syllables than in Latin, and that the copiously vocal elaboration of such a language as Finnish does not necessarily lend itself to amenity or grace of expression. There is ample evidence that the language of the Northern barbarians became less polysyllabic as they became less barbarous. But a philologist's evidence is not necessary. We need only see what Johnson himself could do with twenty-six monosyllables and three words of two syllables. The passage is from the story of Misella in *The Rambler*:

> When he saw my face pale with hunger and my eyes swelling with tears, he spurned me from him and bade me cant and whine in some other place.

By no other means could Johnson have achieved so pathetic an effect. Johnson, and to a greater degree Smollett, like all great stylists, knew the worth of a judicious variety of diction.

At the end of his short history of English Literature from Beowulf to the Bloomsbury intellectuals, Sir Ifor Evans places Lytton Strachey with Swift for pre-eminence in prose style. This is in spite of the fact that Evans has previously said less about Swift's style than about his sexual life. Setting aside the qualities which cannot strictly be considered stylistic (Swift's fierce observant censoriousness and his incomparably effective satirical apparatus), a more quibbling critic might consider that Swift's prose style, with its hedging mysteriousness, its shuffling archly backwards and forwards, its elaborately concessive manner and its facetious circumstance, resembles nothing more than one of those Chinese carvings from a single piece of ivory in which a fretted globe revolves round a fretted globe containing nothing more than a fretted globe which is quite hollow : a highly wrought object but neither beautiful or useful. Surely no joke was ever so ponderously and so protractedly wearisome as the diction of *The Tale of a Tub*! It is in Swift's poems that one must look for the acumen of his style.

Far more important than these attempts to create a patrician style was the movement towards precision of statement. Here there were two important pressure-groups : the up-and-coming men of business and the scientists.

The commercial view of language is a utilitarian one. Words should state as directly as possible a profitable thought. Literature is to be tolerated only so far as it is used to some practical or moral purpose. The tone should be brisk, nonsense should be avoided and hard words reduced to a minimum for the sake of the ladies. "In a play", says Thomas Rymer, "one should speak like a man of business." Language becomes a measurable commodity. Addison, in spite of his objections in principle to monosyllables, was the type of writer on whom the citizens were most likely to bestow their approval. He was direct and profitable. He thought that the basis of wit is Good Sense. He had no time to waste on the flighty and ill-conditioned French. He promises, in his paper on the aims of the *Spectator,* to instil wholesome sentiments into his readers, whom he wishes to rescue from "the desperate state of vice and folly into which the age is fallen".

The physical sciences admittedly come in for a certain amount of affable mockery in eighteenth-century literature. Addison's Virtuoso bequeaths to his family nothing more than three crocodiles' eggs and a recipe for preserving caterpillars. Johnson's Collector treasures up a snail which has crawled on the Great Wall of China. At the Academy of Paputa a blind man is involved in researches concerning the nature of colour. Pope's

Essay on Man opens with a statement of the limitations of
human knowledge:

> Of Man what see we but his station here
> From which to reason, or to which refer?
> Through worlds unnumbered though the God be known,
> 'Tis ours to trace him only in our own.

Yet in spite of many contemptuous references to what Addison
calls "the trifling rarities of the virtuoso", and many expositions
of Man's benighted state, educated opinion in the eighteenth
century had a great respect for the physical sciences. Dr. Johnson spent part of his leisure time in making a number of chemical
experiments, the purpose of which was known only to himself,
up in his lumber-room. According to Mrs. Thrale[2] he would
divert his mind, at times of distress, by making vast mathematical
calculations, such as converting the national debt to a belt of
silver stretching round the earth, and finding out how broad that
belt would be. Gray's letters show a more than trifling interest
in Botany. Throughout 1755, he kept a calendar of such events
as the flowering of the hawthorn and the fall of the ash leaves in
Cambridge, noting the corresponding dates in Upsala and Stratton in Norfolk. Such men as Gibbon attended Hunter's annual
course of lectures on human physiology, and a striking number
of eighteenth-century writers, conforming to John Locke's precedent started life as medical practitioners. The work of the
French Encylopaedists was steadily changing the outlook of English scholars, and such compilations as those supervised by
Smollett popularised the French notions.

So great was the prestige of the new Science that when Pope,
in his *Essay on Man* wanted to give an example of humanity
at its best, he chose Newton. Science demands direct unadorned
statement. In his *History of the Royal Society* (1667) Sprat
had proscribed lying figures of speech and "Enthusiasm" in
writing. "Vague and insignificant forms of speech", Locke had
written, "and abuse of language, have so long passed for mysteries of science: and hard and misapplied words, with little or no
meaning, have by prescription, such a right to be taken for deep
learning and height of speculation, that it will not be easy to persuade either those who speak or those who hear them, that they
are but the covers of ignorance, and hindrance of true knowledge." He had gone on to complain of the damage done to
Philosophy ("which is nothing but the true knowledge of things")

by "the learned but frivolous use of uncouth, affected, or unintelligible terms".[3] Leibniz went so far as to project a Characteristica Universalis: a symbolic language in which each simple idea is represented by an algebraic symbol, the combination of these symbols being regulated by mathematical rules, so that complex reasoning can be carried out by algebraic calculation. In the search for a prose style well adapted to the clear expression of truths in the physical sciences the Augustans forgot that this is not the only purpose of prose, and that there are other styles for other needs. One can hardly complain of Joseph Conrad's lack of quantitive definition or Dylan Thomas' vagueness about measurable qualities. Such was the influence of the Royal Society that the characteristic prose style of the early eighteenth century became even, matter-of-fact and unambitious. The "bellowings and distortions of enthusiasm" had no place in the Newtonian scheme of things. Dr. Johnson went so far as to equate "the prevalence of the imagination" with insanity.[4] In the *Spectator* metaphors were avoided and such similes as were used were most often used humorously. They were drawn for the most part from history, from contemporary affairs or from mechanics, the most esteemed of the sciences, the one on which the Industrial Revolution was to be based, and the one from which Voltaire was to deduce the existence of God.

There was every reason to expect, as a consequence, a severe whittling down of the language in the second half of the eighteenth century. In fact nothing of the sort happened. Hume's scepticism had dispersed many of the old certainties. The neat, cocksure classicism of the preceding generation began to sound less convincing. And the Goths were already at the gates. In 1761, Horace Walpole inveighed against Vanbrugh:

> The style of no age, no country, appears in his works; he broke through all rule, and compensated for it by no imagination. He seems to have hollowed quarries rather than to have built houses; and should his edifices, as they seem formed to do, outlast all record, what architecture will posterity think was that of their ancestors? The laughers, his contemporaries, said, that having been confined in the Bastille, he had drawn his notions of building from that fortified dungeon.

It did not assuage the builder of Strawberry Hill Castle that Vanbrugh himself had been guilty of Gothic lapses, such as the castellated pavilion erected in 1720 at Shotover Park. The year after Walpole's denunciation of Vanbrugh, Bishop Hurd carried the attack into Literature with his *Letters on Chivalry and Romance,* in which he regrets the suppression of the Gothic imagination, with its "world of fine fabling". Addison himself had allowed for a *gusto grande,* a sublime defiance of the rules "which elevates and astonishes the fancy, and gives a greatness of mind to the reader" in the perusal of a noble work.[5] Dr. Johnson teased Mrs. Thrale by preferring Young's descriptions of the night, "as being more forcible and more general", to those of Shakespeare. But he added that, although Young bubbles sometimes very vigorously, "we must not compare your tea-kettle here with the roaring of the ocean". Expanding, he made the further observation that Corneille is to Shakespeare what a clipped hedge is to a forest.[6] A number of writers were breaking down the geometrical temples and belvederes of Augustan prose into more picturesque outlines. The antique phrasing of Gray, the archaisms of Chatterton, the Biblic rhythms of MacPherson's *Ossian,* the development of the Scottish vernacular by such writers as Allan Ramsay, all had their effect. Little Gibbon was stalking the Roman Emperors through the thickets of late Latinity. His first book had been in French, and his first English composition was an abstract of Blackstone's *Commentaries on the Laws.* In a style compounded of Silver Latin sonorities, Gallicisms and informed doubtfulness, his ideas and images multiplied by his studies in Anatomy and Chemistry, he broadened the range of the language to a remarkable degree, creating an idiom for Macaulay and Lytton Strachey. Horace Walpole, flighty, affected, the Evelyn Waugh of the eighteenth century, made up new words and used new constructions with a calculated off-handedness which would have given Addison cause for the most extreme concern and material for a paper. English became like the Latin of Apuleius, as described by Huysmans in *A Rebours* : "sweeping along in a dense flood fed by tributary waters from every province, and combining them all in a bizarre, exotic, almost incredible torrent of words".

There was another influence even more powerful than these. That was the massive but equivocal presence of Johnson himself. Boswell's account of Johnson is all too winning. Johnson's habits, appearance and sharply delivered pronouncements so prompt that half-admiring amusement which we feel when confronted by any kind of eccentricity that we forget that this was by no means the whole Johnson. In the rapid give-and-take of casual conversation, opinions are delivered in an exaggerated form and positions are overstated. Exceptionally brilliant though Johnson's conversation was, it would be unfair to judge him by it. Criticism requires a number of deliberate processes and is not at its best bawled out *ad hoc* in the Mitre. Isaac Bickerstaff, in one of Steele's contributions to the *Tatler,* resists the importunities of a fair and unknown admirer, telling her that he is more truly familiar to her through his writings than he would be if they met. Johnson, the artist at work, is overshadowed by the Johnson off-duty of Boswell. The cudgel, the crooked wig and the shabby clothes, the impatience and prejudices, the very gruffness and generosity of Boswell's Johnson distract the attention from the intelligent sensitivity of Johnson the stylist. What a contrast there is between the oratorical grandeur, the spiritual pomp, of Johnson's fastidious periods, accumulating with all the sonority of late Latin, and the slovenly, unwashed old man of the biography! Then there is the hidden Johnson, the Johnson of the opium and the distillations, the Johnson who loved to travel at great speed on horseback or by post-chaise, the Johnson of echoic luminous passages and matador-like precision of statement.

Since the style of Smollett has many affinities with that of Johnson, it may be as well to consider them jointly. They both wrote in a way which has been dismissed by Macaulay as "systematically vicious". Macaulay's chief objection to it is that in it sentences are translated out of English into "Johnsonese" (a manner of writing characterised by a partiality for terms having their origin in Latin or Greek, by forced embellishment and by the wasting of big words on little things). It is only fair to let Johnson explain what he meant to do. In the last *Rambler* he lists what he considers to be the qualities of a good style. They are aptness, polish, variety, grammatical purity, choice construction and harmony of cadence. "When common words were less pleasing to the ear, or less distinct in their signification" he has used rarer words. Johnson was in fact restoring the language, after a period of austerity, during which mere platitude was degenerating into downright insignificance, to its old richness. He was making a new claim for artistry, the music of words, originality. Above all, he attempted that precise definition of sensation and experience which is one of the most important functions of literature. His expression is commonly tight, just and pithy. It is his thought which is complicated. It would be hard to match the concise adequacy of his observations that "merit rather enforces respect than attracts fondness" and that old men prefer to do business by "slow contrivances and gradual progressions". In the statements, "The attention naturally retires from a new tale of Venus, Diana and Minerva" and "The character of Diogenes has never excited any general zeal of imitation", one is surprised not by the extravagance of the expressions employed, but by their economy. When Johnson uses Latinate words, as in his description of savages who "are either corroded by malignant passions or sit stupid in the gloom of perpetual vacancy", he uses them with a vivid awareness of their etymological implications, and burlily couples them with straight Saxon terms. Even the famous parallel or antithetical clauses (suggested, perhaps, by Latin inscriptions on tombs) give an effect of sureness, and contain nothing redundant. Rounding each clause one obtains a new prospect. "The causes of good and evil are *so* various and uncertain, *so* entangled with each other, *so* diversified by various relations, and *so* much subject to accidents *that* . . ." by the time the reader comes to the word "that", he has been given a very concise account of the complicated causes of good and evil. The epigrammatic closeness of it may account for Macaulay's aversion from the style of Johnson. Macaulay's art was one of expansion, Johnson's one of contraction.

In spite of his well-known love of practical jokes, one cannot plausibly present the old lexicographer as some sort of fertility god, rollicking over the level Georgian sward and scattering largesse from his cornucopia-like hearing-trumpet. His ghost resolutely declines to play the part. Nevertheless, the enrichment of our language in the late eighteenth century owes more to Johnson than to any other man. Although Smollett was a lesser stylist than Johnson, the main characteristics of his style are similar: exact choice of words, knowingness of expression, ironical intonation, metaphorical device and rhythmic dexterity. Each of these characteristics will now be examined in turn.

Fathom and a number of companions, including a German count and an English knight, having grown "whimsical" under the influence of Burgundy, decide to visit the house of "an obliging dame, who maintained a troop of fair nymphs for the accommodation of the other sex". On their arrival, a question of precedence is raised by the count and the knight, who have both decided upon the same girl. The count appeals to his fellow-visitors:

> Before the company had time or inclination to interest them-selves in the quarrel, his opponent observed that no person who was not a mere German would ever dream of forcing the inclina-tions of a pretty girl, whom the accidents of fortune had sub-jected to his power.[7]

By the use of the words "observed", "pretty girl" and "accidents of fortune" in this low situation Smollett contrives the effect of an indignant and mouthily confused young man whose sense of decency has been ludicrously wronged.

Commander Trunnion's horse runs away with him, and he resolves to hold on as tight as he can until Providence intervenes on his behalf:

> With this view he dropped his whip, and with his right hand laid fast hold on the pommel, contracting every muscle in his body, to secure himself in the seat, and grinning most formid-ably in consequence of this exertion.[8]

Pretending to be impressed by the formidability of Trunnion's grin, as if it was of any importance in such a contingency, Smollett introduces the phrase "grinning most formidably" with comic dexterity.

On his travels Peregrine Pickle encounters a doctor who esteems the classics so highly that he decides to give a feast at which Ancient Roman delicacies, such as dormice stewed in syrup, are to be served. He has difficulty in obtaining a cook:

> By this communicative painter, the guests understood that the doctor had met with numerous difficulties in the execution of his design; that no fewer than five cooks had been dismissed, because they could not prevail upon their own consciences to obey his directions in things that were contrary to the present practice of their art.[9]

"They could not prevail upon their own consciences" suggests the affronted professionalism of the cooks and the monstrosity of the demands made upon them.

Pickle manages to persuade the painter Pallet to attend a masquerade dressed as a woman:

> Among the masks was a nobleman, who began to be very free with the supposed lady, and attempted to plunge his hand into

her bosom : but the painter was too modest to suffer such indecent treatment.[10]

Here again the humour owes much to the apparently unstudied phrasing, the calm consequence (expressed so briefly) of "began to be very free with the supposed lady, and attempted to plunge his hand into her bosom". The painter's acceptance of his role is implied by the statement that he "was too modest to suffer such indecent treatment".

In *Pickle* Smollett remarks on the French habit of gesticulation :

Indeed, I have known a Gascon, whose limbs were as elegant as his tongue : he never mentioned the word sleep without reclining his head upon his hand; when he had occasion to talk of a horse, he always started up and trotted across the room, except when he was so situated that he could not stir without incommodating the company, and in that case he contented himself with neighing aloud : if a dog happened to be the subject of his conversation, he wagged his tail, and grinned in a most significant manner.[11]

The use of the expressions, "contented himself with neighing aloud" and "wagged his tail and grinned in a significant manner", makes all the more evident the self-satisfaction of the accomplished Gascon.

In the straight-faced style of humour, the air of not knowing what all the fuss is about, Smollett excelled. Let us consider the surprised mock-objectivity of the following passage, which concerns Commodore Trunnion's response to a preposterous request :

Mrs. Grizzle, falling on her knees before him, conjured him with many pathetic supplications to hear and grant her request, which was no sooner signified, than he bellowed in such an outrageous manner that the whole court re-echoed the opprobrious term bitch, and the word damnation, which he repeated with surprising volubility, without any sort of propriety or connection.[12]

By the knowingness of his phrasing, Smollett suggests that the scene is beyond his comprehension, although he helpfully points out that "bitch" is an opprobrious term and that "damnation" is a word. Beyond that, he fears, he cannot be of assistance, since the repetitions lack "any sort of propriety or connection".

The same artful simplicity is to be found in Smollett's account of the doings of that foolish painter, Pallet. At the Banquet in the Manner of the Ancients, Pallet "testified his abhorrence of the sow's stomach", which he wittily compared to a bagpipe, and hearing roasted pullets mentioned, "eagerly solicited a wing of a fowl". Here "eagerly" is the salient word, emphasising the painter's pronounced inclination towards more conventional food than fricassees of snails or pork-and-honey pies. Nor is Pallet the amorist better equipped than Pallet the gastronome for the unexpected. In the course of one of the crowded bed-room-scenes in *Peregrine Pickle*, Pallet encounters his inamorata's Confessor, who has been keeping watch:

> Finding the door unlatched, his suspicion was confirmed, and he made no scruple of creeping into the chamber on all fours; so that the painter, having stripped himself to the shirt, in groping about for his Dulcinea's bed, chanced to lay his hand upon the shaven crown of the father's head, which, by a circular motion, the priest began to turn round in his grasp, like a ball in a socket, to the surprise and consternation of poor Pallet, who having neither penetration to comprehend the case, nor resolution to withdraw his fingers from this strange object of his touch, stood sweating in the dark and venting ejaculations with great devotion.[13]

One notices the innocent manner of this passage: factual ("by a circular motion"), explanatory ("like a ball in a socket") and admiring ("venting ejaculations with great devotion"). Smollett employs a similar comic objectivity in his treatment of Winifred Jenkins. Tabitha Bramble complains of Humphry Clinker's indelicacy in appearing before her in split breeches: "Mrs. Winifred Jenkins confirmed the assertion, with respect to his nakedness, observing, at the same time, that he had a skin as fair as alabaster."

The sustained use of metaphors, which Bishop Sprat had condemned as specious trickery, is an outstanding (and, for his time, singular) characteristic of Smollett's style. This metaphor, from *Peregrine Pickle*, is particularly apt and well developed:

> He projected a thousand salutary schemes of deportment, but, like other projections, he never had interest enough with the ministry of his passions to bring any one of them to bear.

Equally beautifully sustained is the metaphor with which Smollett describes Count Fathom's attack on Elinor:

> She knew herself in a strange place, destitute of all resource but

in his generosity. She loved his person, she was dazzled by his rank; and he knew so well how to improve the opportunities and advantages he derived from her unhappy situation, that he gradually proceeded in sapping from one degree of intimacy to another, until all the bulwarks of her chastity were undermined, and she submitted to his desire; not with the reluctance of a vanquished people, but with all the transports of a joyful city, that opens its gates to receive a darling prince returned from conquest.[14]

In his short reflective passages, especially in *Ferdinand, Count Fathom*, Smollett's style is reminiscent of the sober explanatory perceptiveness of Locke, but has more imaginative flourish than Locke permitted himself. He has all the thoroughness of exposition which might be expected from a man who went through 1,800 pages of a book called *Roma Antica E Moderna* to find material for 14 pages of his own *Travels*.[15] At the same time, when he describes Baynard's estate, reduced by his wife's improvements to "a naked circus of loose sand", when he depicts in *Reproof*, "the giggling minx half-choked behind her cards", he exemplifies the compression of phrase which enabled him to be thorough with the greatest economy of words.

Next to Johnson himself, Smollett was the great eighteenth-century master of prose rhythm. The degeneration of Peregrine Pickle is recounted in almost fugue-like form thus:

EXPOSITION : *The struggle between his interest and love produced a perplexity which had an evident effect upon his behaviour;* DEVELOPMENT : *he became pensive, solitary, and peevish, avoided all public diversions, and grew so remarkably negligent in his dress;* CODA : *that he was scarce distinguishable by his own acquaintance.* (Did Smollet learn from Johnson or Johnson from Smollett? The dates are certainly on Smollett's side. When *Roderick Random* was published, Johnson was a little-known writer at work on the *Dictionary*.) Reference has already been made to the fact that, almost alone amongst the great prose-writers of the eighteenth century, Smollett was a lover of music. Certainly nobody insensitive to the effects of sound-arrangement could have written the account of Fathom's seduction of Celinda, with its cumulative rhythm, inexorably pressing forward to the assured finality of the generalisation :

Such a commerce between two such persons of a different sex could not possibly be long carried on, without degenerating from the platonic system of sentimental love. In her paroxysms of dismay, he did not forget to breathe the soft inspirations of his passion, to which she listened with more pleasure, as they diverted the gloomy ideas of her fear; and by this time his extraordinary accomplishments had made a conquest of her heart. What therefore could be a more interesting transition than that from the most uneasy to the most agreeable sensation of the human breast?[16]

Smollett's accomplishments as a stylist, then, were not limited to the sarcastic placing of words. If some scholar could be prevailed upon to collect the statistics, I conjecture that he would find that the vocabulary used by Smollett is wider than that of any other eighteenth-century English writer except Johnson, who did, after all, have the advantage of having compiled a dictionary. Scottish Grammar School education in the eighteenth century consisted of a copious reading of Latin, and nearly all the lessons were conducted in that language. Whilst Smollett revolted against this imposed classicism, he retained the vivid awareness of the etymology and the consequent imagery of English words which Pater, a century later, was to insist upon in his paper on Style. Words, selected and applied with a subtle particularity, formed Smollett's equipment for anatomising and classifying Man. With them he fashioned the imposing combinations and rhythms which he could use at will for the most serious purposes.

CHAPTER XII

THE GENEROUS INDIGNATION

Voltaire, hiding between two flights, attacks all irrationally organised mankind. Juvenal, writing in some Egyptian waste safe from the Empire, attacks all organised mankind. Swift, hounded by his own temperament into a seclusion in which he still could not escape from himself, attacks mankind as such. In an age of authority, authors who direct their satire at society are seldom greatly esteemed. Few satirists of the age of the Grand Monarchs were so venturesome as Juvenal, Voltaire and Swift. *Don Quixote* is not a satire on the way of the world but on an aged lunatic who does not understand the way of the world. Quixote and Sancho Panza are in fact very reasonably treated by the temporal powers, and Sancho is given a governorship. This he renounces as he does not wish to rise above his station. Scarron, as befitted the husband of the future Mme. de Maintenon, excluded social criticism from his *Roman Comique*. With the first hint that something might be wrong with society, in Le Sage's *Turcaret*, came official prohibition. When the state is absolute, it is considered more proper, and found to be much safer, to satirise individuals. Even such writers as Addison, who thought that personal satire was in poor taste, and did attempt a consideration of society, deal with its foibles rather than its iniquities. They believed in Providence and the rightness of things, and thought that the Law and the Church were adequate to deal with anything that went seriously wrong.

Pope is the outstanding example of a conservative who satirises individuals rather than society. Like Horace, Pope builds his satires around himself, and like Juvenal he uses every trick of venomous allusion. To this extent alone Pope is like Horace and Juvenal. What he did not perceive was that Horace's autobiographical references are only nominally so. They were introduced for artistic reasons and not because Horace wanted to talk about himself. Horace uses himself as a peg to hang something else upon—an evocation of the countryside in which he grew up, an impression of the vexations of travel—just as at other times he used an amphora or the Consul Manlius. Pope did want to talk about himself, and concluded that he had the sanction of classical antiquity for doing so. Thus such a poem as the *Epistle to Dr. Arbuthnot* is directly concerned with ephemeral matters, with current literary trifles and Pope's private circumstances. It can be studied only archaeologically, with much digging in footnotes, and, like all poems which provide an autobiographical record of fact rather than of sensation, is of most value to those who are closely interested in the author's career. Pope has taken this interest for granted. He tells us in detail about his estate at Twickenham, about his relations with actors and publishers, about his ancestors and about how good he was to his old mother. He draws a contrast between his fussy little establishment at Twickenham and the pinched draughty strivings of Grub Street, a contrast which puts nobody so much to shame as Pope.

He imitates Juvenal's methods as well, without having Juvenal's reasons for adopting those methods. The crowded personal allusions of Juvenal, although they seem to be the piled-up indiscriminate invective of an angry man, always sharpen the point of the satire in which they are placed. They show how vile and yet how ludicrous the vice in question is and light up its every ramification. The allusions are not so much to private persons as to practitioners of a vice who happen to be private persons. A knowledge of their identity outside the Satire is rarely necessary. We need no footnotes to explain the point of Juvenal's references to Posthumus or to Fuscus's wife. Juvenal's reference is self-sufficient. In the *Epistle to Dr. Arbuthnot* little of the satire can stand by itself. We need continuous extraneous information, we need to know who Sporus was and why he should be whispering at the ear of Eve and why he was now master up, now miss. Pope's references are too topical, too limited in their application, too often a matter of otherwise unexceptional people who had annoyed Pope. They are hardly even castigated as practitioners of a vice. They are just pitchforked together without any unity of purpose except such unity as can be discovered in a general massacre. At least a massacre was intended. Hervey survived, to say of the character of Sporus that "a rotten egg more or less, after so many thrown, was of no consequence to me".

It is this same Hervey, epileptic, starving himself and weakening his under-nourished constitution with regular purges and doses of quinine, rising early and going to bed late in order to devote his days to the strenuous persuasion of people whose abilities he despised, painting his face to look less ghastly, a sceptic and a friend of Dr. Middleton, it is this Hervey who emerges, with Swift and Smollett, as one of the three severest *social* satirists of the time. He received little credit from Smollett, who refers to him in his *Continuation of a History of England* as "pert, frivolous and frothy", but then Smollett did not know of Hervey's secret *Memoirs*. Hervey's satire came from inside the fashionable world whilst the satire of Swift and Smollett came from outside. Shruggingly collaborating with Walpole, Hervey was too weak to resist the corruption of his age but too intelligent not to perceive its extent. With a style expressly formed for ridicule, for the apparently whimsical weighing of absurdities, he is sometimes more damning than either Swift or Smollett.

All three felt discontented with the organisation of society in the eighteenth century. Smollett in particular made it clear from the start that he is primarily a social satirist, prefacing *Roderick Random* with a statement that he aims to arouse "that generous indignation which ought to animate the reader against the sordid and vicious disposition of the world". The range of his satire has already been indicated. We shall be engaged here in a study of his satirical technique, considered in conjunction with the techniques of Swift and Hervey. We shall see that there were a number of devices which they used in common, and that, contrary to the common view, Smollett was far from lacking subtlety in his employment of these devices.

1. *The Pretended Conviction that Black is White*

In the account of his native country which Gulliver renders to the Houyhnhnms, he observes that "very many men among us were bred from their youth in the art of proving, by words multiplied for the purpose, that white is black and black is white". In order to make black indisputably and hatefully black, Swift frequently claims to be convinced by such proof. He writes from the opposite side in a judicious, Latinate manner which sometimes relaxes into honest, forthright idioms and sometimes (although the usual mood is one of placid acquiescence) starts up into all the fervour of passionate conviction. His irony is the product of strict self-control. Never do the primly cocked features contract with the rage and disgust which he really feels. He plays the devil's game for him in a way the devil never thought possible, and supplies a damning vindication of evil. Swift's view of society is that of the king of Brobdingnag and the Houyhnhnms, but it is a view against which he makes his puppet, Gulliver, protest. It must not be supposed that Swift's satire is the mere crude substitution of yea for nay. That is no more than the point at which his peculiar technique starts.

In the *Modest Proposal* Swift lends his anxiously helpful support to English policy in Ireland, which was one of expediency rather than humanity. Choosing the most inhuman project he can think of (the sale of Irish children as butcher's meat) he provides statistics, expert cannibal opinion and an appraisal of the economic possibilities. Similarly, in the *Tale of a Tub* he encumbers the bigot Peter with too whole-hearted an approval. Peter's ridiculous search for an anagram of the word "shoulder-knot" in the Bible is thrown upon a cosmic screen, becoming proportionately more ridiculous, when Swift sets down his failure to find the letter K to the malignity of "that same planet, enemy of their repose".[1] In much the same way Swift's fear that the wits of the age "should find leisure to pick holes in the weak sides of religion and government", with its suggestion of dangerously idle Titans, makes the wits look all the smaller.[2] Swift bestows his fatal cordiality upon the critics of Homer too. He searches out their crucial weakness (their assumption that Homer is to be treated as an encyclopaedia and accordingly censured for his inaccuracies about matters of fact) and puts it forward as the proposition, "whereas we are assured that he designed his work for a complete body of all knowledge, human, divine, political and mechanical".[3] So straight-faced is Swift in the use of this device that a foreign writer compared the state of Ireland, where a dignitary of the Church could suggest so horrible a remedy as the eating-up of little children, to that of Jerusalem when it was besieged by Titus.

Hervey too is a skilful administrator of the demolishing pat-on-the-back, the helping hand which pulls a man off his feet. He records that Sir William Yonge was advised to vote on the king's side in Parliament as assiduously as if he was still paid to do so.[4] He mentions that even the joy with which George II heard of the death of his father could not at first reconcile him with Sir Robert Walpole.[5] He comments on the resolution of the king and queen in dealing with the Prince of Wales : "The truth was, they both hated their son to that immoderate degree that they would rather put themselves to inconveniences than make him easy."[6] However, Hervey must say for the Prince of Wales that he "never forgot an injury or remembered an obligation".[7] Hervey points

out the domestic sentiment of George II in choosing Lady Deloraine, the wife of Duke William's tutor, as his mistress. The king
decided "not from any violence of passion, but as a decent,
natural and unexceptional commerce, to make the governess of
his two youngest daughters his whore . . . and the guardian
director of his son's youth and morals his cuckold".[8]

This device calls for a degree of phlegm and self-control which
one does not suppose Smollett normally to have been endowed
with. That he can use it with great effect, even when his most
serious convictions are concerned, proves that he is more complex
an artist than most critics have suggested. Smollett detested war.
He campaigned strenuously for a European peace in his ill-fated
British Magazine. In a note on the battle-scene in *Candide* he
recommends Voltaire's account to "the consideration of those
who are such sanguine advocates for the continuation of war".[9]
Yet he is prepared like an athlete to withdraw from his original
position in order to give himself a longer run and a more impressive leap. Describing, in *Roderick Random*, the Carthagenan
expedition, he mentions that, although the sailors were in the
tropics, they were rationed to two pints of water each per day.
He comments that there was no scarcity of water, since every
ship had enough aboard for a six months' voyage, "but this fast
must, I suppose, have been enjoined by way of penance on the
ship's company for their sins; or rather to mortify them into a
contempt of life, that they might thereby become more resolute
and regardless of danger". It is absurd, he expostulates, to protest
that there was a great loss of life because of the scarcity of food
and water. Admittedly the idle transport ships could have fetched
provisions from Jamaica, but one is bound to say that "those
who died went to a better place, and those who survived were
the more easily maintained". The idiocy of this argument only
slightly exaggerates the idiocy which was licensed, indeed ordained, by the State during the course of the expedition. From
what is known of the Duke of Newcastle, the "venal drudge" who
set the expedition in motion, one can almost believe him capable
of putting Smollett's argument forward, an argument which
Smollett rounds off with one of his characteristic ironical
crescendoes :

> After all, a sufficient number remained to fall before the walls of
> St. Lazar, where they behaved like their own country mastiffs,
> which shut their eyes, run into the jaws of a bear, and have their
> heads crushed for their valour.[10]

It is with the same subject, war, and in the same manner that Smollett begins his grand indictment of human folly in *Ferdinand, Count Fathom*. The hero's mother ("five times a widow in one campaign") follows Marlborough's army, "supplying the ranks with the refreshing streams of choice Geneva, and accommodating individuals with fresh linen, as the emergency of their occasions required". Nor is this her only pursuit. She dispenses her favours liberally to the troops, "in order to sweeten the toils and dangers of the field". So profitable does she find her double occupation that, during a lull in the fighting, she prays without ceasing that Europe may "speedily be involved in a general war". She moves east with the Austrian army, and actually participates in the fighting against the Turks. She goes round the battlefields with a dagger and a bag, "in order to consult her own interest, annoy the foe, and exercise her humanity at the same time" by stabbing and plundering the wounded, thus easing them of "the pain under which they groaned". Nor is she willing to withhold from the wounded Austrians the compassion which she bestows on the enemy.[11]

No doubt it is the same spirit of generosity which her son Ferdinand shows later in the novel, when, having stolen Elinor's purse on the coach, he "not only discharged what she owed for her place, but likewise procured for her an apartment in the house to which he himself had been directed for a lodging, and even hired a nurse to attend her during a severe fever, which was the consequence of her disappointment and despondence". Ferdinand is so anxious to win her heart that he is willing "to extend his charity to the last farthing of her own money".[12]

Although these are the most powerful examples of the device of excoriating sympathy in Smollett, they are not the only ones. There is his compliment to the English residing in Rome, who have hit upon such bad manners "without any assistance from France, Italy or Lapland".[13] There is the suspicion which the English feel towards the linguist Fathom, "inasmuch as no person would take the pains to learn such a variety of gibberish, except upon some sinister intent". Perhaps most tart of all, there is the description of the Debtors' Prison as "the author's never-failing goal; a place of rest appointed for all those sinners whom the profane love of poesy has led astray".[14]

2. *The Assumption that Human Weakness is Axiomatic*

Satirically allied to the complacent approval of wrong in the work of Swift is his impudent taking-for-granted of the malignity of human beings. In the verses on his own death, he accepts as a matter of fact, calmly, the maxim that there is something pleasing in the misfortunes of others, even though they are our best friends:

> They hug themselves and reason thus,
> It is not yet so bad with us.[15]

There is a similar couplet in *Cadenus and Vanessa*:

> I'm sorry Mopsa breaks so fast;
> I said her face would never last.[16]

In these two poems he mocks a distasteful human characteristic by taking it as axiomatic. The great practitioner of this satirical device is Voltaire. After the battle in *Candide* between the Bulgarians and the Abares, the Bulgarians commit atrocities in Abare villages and the Abares commit atrocities in Bulgarian villages. The interchange is brought about by the loss of some thirty thousand men. Both kings order the Te Deum to be sung.[17] Later after the earthquake at Lisbon has killed so many people the Church decides to placate God by killing some more at an *auto de fe,* "it having been decided by the University of Coimbra that burning a few people alive by a slow fire, and with great ceremony, is an infallible secret to prevent earthquakes".[18]

Mockingly determined to take the world at its own valuation, Swift often describes how an evil quality is actually cultivated because of its social usefulness. These descriptions are by implication a satire on society. The three brothers in the *Tale of a Tub* conscientiously adjust themselves to fashionable life: "they drank and fought and whored and took snuff".[19] The diminuendo, "and took snuff" suggests the joyless self-consciousness of these indulgences, which the brothers allowed themselves only in order to rise in a world which regarded them as the attributes of a gentleman. Gulliver's acquaintance, Munodi, is "nearly related to the king and for that reason alone used with respect", for that reason alone because Munodi persists in farming his land so that things do in fact grow, and pays no attention to the impractical projects of the Laputan Academy, a place where, for example a blind man is investigating the nature of colour. Gulliver himself is despised by the intellectuals of Laputa because he can walk about safely without the aid of a "Flapper". On his visit to Glubbdubdrib Gulliver rightly concludes that had statesmen and generals been so magnanimous as historians lyingly say, they would never have been successful.[20]

Hervey, with his blasé honesty, delicately analysing each new situation at a court engaged in continual and largely purposeless manoeuvre, also takes human weakness as axiomatic. He takes every opportunity to exploit the particular (the Civil List of 1727 or the king's affair with Mme. de Walmoden) so that it takes on a wry universal significance. The exclamation, "What fools these mortals be!" is always softly on his lips.

A good example of Hervey's Racine-like compression is in his account of the proposed Ministry of Sir Spencer Compton, who was "equally ambitious of and unfit for" the office of First Lord of the Treasury. It is presented as the solemnest of farces. Sir Robert Walpole, temporarily out of office because the king detests him, but about to resume the premiership for another fifteen years, tells Sir Spencer Compton, whose ascendancy lasts for a few days, "My time has been, yours is beginning". (Presumably Hervey, like Thucydides, made up the speeches in his historical narrative, and this stroke of dramatic irony is Hervey's own.) Compton, at a loss how to draw up his formal address to the king, asks Walpole to write it for him, and even calls him into the audience chamber to help when the king, as Walpole intended, finds fault with it. Walpole, before his "caretaker government" is dissolved, hurries through legislation to increase the royal family's allowance. The king shakes his head, and says that undoubtedly Walpole is a better public speaker than Compton, and makes Walpole his minister. Thereafter the royal family are so expertly managed by Walpole that, whilst he is directing them, they are convinced that they are directing him. The queen even congratulates her husband on "a prudent and happy choice of minister to do what they had vainly fancied they could do alone". All the time, the attitude of Walpole's ministry to George II is exactly the same as Queen Caroline's to the Prince of Wales: "There he is, he must be king, and we will make the best we can of him, though we cannot make him as good as we would."[21] Yet this same foxy Walpole is in the long view as foolish as all the others. Weary of daily wheedling and intrigue, he longs to retire to enjoy his considerable substance at Houghton, but cannot bring himself to relinquish the power of his great office. Believing that money is all-important and that every man has his price, he exhausts himself in a post to which he has no financial inducement. He tells Hervey that that ease and safety are considerations which outweigh all others in his mind, then continues to spend his days in laborious and vexatious intrigues which expose him to danger every hour of his life.

When one reads Hervey's story of the licence which George II permitted himself amongst the fine ladies of his court (Mrs. Bellenden, Lady Suffolk, the Countess of Yarmouth, Lady Deloraine), the docility of these ladies and the complaisance of their husbands, one is reminded of similar episodes in Suetonius (an author whom Hervey alludes to more than once), of Nero's construction of a row of brothels for his use on the way down the Tiber to Ostia, each brothel containing a noblewoman. It is clear that George II attained at least one kind of absolutism. Yet for the purposes of satire the king is axiomatically absurd and Hervey therefore treats the king's amours with a shrugging nonchalance, as if their frequent inanity was only to be expected. The husband of Mrs. Howard, one of the king's mistresses, threatens to reclaim her (although he does not want her) unless the king pays him money. The king, who is tired of Mrs. Howard, and very willing to relinquish her, is obliged to pay, partly for form's sake, but mainly to please the queen, who is afraid that Mrs. Howard will be replaced by somebody more dangerous. In this way the king parts with money, which he does like, in order to retain Mrs. Howard, whom he does not. This exercise in stately foolishness is followed by the episode of Mme. de Walmoden, the king's Hanoverian mistress, who engages the king's fancy so much that on his return from Germany he hangs his wife's drawing room with portraits of her.

Meanwhile Queen Caroline submits to indignities, flaunting unfaithfulness and boredom. "She was generally seven or eight hours tête-à-tête with the king every day, during which time she was generally saying what she did not think, assenting to what she did not believe, and praising what she did not approve."[22] She longs for him to visit Hanover because of the "conjugal fatigue" of entertaining him for twenty hours out of the twenty-four. All this she endures so that the public will think that she makes decisions of state. The truth is that she does not. Like Hervey himself, she is merely Walpole's instrument, but unlike Hervey, she does not know it. Snubbed continually by the king, who even during her last illness mixes irritation with his tears, she spends her nine years as queen in the aggrandisement of Walpole.

Since the king is what he is, the marriage which he arranges for the Princess Royal is naturally a ridiculous one. Hervey records it with a flourish:

"There is one of two inconveniences which generally attends most marriages; the one is sacrificing all considerations of interest and grandeur for the sake of beauty and an agreeable person; and the other that of sacrificing all consideration of beauty and person to interest and grandeur. But this match unfortunately conciliated the inconveniences of both these methods of marrying."[23]

The word "unfortunately" is particularly deftly employed, since the marriage was not a matter of chance but the result of long circumspect negotiation.

It is a mad world, Hervey implies. Men are always willing to exchange a real for an imaginary advantage. Their ponderous foolery creates all sorts of intermediaries between will and action. Because everyone was angling for the favour of the king, the only motion ever to be carried in the Commons with only one vote against it (and that by a political eccentric) was the Civil List of 1727, of which nobody approved. "No one thought it reasonable yet no one opposed it; no one wished for it, and no one voted against it." It was carried "without two opponents or two well-wishers".[24]

They are all fools: the queen and Prince Frederick, with their vindictive exchanges of dutifulness; Princess Emily, "who managed her affairs so well as to have lost entirely the confidence of her mother without having obtained the friendship of her brother"; Sir Spencer Compton, inordinately proud of the peerage which he has been given because it is dangerous to have him in the Commons; Bubb Dodington, with his "je ne sais quoi of displeasing". The king is a fool, Walpole is a fool. And the greatest fool of all, Hervey calmly notices, is Hervey, tired out and listening, nourishing himself with the impossible hope of succeeding Walpole, stretching his abilities night and day in order to keep up his position as "a dignified cipher".

The phlegmatic assumption which Swift and Hervey made was an insolent one, and for the sake of insolence even Smollett was willing to write coolly, and with an apparent absence of spleen, about things which really made him angry. The epistolary form, which forces the novelist to be at least overtly detached and to let the characters explain (or, unknowingly, expose) themselves, is cunningly used by Smollett in *Humphry Clinker* and elsewhere. One example is Lord Grizzlegrin's letter to Ferdinand,

Count Fathom. Fathom has to pay £1,500 damages for adultery. Not having the money by him, he writes to several men of quality whom he knows, asking them to lend it to him. Grizzlegrin replies, deploring the barbarous punishment: "Egad, at this rate no gentleman will be able to lie with another man's wife, but at the risk of cursed prosecution!" He exhorts Fathom to strive to forget "this disagreeable circumstance", declares his mortification at not being able to help him, and gives his opinion that "a man of Count Fathom's figure and address can never be puzzled for the want of such a paltry sum". In conclusion he looks forward to seeing Fathom the next day at White's.[25]

Another successful exercise in detachment, in which Smollett takes the wickedness of the world as axiomatic, is the fortune-telling episode in *Peregrine Pickle*. Crabtree, Pickle's cynical friend, sets up as a fortune teller in order to find out more about the private affairs of persons of fortune. As he is consulted "in all cases of law, physic and trade, over and above the ordinary subjects of marriage and fornication", he becomes almost as well-informed as Le Sage's Asmodeus. Indeed, the survey of elegant society in this part of the novel is rather like *Le Diable Boiteux*. Two visitors are interested in other people's expectation of life. One is a clergyman. The object of his interest is the incumbent of the parish to which he hopes to succeed. The other is a financial speculator who has insured the life of a young nobleman, "being thereto induced by the affirmation of his physician, who had assured him his patient's constitution was so rotten that he could not live one year to an end".

> He had nevertheless, made shift to weather eighteen months, and now seemed more vigorous and healthy than he had ever been known; for he was supposed to have nourished a hereditary pox from his cradle.[26]

Alarmed, the financier proposes to sue the physician for false intelligence. The incidental manner in which the evidence (the grim piece of calculation, the hereditary pox and the intended law-suit) is presented makes the degeneracy of the age seem a commonplace, something so obvious that Smollett hardly thinks it worthwhile to mention it.

In the same matter-of-fact fashion Smollett describes how, after the severities of the assault on St. Lazare, Roderick Random's ship is taken over by the well-connected fop, Captain Whiffle. Whiffle is anxious to leave the tropics because the sun is destroying his complexion. He arrives in his ten-oared barge,

> overshadowed with a vast umbrella, and appeared in everything
> the reverse of Oakum, being a tall, thin, young man, dressed in this
> manner : a white hat, garnished with a red feather, adorned his
> head, from whence his hair flowed upon his shoulders, in ringlets,
> tied behind with a ribbon. . . . But the most remarkable parts of
> his furniture were, a mask on his face, and white gloves on his
> hands, which did not seem to be put on with an intention to be
> pulled off occasionally, but were fixed with a curious ring on the
> little finger of each hand. In this garb, Captain Whiffle, for that
> was his name, took possession of the ship, surrounded with a
> crowd of attendants, all of whom, in their different degrees,
> seemed to be of their patron's disposition; and the air was so
> impregnated with perfumes, that one may venture to affirm the
> clime of Arabia Felix was not half so sweet-scented.[27]

He cannot bear the way the sailors smell of tobacco, so when
Random comes to attend him he bids him approach gradually,
"that his nose might have intelligence, before it could be much
offended" :

> I therefore approached with great caution and success, and he
> was pleased to say, "Ay, this creature is tolerable". I found him
> lolling on his couch with a languishing air, his head supported
> by his valet-de-chambre, who, from time to time applied a
> smelling bottle to his nose. "Vergette," said he in a squeaking
> tone, "dost thou think this wretch (meaning me) will do me no
> injury? May I venture to submit my arm to him?"[28]

Shortly before Whiffle's arrival, an epidemic fever (occasioned
Smollett says, by the heat, the rotten provisions, the lassitude of
the crew and the stench of the dead), had raged on board with
such violence that three-fourths of those whom it invaded died
in a deplorable manner. Random has been obliged to lie amongst
the sick in the cock-pit, which reeked of decayed food. Smollett
does not point the moral. The contrast in itself is enough, and
by treating the incident as if it was an everyday occurrence he is
able to suggest that this is the way of the world.

3. *Minute Observations Recorded with Apparent Objectivity*

Swift, as a mock-apologist, keeps to all the conventions of
apology. He studies his subject with the utmost diligence.
Indeed, so that no blemish shall escape his search, he is always
ready to go over the subject with a magnifying glass. His habit

of censorious observation was naturally strong. He once told a friend that since they had sat down to dinner the servant who was waiting on them had committed fifteen faults. It is not the mere negation of customary precept and example which distinguishes the *Directions to Servants* and *Polite Conversation*. In *Directions to Servants* it is the intricate flunkey-lore, the omniscience below stairs. Likewise, in *Polite Conversation* it is the ruthless setting-down in turn of every horrifying vulgarity of which the company is guilty. The *Modest Proposal* is a careful enumeration of the advantages of eating children. The hair-by-hair comparison between a man and a Yahoo results in two conclusions about their difference: that men do not have hair on the back of their hands (which is questionable) and that Yahoos do not engage in unnatural vice.[29]

The objective manner takes on a malevolent grace in the hands of Hervey, who uses it in detailing the reasons why people thought that the Duke of Newcastle was a fool ("either by their own observation or the deference which they paid to the opinion of the public") and that Lady Trevor had an unattractive face ("the most virtuous forbidding countenance that natural ugliness, age and smallpox ever compounded"). He is painstakingly exact in recording why the king and queen hated the English ("king-killers and republicans") who had made them king and queen, and the Whig party, which kept them so.

Hervey is subtle in the futilities of court life. The king is returning from Hanover, where he has been gallanting with a new mistress. There is a violent storm in the Channel. It is feared that the king is lost. The Prince of Wales celebrates. Sir Robert Walpole is melancholy and reflective. Hervey, at Walpole's request, advises the queen how she can gain an ascendancy over the mind of the Prince of Wales. There is great discussion over whether the queen should appear in public or not. Meanwhile the king is taking his ease at Helvetsluys, from which port he has not stirred. Another flurry takes place when the Prince of Wales requests an interview with his father. Everyone makes guesses about what will happen. Vexed discussions take place about whether Dodington or Chesterfield is at the back of whatever it is. A cabinet meeting is held, and Walpole hastens to the royal parents with advice. The interview is granted. The prince approached with his simple question: Does the king not think that it is time that the prince was married?

Smollett uses the same satirical precision in his account of the fatuous yet tragic mismanagement of the expedition to Carthagena:

> A day or two after the attempt on St. Lazar, the admiral ordered one of the Spanish men-of-war we had taken to be mounted with sixteeen guns, and manned with detachments from our great ships, in order to batter the town. Accordingly, she was towed into the inner harbour in the night, and moored within half a mile of the walls, against which she began to fire at daybreak; and continued about six hours exposed to the opposition of at least thirty pieces of cannon, which at length obliged our men to set her on fire, and get off as well as they could in their boats.

Smollett lists the various explanations suggested for this "stroke of policy", dismissing as irreverent the notion that the admiral thought he could gain anything by it:

> Some entertained such an irreverent opinion of the admiral's understanding, as to think he expected the town would surrender to his floating battery of sixteen guns. Others imagined his sole intention was to try the enemy's strength, by which he should be able to compute the number of great ships that would be necessary to force the town to a capitulation. But this last conjecture soon appeared groundless, inasmuch as no ships of any kind whatever were afterwards employed on that service. A third sort swore, that no other cause could be assigned for this undertaking, than that which induced Don Quixote to attack the windmill.[30]

In his grand ironical build-ups Smollett often employs well-chosen detail. In *Ferdinand, Count Fathom* he depicts the hero's "great tranquillity and inner satisfaction" as he makes off with a pair of saddle-bags containing what he believes to be jewels, "the spoils of sundry dupes". Fathom arrives at an inn, enjoys "a very comfortable refreshment of sleep, with his bags under his pillow", and eats a hearty meal. When he has eaten he lets his fancy dally upon the "happy presages and ideal prospects of his future fortune", and decides to re-examine "the fruits of that success which had hitherto attended his endeavours". He opens the bags and finds "neither more or less than a parcel of rusty nails, disposed in such a manner as to resemble in weight and bulk the movables he had lost".[31]

There is nothing here in the style of Fielding's post-mortem on the death of Captain Blifil in *Tom Jones,* no sagacious reflecttion, no quotation from Horace. Smollett contents himself with

observing that one may "easily conceive the milkiness of resignation" with which Fathom bears his loss. Smollett knows when
he has said enough. When Louis XV appears momentarily in
Roderick Random, Smollett wastes no rhetoric on the king's
human frailties. He merely states that Random "had the honour
of seeing His Most Christian Majesty eat a considerable quantity
of olives".[32] The stringent, poised contempt of the juxtaposition
lays low, with a single stroke, whatever notions of glory Louis
XV may have had. Facts, if cleverly enough managed, can
always speak for themselves.

4. *The Realistic Treatment of Ideal Concepts*

The grandiose classical jargon of Grub Street, and the fashion
for imitating the poetic forms of the Greek and Latin writers,
gave many opportunities to the eighteenth-century satirist. Swift
has a Pastoral in which Corydon and Phyllis dig potatoes and
weed in the rain, and in *The Dean Reasons* he pauses to do the
Heroical Epistle to death with the lines:

> Here poor Pomona sits on thorns
> And here neglected Flora settles
> Her bum upon a bed of nettles.[33]

There were few things which pleased Swift better than to bring
low a poetic convention. In the *Beautiful Young Nymph Going to
Bed* Swift parodies the stock poetic response to the sight of a
woman shedding her clothes—Spenser's description of the des-
poilation of Selena is an example of a flourishing erotic genre. As
Swift's young nymph undresses she becomes not more beautiful
but more grotesque. Swift has already practised this sort of thing
when he changed Cowley's gallant *Clad All in White* into his
own *Clad All in Brown* and followed Cowley's pattern with
appropriate substitutions.

Life has its conventions too. In the *Verses on the Death of Dr.
Swift,* Swift sets about the shams of fashionable mourning by
making the ladies of his acquaintance lament his death as they
play cards. Reality breaks through a heroic convention in *Clever
Tom Clinch Going to be Hanged* (a title in itself satiric). Swift
relates with approval how Tom Clinch dispensed with the pious
last speech usual at public executions:

> The hangman for pardon fell down on his knee;
> Tom gave him a kick in the guts for his fee.[34]

The idea that a Christian should be grateful for punishment, and indeed seek it out, is converted in the *Tale of a Tub* into Jack's "Madam, shall I entreat a small box on the ears from your lady's fair hands?"[35] A small box on the ears—Jack is too humble to ask for more.

Whilst Swift takes a grandiose concept and levels it down, Smollett emphasises the baseness of an action by elevating it to a plane where it cannot but appear ridiculous. Fathom is born on the move in a gin-wagon, so that "the task of determining to what government he owed his allegiance would be at least as difficult as that of ascertaining the so much contested birthplace of Homer". His mother, who goes round the battlefields of Europe stabbing and robbing the wounded, is referred to as "our English Penthelisia" and "this modern Amazon". The aga whom she slaughters in this squalid way is described as having his destiny thus fulfilled. He evokes the name of Allah three times, and expires.

The implication of the battle scenes in *Ferdinand, Count Fathom*, is that this is what the "illustrious" Prince Eugene's victories amount to. The difference between Fathom's mother and other war-profiteers is only one of scale. She is active in a small way and on the spot. In the Carthagenan episode of *Roderick Random* Smollett deals with two other death-mongers, whose wickedness is greater because their power is greater. The sick and wounded are crowded together on so-called hospital ships, without medical attention and with so little space that "the miserable patients had not room to sit upright in their beds" :

This inhuman disregard was imputed to the scarcity of surgeons; though it is well known that every great ship in the fleet could have spared one at least for this duty; an expedient which would have been more than sufficient to remove this shocking inconvenience. But, perhaps the general was too much of a gentleman to ask a favour of this kind from his fellow chief, who, on the other hand, would not derogate so much from his own dignity as to offer such assistance unasked; for I may venture to affirm, that, by this time, the Demon of Discord, with her sooty wings, had breathed her influence upon our counsels; and it might be said of these great men (I hope they will pardon the comparison), as of Caesar and Pompey, the one could not brook a superior, and the other was impatient of an equal; so that, between the pride of one, and insolence of another, the enterprise miscarried,

according to the proverb "Between two stools, the backside falls
to the ground".[36]

As one reads this courtly narrative, with the drily and deliber-
ately inappropriate tableau of Caesar, Pompey and the figure of
Discord, one remembers all the time what Smollett has said about
the clamorous distress of the common seamen. Smollett has in-
vested the coarse old proverb at the end of the passage with a peculiar venom. Its acquiescent mildness represents the defeated shrug
of a man who can find no limit to human stupidity, and who
finds sanity has no place in a world run by such heroes as these.

5. *Internal Satire within a Satirical Supposition*

Like the fleas of his playful quatrain, Swift's satire often
carries further satire on its back. Within a satirical supposition a
further satirical supposition is made. In the *Directions to Servants*
he advises the maid upon the choice of lovers. One of the candidates will be the chaplain, but he is only to be taken "if you are
big with child with my lord".[37] The primary satire is on the
viciousness of chaplains. The secondary satire is on what fools are
made of chaplains. In fact there is a third all-embracing satire
on the easy virtue of the maid. Swift also has advice to give the
footman, who is told that it is particularly pleasing in a "sightly
young fellow" for him to breathe in his mistress' face.[38] In
other words, not only is the habit permissible, but also, in a
dashing young flunkey, seductive. The *Physician's Love Poem* is
primarily a satire on a pedant who writes in terms of his bodily
functions, and secondarily a satire on man, who is so dependent
on his mean inside. More lightly, Swift contests not only the
future but also the present reputation of John Dryden by affirm-
ing his existence, "which I have upon the word of a sincere
man", in the Dedication of the *Tale of a Tub*.

The complications of a court where the only person who did
not have to bear the ill-humour of the king was the Prince of
Wales, who was fortunate enough not to be "on a footing of
being spoken to by his father", the hypocrisies and circumlocu-
tions, gave Hervey every chance to use compound satire. He
had, for example, to learn the art of baulking and exasperating
a royal personage in a letter which ended with wishes for his prosperity and happiness, and assurances of unalterable affection. He
had to busy himself with the intricate situation of writing such a
letter on behalf of Mrs. Vane, who was sleeping with Hervey, to
the Prince of Wales, who (to her relief) no longer wanted her as

a mistress—writing away and recollecting that she had once jilted Hervey for this same Prince of Wales. There was primary and secondary satire in almost everything which took place. The Prince of Wales is "as false as his capacity would allow him to be". The queen wishes that she had never given birth to him. "Pray, mama," interrupts Princess Caroline, "do not throw away your wishes on what cannot happen, but wish that he may crever, and that we may all go about with smiling faces, glad hearts, and crepe and hoods for him."[39]

The Princess Royal takes every opportunity to point out her father's faults, "and wherever these were small enough to admit of it she would magnify them".[40] The Prince of Wales is angry when the Princess Royal marries before him, "but upon her presuming to be with child he was quite outrageous".[41] Newcastle runs about with "a bundle of papers as big as his head and with little more in them".[42] Whilst all this is taking place the courtier-moles "are always drudging on in their interested little paths without seeing".

Smollett uses compound satire in a more diffused way than either Swift or Hervey, sometimes sustaining whole episodes with it. The inner contradiction of a Capuchin friar who marches along with Roderick Random singing "an infinite number of catches on the subjects of love and wine" is further complicated when the priest-turned-libertine turns priest again to hear the confession of the girl whom he has spent the night with.[43] Tabitha Bramble is converted to Methodism by the postillion who so affronts her with the sight of his bare posterior. In the belief that he is bankrupt the philosopher Cadwallader Crabtree contemplates suicide, but "his unwillingness to oblige and entertain his fellow-creatures hindered him from practising that expedient".[44] A reprehensible passage, left out of the second and subsequent editions of *Peregrine Pickle,* relates how, at the banquet in the manner of the ancients, the count tipsily made love to the baron "with such expressions of tenderness as scandalised the virtuous painter, who, conscious of his own attractions, was alarmed for his person, and staggered in great hurry and discomposure into the next room, where he put himself under the protection of Pickle".[45] Compound satire forms part of Fathom's education when, as a boy, he learns how to confess what he really has done, in such a manner that it is thought that his confession is a noble lie to shield someone else.[46]

In the foregoing examples Smollett uses the device quizzically, but he could also make it serve an intent purpose. He used every possible method to ridicule and deplore the Carthagenan expedition, which he was determined should not be forgotten, this one among the others:

> This piece of conduct, in choosing a camp under the walls of an enemy's fortification, which, I believe, never happened before, was practised, I presume, with a view of accustoming the soldiers to stand fire, who were not as yet much used to discipline, most of them having been taken from the plough-tail a few months before.[47]

So, on comparing Smollett's satirical technique in with that of two of the subtlest writers of his age, one finds that he was a highly conscious artist—a discovery which is borne out by an examination of his style. It remains necessary to make allowances, as always, for his extreme individualism. Hervey lacked the prompting anger of Swift and Smollett, and in Swift and Smollett anger took different forms. We know that it was Swift's manner, when he had set the table roaring, to contemplate the merriment with a severe and inquiring face. What those features, contemplative, faintly acid, never revealed was the cruel indignation which, to the last, lashed his heart without intermission. In contrast to the militant social attack of Smollett, Swift's satire moves in a cloud of pious avowals and expressions of diffidence.

Swift hated rhetoric and sentiment, and irony gave him a medium without rhetoric or sentiment for his colossal disdain. It also indulged the private humour of a man who, in his youth, had been obliged to bear in silence with much pomposity and arrogance from men of great place. There was a great deal of natural concealment in Swift. He never laughed, preferred to avoid pleasing people (unless they could further his projects) and, although a dignitary of the established Church, prayed in secret like an early Christian. He lived cautiously, weighing chances and insinuating his way. Only when he had made sure that he could not be dispensed with did he reveal his inner intractability. Smollett, on the other hand, led a life of sustained defiance in the interests of which he even went to prison. It is only momentarily and for the sake of a definite effect that he ever hides his intentions. To him irony was an occasional weapon, to Swift it was a way of life. Whilst Swift withdrew into his own sombre disgust, Smollett, ardent, extravagant and quarrelsome, took on all comers.

Swift seldom put himself forward as a reformer. When he did, it was on a trivial scale, as in the affair of Wood's half-pence. Mankind was a bad job and there was nothing that could be done about it. "Do not the corruptions and villianies of men eat your flesh and exhaust your spirits?" he once asked a startled ecclesiastic friend. His attitude to Authority was equivocal. The first blow to his pride in himself was when he was sent as emissary to William III to promote triennial parliaments, and he found that his laboriously drawn-up arguments could not shift the king, who had made his mind up already and did not want to listen. This was not the only occasion on which he swallowed a humiliation for the sake of his career. Once when he had every reason to know best, since the discussion concerned the authorship of the *Tale of a Tub,* a bishop silenced him with the remark that he was "a very positive young man". These incidents may account for the elaborately concessive style of Swift's satire. It is the quirk of a man who knows best but may not say so, because he has sold himself to the world.

Here again Smollett differs from Swift. The whole point of Smollett's assault on the existing order is that the existing order can, by human endeavour, be changed. Smollett is a reformer of a type more common in the Victorian period than his own. He is an eighteenth-century Radical. He arraigns society in the terms in which Sir Launcelot Greaves arraigns Justice Gobble:

Instead of protecting the helpless, restraining the hands of violence, preserving the public tranquillity, and acting as a father to the poor, according to the intent and meaning of that institution of which you are an unworthy member; you have distressed the widow and the orphan, given a loose to all the insolence of office, embroiled your neighbours by fomenting suits and animosities, and played the tyrant among the indigent and forlorn.[48]

Swift's satire is like the finely wrought intimation of a classical prelude, or a late Egyptian statuette, the body cylindrical although dallied upon by small variations of curve and slow hints of contour, the face and hands alone being chiselled out in detail. Smollett's satire is like some mad swingeing Romantic scherzo, or an engraving by Dürer, with every wrinkle in a face and every fold in a drapery asserted, every flower formed with botanical verve, every twig and pebble bitten hard into the copper plate in his zeal to bear honest witness. Yet, as in the engraving by Dürer, there is more than a regard for Truth, there is an enthusiasm for it.

CHAPTER XIII

NOR HEED THE STORM

THE COMPOUND CRUELTIES of Smollett's last illness were recorded a little histrionically by an Italian doctor called Gentili. He died, says Gentili, "without trying to help himself", died with a coughing disgust.

Often, in reading the English writers of the eighteenth century, one becomes suddenly aware of the glands and paroxysms under the *jabot* and the bullioned waistcoat, of the brute cry breaking into the set-piece. One thinks of Johnson's "Mens turbata. It snowed all afternoon". Of Swift, interrupting Stella's exequy, with, "My head aches, I can write no more". Of Hume, playing a game of backgammon to divert himself from the disagreeable sense that he is "in the most deplorable condition imaginable, environed with the deepest darkness, and utterly deprived of the use of every member and faculty".[1] Smollett's wary balances and his nice diction are waterflies on the flood of his contempt and despair. Nature to him, is not "supremely fair and sovereignly good", as it was to Shaftesbury.[2] Nature destroys, man attempts to save:

> Mr. Morgan being nettled at this treatment, told him, his indignation ought to be directed to God Almighty, who visited his people with distempers, and not to him, who contributed all in his power towards their cure.[3]

At its best Nature is wholly indifferent to the insect sorrows of mankind. Too impatiently angry to comment on them, Smollett points to this and that instance.

Because of their geographical position these people are assigned at birth to consumption:

> Many people here have scorbutical complaints, though their teeth are not affected. They are subject to eruptions on the skin, putrid gums, pains in the bones, lassitude, indigestion, and low spirits; but the reigning distemper is a marasmus, or consumption, which proceeds gradually, without any pulmonary complaint, the complexion growing more and more florid, 'till the very last scene of the tragedy.[4]

This is how the invalids at Bath are permitted to use their talents :

> In the forenoon, they crawl out to the rooms or the coffee-house, where they take a hand at whist, or descant upon the General Advertiser; and their evenings they murder in private parties, among peevish invalids, the insipid old women. This is the case with a good number of individuals, whom nature seems to have intended for better purposes.[5]

This is what bereavement does to the manhood of Renaldo :

> His hair hung in dishevelled parcels, his cheeks were wan, his looks ghastly, his vigour was fled, and all the glory of his youth faded.[6]

But Fathom is cleverer than Renaldo, Fathom can surely fend for himself. What happens to Fathom?

> He was worn to the bone either by famine or distemper; his face was overshadowed with hair and filth; his eyes were sunk, glazed, and distorted; his nostrils dilated; his lips covered with a black slough; and his complexion faded into a pale clay-colour, tending to a yellow hue.[7]

This is an old gentleman with gout, waking from nightmares to worse than nightmares :

> Had it been simply waking, he would have been obliged to them for the noise that disturbed him; for, in that case, he would have been relieved from the tortures of hell-fire, to which, in his dream, he fancied himself exposed : but this dreadful vision had been the result of that impression, which was made upon his brain by the intolerable anguish of his joints; so that when he waked, the pain instead of being allayed, was rather aggravated by a great acuteness of sensation.[8]

These were the consequences of a little piece of foppery :

> A Frenchman will sooner part with his religion than with his hair, which, indeed, no consideration will induce him to forego. I know a gentleman afflicted with a continual head-ache, and a defluxion on his eyes, who was told by his physician that the best chance he had for being cured, would be to have his head close shaved, and bathed every day in cold water. "How (cried he) cut my hair? Mr. Doctor, your most humble servant!" He dismissed his physician, lost his eye-sight, and almost his senses, and is now led about with his hair in a bag, and a piece of green silk hanging like a screen before his eyes.[9]

This is how a young man of uncommon ability was disposed of in the tenth part of a minute:

> When I was a very young man, I remember to have seen a person suffocated by such impertinent officiousness. A young man of uncommon parts and erudition, very well esteemed at the university of G——ow, was found early one morning in a subterranean vault among the ruins of an old archi-episcopal palace, with his throat cut from ear to ear. Being conveyed to a public-house in the neighbourhood, he made signs for pen, ink and paper, and in all probability, would have explained the cause of this terrible catastrophe, when an old woman, seeing the wind-pipe, which was cut, sticking out of the wound, and mistaking it for the gullet, by way of giving him a cordial to support his spirits, poured into it, through a small funnel, a glass of burnt brandy, which strangled him in the tenth part of a minute.[10]

Life gives no respite to the weak and over-fond Elinor. She is bludgeoned into a merciful insensibility:

> When she recovered the use of her senses so well as to reflect upon her forlorn condition, she was seized with the most violent transports of grief and dismay, by which her brain was disordered to such a degree, .that she grew furious and distracted, and was, by the advice and assistance of the Tyrolese, conveyed into the hospital of Bethlem; where we shall leave her for the present, happily bereft of her reason.[11]

The long progress of Monimia's sufferings leads only to her obliteration. The distresses which she has undergone so enfeeble her that even a change of fortune serves only to disorder her mind. Prostrate, she falls into a deathlike coma.[12]

The battle of Carthagena, the crucial event in Smollett's life, furnishes him with the image of the lonely human soul struggling. Random, gasping for breath in the coils of a violent fever, sees "six or seven thrown overboard every day, who died of the same distemper", and is visited by the ship's chaplain, who makes various learned distinctions about what is needful for Random's salvation, then returns to drink grog with the other officers in the ward-room. The ship's physician does not even know where Random is:

> In the meantime, being in great danger of suffocation, I started up in a kind of frantic fit, with an intention to plunge myself into the sea; and as my friend the serjeant was not present, would have cooled myself to some purpose, had I not perceived a mois-

ture upon my thigh, as I endeavoured to get out of my hammock. The appearance of this revived my hopes, and I had reflection and resolution enough to take advantage of this favourable symptom by tearing the shirt from my body, and the sheets from my bed, and wrapping myself in a thick blanket, in which enclosure, for about a quarter of an hour, I felt the pains of hell; but it was not long before I was recompensed for my suffering by a profuse sweat, that, bursting from the whole surface of my skin, in less than two hours relieved me from all my complaints, except that of weakness, and left me as hungry as à kite.[13]

To the struggle, Smollett suggests, Man can bring only a dominant, belligerent stoicism. In *Humphry Clinker* Smollett quotes with approval the example of a certain eccentric called Mr. H:

Being taken with a suppression of urine, in imitation of Pomponius Atticus, to take himself off by abstinence; and this resolution he executed like an ancient Roman. He saw company to the last, cracked his jokes, conversed freely, and entertained his guests with music. On the third day of his fast, he found himself entirely free of his complaint; but refused taking sustenance. He said that the most disagreeable part of the voyage was past, and he should be a cursed fool indeed to put about ship when he was just entering the harbour. In these sentiments he persisted, without any marks of affectation; and thus finished his course with such ease and serenity, as would have done justice to the firmest stoic of antiquity.[14]

In a letter to William Hunter, written when Smollett was very ill in 1767, Smollett describes himself as "still crawling on the face of the earth", and refers humorously to the "ridiculous use" which he has made of his ulcerated right arm "in writing such a heap of absurdities". He adds that his circulation is beneficially stimulated by the attacks made upon him by the writers of Grub Street. Fifteen years previously, in the *Essay on the External Use of Water,* he had noted the vivifying power of anger:

If the intention is to induce a strong contraction to the solids (of the nervous system) nothing more effectually accomplishes that aim than such treatment as inspires the passions of anger and fear . . . I have known a gentleman who was paralytic to a deplorable degree, enraged to a perfect use of all his limbs whilst his anger predominated.[15]

Smollett illustrates the principle in his amusing and touching account of Dick Distich, alehouse satirist, drunken incorrigible and almost a minor poet, at the "peculiar virulence" of whose disposition even Sir Launcelot Greaves cannot forbear to smile. It is certainly anger which keeps Dick Distich going. He and the equally little-known Ben Bullock had decided to savage the scarcely heeding town :

> "Ben Bullock and I," said he, "were confident against the world in arms—did you never see his ode to me beginning with 'Fair blooming youth'? We were sworn brothers, admired and praised and quoted each other, sir . . . I tell you, sir, Ben Bullock and I had determined to crush all that were not of our own party."[16]

In fact, because of his excessive turbulence, Dick Distich is consigned to a private madhouse, and Ben Bullock, it seems, makes a profit from his friend's discomfiture by alluding sentimentally to it in his verses. This incenses Dick Distich, and inspires his unforgettable reply when Sir Launcelot asks if there is anything he can do for him : "If you see Ben Bullock, tell him I wish he would not dedicate any more of his works to me. Damn the fellow, he has changed his note, and begins to snivel."[17] For his part, he sticks to his former maxim, will die hard, and defies the world. Then he settles down to composing some "keen iambics" against a fellow-prisoner who has blackened his eye. Of course, Dick Distich is not really mad ("I was never otherwise than drunk or maudlin") and ones passing acquaintance with him in *Sir Launcelot Greaves* is, although all too brief, enough to make one glad that the knight secures his release later on.

Smollett, like Hume and Hartley, accepted a materialistic philosophy with the greatest unwillingness, but accepted it just the same. He was a materialist by conviction temperamentally opposed to materialism. With honesty and courage he drew each terrible conclusion, not because he wanted it to be true, but because he refused to disavow the intelligence which told him that it was true. His conception of Man, trapped in the flesh and in supplication before a merciless Nature, is entirely pessimistic, but bravely, grimly pessimistic. He has the will to contend, to make a stand. There is nothing passive in Smollett. He is loud in his anger, and gives defiance. In the perhaps too grandoise words of his *Ode to Independence,*

> Thy steps I follow with my bosom bare,
> Nor heed the storm that howls along the sky.

"The spleen" (melancholia or, as it was sometimes called in the eighteenth century, "the English malady") was often a symptom of the strain put on religious faith by the new "mechanical" philosophy, of which Hobbes and Locke deviously and Hume directly were exponents. "The sceptical cobweb", which is what he called Hume's *Treatise of Human Nature*, caused poor Boswell many bouts of melancholia.[18] There is no doubt that Smollett's acceptance of this philosophy made his view of life gloomier. This is all the more pathetic in that the philosophy can be proved to be unsound. That men should pursue a fallacy just in order to be made miserable by it is indeed unfortunate.

Hobbes' whole system is based on a laughably crude, quasi-scientific contention about the nature of the Universe, which he says is composed of matter and motion.[19] Any modern physicist could tell him that matter is a form of motion. Hobbes goes on to make a self-contradictory proposition, in which Hume later seconds him : he denies the reality of the external world except as perceived through Man's mind,[20] yet describes perception as being the pressure of an external object upon the appropriate organ of sense.[21] The decision and downright shrewdness of his manner allows him to pass off his perverse book as wisdom. His hypothetical state of nature ("a war of every man against every other man") has not been found to exist. On the contrary, the principle of mutual aid has been discovered, not only in the most primitive societies, but amongst animals as well. Few men indeed are anxious for "power after power", and those, such as the early Roman Emperors, who obtain despotic sway undergo, as Tacitus nobly phrases it, the inner torments which are the inherent retribution of tyranny, the lash-marks left on the soul by fear and rage.

The despondency into which Hume's own philosophy threw him is well known, as is the conclusion to the second book of his *Treatise*, in which he pronounces his own faculties to be weak and disordered and inadequate to his inquiries, and pitifully complains of the depressing thoughts "which the present subject furnishes me with an abundance".[22] His despondency was needless. The one assumption on which its large and systematic structure was reared, the assumption that, granted sufficient knowledge, everything can be explained in terms of cause and effect, had already been shown by Spinoza to be an untenable one. It is true that Hume admits that he cannot prove the proposition "that nothing can begin to exist without some productive principle", but he certainly believes this. In one of his letters he writes :

I have never defended the absurd proposition that a thing can come into being without a cause : all I maintained was that our certainty of the falsehood of this proposition arises neither from intuition nor demonstration, but from some other source.[23]

In his *Treatise* he refers to "that famous atheist", Spinoza, but refuses to enter further into the "gloomy and obscure regions" of Spinoza's "hideous hypothesis".[24] This suggests that Hume, like many another, was more familiar with Spinoza's name than with Spinoza's writings. It is a pity that Hume averted his face at the threshold. Had he indeed entered, he would perhaps have discovered, and Smollett after him, not gloom and obscurity, but an affirmation in the clearest terms that all is well.

Besides this objection to Hume's main argument, there are various details of the *Treatise* which can well be disputed on Hume's own terms. These concern the nature of thought and so had a special bearing on Smollett's view of Man. As Spinoza regarded matter and thought as two different aspects of the same thing, he was not under an obligation, as a Determinist is, to explain how matter can think. Hume evades the obligation by referring it to the scientist : "The examination of our sensations belongs more to anatomists and natural philosophers than to moral ones."[25] Thus he makes thought ultimately a question of anatomy, since he considers thought to be only the "faint image" of sensation : "When I shut my eyes and think of my chamber, the ideas I form are exact representations of the impressions I felt." Such a statement disallows the selectivity of the memory, which is due to thought preceeding and qualifying sensation. The same lack of subtlety is shown in Hume's challenge to the reader (a challenge based on a failure to distinguish between reflection and simple awareness), to "show a simple impression that has not a correspondent idea", or vice versa. From this challenge he proceeds to his general proposition : "All our simple ideas in their first impression are derived from simple impressions, which are correspondent to them, and which they exactly represent."[26] He anticipates the notion of Condillac's statue by insisting that the sensations from which thought is derived depend upon the faculties which receive them. Therefore, when a person is born blind or deaf, he forgoes not only impressions but also the correspondent ideas. Even if we accepted Hume's account of thought, we could contest this particular statement on the grounds that the same ideas (as distinct from perceptions) could be attained by the use of other faculties. Indeed, in describing

the impressions of one faculty, we often use the terms appropriate to another faculty, such as the words "sharp" and "clear".

So decidedly does Hume insist that upon the sensory deriva-
tion of thought, so emphatically does he deny the existence of
innate ideas, that he cites the "care and nicety" with which a
bird chooses the place and materials for its nest as a proof of the
bird's "sagacity" and powers of reflection.[27] Yet he frequently
and inconsistently mentions the effects of "Nature". Nature sets
him off on his inquiry: "Nature, by an absolute and uncontrollable necessity, has determined us to judge as well as to breathe
and feel."[28] Nature extricates him from the difficulties which are
brought about by that inquiry: "Most fortunately it happens,
that since reason is incapable of dispelling these clouds, Nature
herself suffices to that purpose."[29] By such inconsistency Hume
unwittingly allows his own philosophy to be untenable.

In spite of Smollett's imposing medical connections and the
flattering testimony of Dr. John Moore, there is much evidence
that Smollett's practical skill as a doctor was only great enough
to enable him to misapply Hume's theories to his own misunderstanding of the medicine of his time. What little is known about
Smollett's professional practice is not to his credit, and a distinguished modern physician, after an exhaustive examination
of the relevant passages in Smollett, declares that there is no
evidence that Smollett possessed a scientific mind.[30] In the *Essay
on the External Use of Water* the cure of wens by application
to the hand of a hanged man is "cited not as a superstitious
belief but in all seriousness". Smollett adopts Galen's system and
terminology, owes little to the scientific work of his day in his
physical observations and shows scarcely any interest in the development of medicine. Although he spent thirteen years, at least
intermittently, as a physician, "there is no allusion in Smollett
which might suggest interest in the pathology of his time". He
considers blood-letting to be a serious remedy, especially for the
many hysterical seizures which he describes. His account of the
workings of the dropsy, as in the story of the death of Roderick
Random's grandfather, is inaccurate, as is his attribution of
tuberculosis to the drinking of brackish water.[31] One of Smollett's errors in diagnosis is intensely pathetic. At a time when he
was dying of consumption he described himself as labouring
under an asthmatic disorder.[32] Indeed he quarrelled with a
French doctor, to whose ignorance of Latin he took exception,
who told him the truth, and who added that the theory in

Smollett's own explanation of his illness was an idle one.

Because of his doctrinaire following of materialist theory, Smollett was guilty of the same sort of over-simplification as Zola made about heredity in the Rougon-Macquart novels. A hesitant new notion of physical science, crudely understood, was interpreted in an exaggerated form and as if it was incontestable truth. Hence an excessive stress on the effects of physical circumstances, and conversely on the physical manifestations of thought and feeling. The terrified Pallet escapes from the Bastile "with each particular hair crawling and twining like an animated serpent".[33] This excessive stress has often been discerned in Smollett, but previously it has always been attributed to a mere taste for caricature on his part. It was, as we have seen, part of something more systematic than that. The system was wrong, but so was Dante's and nobody thinks the less of Dante for it.

We have examined the philosophical contentions behind the pessimistic view of life which Smollett adopts. But there were more urgent and immediate reasons for his pessimism in the circumstances of his own life. The miseries of authorship at the time when Smollett was trying to make an independent living as an author have been ruefully described by Oliver Goldsmith. A writer must necessarily be a sensitive creature, "of feelings so exquisitely poignant as to agonise under the slightest disappointment". This is certainly true of Smollett. Yet this delicate instrument is exposed to the most brutal of shocks:

> Broken rest, tasteless meals, and causeless anxiety shorten his life, or render it unfit for active employment; prolonged vigils and intense application still farther contract his span, and make his time glide insensibly away.

Goldsmith considers the lives of some of the most promising writers of his time:

> It is enough that the age has already produced instances of men pressing foremost in the lists of fame, and worthy of better times; schooled by continued adversity into a hatred of their kind, flying from thought to drunkenness, yielding to the united pressure of labour, penury and sorrow, sinking unheeded, without one friend to drop a tear on their unattended obsequies, and indebted to charity for a grave.

In order to survive, the writer must sacrifice his literary pretensions, deny his own talents and become a mere journalist:

The author, when unpatronised by the great, has natural recourse to the bookseller. There cannot be perhaps imagined a combination more prejudicial to taste than this. It is the interest of the one to allow as little for writing, and of the other to write as much, as possible. Accordingly tedious compilations and periodical magazines are the result of their joint endeavours. In these circumstances, the author bids adieu to fame, writes for bread, and for that only imagination is seldom called in.[34]

"Tedious compilations and periodical magazines" are exactly what Smollett was obliged to devote his abilities to during the period 1753–63, those desperate ten years which culminated in the death of his daughter, Elizabeth, and the collapse of his own health. Already in 1759 he was writing, "I have toiled myself into an habitual asthma. . . . To tell you a secret my constitution is quite broken". To add to his distractions, during the following year he was tried and sent to prison for three months for a libel on Admiral Knowles in a periodical which he had just started.

The only person he asked for help was Chatham, whom he much admired and to whom he dedicated his *History of England*; and Chatham disappointed him. During Chatham's Ministry of 1758–60 Smollett made several attempts to obtain the consulship at Madrid. Because of the libel on Admiral Knowles and perhaps because of Smollett's opposition to the war with France ("a cruel game of blood, in which even triumph is embittered"), Smollett's application was declined. That the denial did not abate Smollett's admiration for Chatham can be seen from the pathetic pride with which he carried with him on his travels Chatham's letter of thanks for the dedication, which was found amongst Smollett's effects after his death in a trunk at Leghorn.[35]

An even more touching relic is Smollett's personal copy of the *Travels* in the British Museum, which contains insertions in his own hand. Amongst them is his translation of the account of his illness which he sent to Dr. Fizes in Latin. He describes himself as being "very subject to rheums, accompanied with fever, dejection and difficulty in breathing. The least alteration of the weather towards cold or moisture, change of dress, the smallest excess in point of exercise, whether on foot or horseback, or in a carriage, occasions fresh commotions in the animal economy. The nervous system, being extremely irritable, undergoes a variety of spasms . . . and all night long the heat, restlessness, anxiety and asthma prevail . . . The patient's flesh wastes apace, and his strength continues to decay." Confronted with such evidence as this, it would be impertinent to deny a man his right to find fault with life. There is no doubt that Smollett's ill-health was a pitiful affliction to him, the more so in that he paid so much attention to it. Addison, Fielding and Goldsmith, all of whom had worse health and shorter lives, were far less pre-occupied by their physical condition. Addison in fact merrily (and with greater scientific objectivity than Smollett) dismisses the human inside as a "bundle of pipes and strainers". Yet there must have been certain compensations for Smollett. The most independent of authors, he must have taken a fierce pride in his vigorous and successful exploitation of his own powers, especially when he used them to challenge the social injustices which he so detested. Unsubmissive, he could always outface the world with the accurate and riddling fluency of his anger. No one who used words with such a loving regard as he did could have failed to delight in the material in which he was working, nor can a man with such a vivid sense of the comic have found life wholly dismal all the time. The very toil to which he submitted himself must have had its value in distracting his mind from his personal anxieties. Above all, as an eighteenth-century Stoic, he was well aware that the pang which cannot be endured soon ends life and itself.

The taut energy of his own resistance to external forces—sickness, wordly failure, bereavement—fluxes through Smollett's novels. It ennobles certain of his characters. Lismahago, impoverished and scalped, is still ready to dispute an assertion or to pick a quarrel. Bramble is never so composed as when he risks drowning. Mrs. Williams, though nearly trodden into extinction, still has the courage to begin a new life. Even Fathom takes on a kind of nobility in the end, in his lopsided attempts to save his maimed fortunes. Surely the *certain ferocity* which gleams in imprisoned Pickle's eye is the fire which Prometheus brought down from heaven, the fury which drives Man to hammer out a way of life which, in Smollett's view, Nature never intended. A lazaret founded, an abuse stamped out, a pernicious custom extirpated: though the battle can never be won, these are outposts from which further advances can be made.

Perhaps, then, there was something which we missed when we looked at the allegorical frontispiece. Let us look at it again, more closely. We have already recognised, in the group of sages, the primly percipient face of Hume, the blue-chinned grin of Voltaire. We have recalled that the astrolabe, the truncated rhomboid and the balances, which bedeck one margin, are emblems of measure and order. As we scan the embellished page in search of a new detail, our eyes fall upon the looking glass. By a fine stroke of his art, the engraver has wrapped the statue in a sheet of fire. What is this strange fire? Deep in emblematical secrets, we reply, "It is the flare of Man's defiance to his lot".

NOTES

Chapter I

[1] F. W. Boege : *Smollett's Reputation as a Novelist*, p. 4. Dr. Boege is an American scholar to whom I have been greatly indebted in writing the earlier part of this chapter. It is impossible to better his survey.

[2] ibid. pp. 10–15.

[3] ibid. p. 30.

[4] ibid. p. 50.

[5] ibid. pp. 84–98.

[6] ibid. p. 71.

[7] ibid. p. 82.

[8] ibid. p. 81.

[9] ibid. p. 80.

[10] ibid. p. 105.

[11] ibid. p. 106.

[12] *The Nineteenth Century*, V(1879) p. 30. This is the only important reference to Smollett, so far as I know, which has escaped Dr. Boege's attention.

[13] Beoge : op. cit., p. 111.

[14] ibid. p. 76.

[15] ibid. pp. 135–7.

[16] ibid. p. 116.

[17] ibid. p. 125.

[18] T. G. Smollett : *Advice, a Satire*, l. 130.

[19] W. Hazlitt : *Works*, VI, p. 116.

[20] E. S. Noyes : *Letters of Smollett*, p. 80.

[21] ibid. p. 35.

[22] Smollett : *Travels*, p. 10.

[23] A. S. Turberville : *Life in Johnson's England*, I, p. 48.

[24] Smollett : *Roderick Random*, ch. 18.

[25] ibid. ch. 24.

[26] L. Knapp : *Tobias Smollett*, p. 32.

[27] Turberville : op. cit., I, p. 53.

[28] *Roderick Random*, ch. 31.

[29] Smollett : Dedicatory epistle to *Ferdinand, Count Fathom*.

[30] Boege : op. cit., p. 49.

[31] Introduction to *Roderick Random*.

32 Smollett : *Peregrine Pickle,* ch. 97.
33 Introduction to *Roderick Random.*

Chapter II
1 L. Knapp : *Tobias Smollett,* p. 298. Dr. F. Poynter, of the Wellcome Institute of Historical Medicine, who has kindly read this chapter through, comments that all the symptoms mentioned by Gentili are the result of physical over-sensitivity. Asthma is over-sensitivity of the respiratory organs, diarrhoea is over-sensitivity of the colon. Dr. Poynter's diagnosis of Smollett is the same as Smollett's diagnosis of Matthew Bramble.
2 Turberville : op. cit., II, pp. 269–70.
3 J. Moore : *Works of Smollett,* I, p. 151
4 J. Crombie : *History of Scottish Medicine,* I, p. 354.
5 J. Moore : *Works of Smollett,* I, p. 83.
6 A. F. Fergus : *The Glasgow School of Medicine,* p. 11 *et seq.*
7 D. Guthrie : *History of Medicine,* p. 196.
8 F. H. Garrison : *History of Medicine,* p. 358.
9 D. Guthrie : op. cit., p. 178.
10 Smollett : *Roderick Random,* ch. 7.
11 G. R. Mather : *John and William Hunter,* passim.
12 ibid, p. 84.
13 J. Thomson : *Life of William Cullen,* I, p. 284.
14 S. R. Gloyne : *John Hunter,* passim.
15 W. J. Maloney : *George and John Armstrong,* passim.
16 J. Armstrong : *The Economy of Love,* p. 10.
17 ibid. p. 4.
18 ibid. p. 29.
19 ibid. p. 7.
20 ibid. p. 37.
21 ibid. p. 42.
22 *Advice, a Satire,* ll. 91–94 and ll. 103–110.
23 J. Moore : *Medical Sketches,* p. 204 *et seq.*
24 ibid. p. 68.
25 ibid. p. 204 *et seq.*

Chapter III
1 Smollett : *Continuation of the Complete History of England,* IV, p. 460.
2 E. S. Noyes : op. cit., p. 104.
3 Smollett : *Continuation of the Complete History of England,* IV, p. 460.
4 O. Goldsmith : *The Present State of Polite Learning,* ch. 8
5 L. Martz : *Later Career of Tobias Smollett,* p. 8.
6 A. Pope : *Essay on Man,* Ep. I, sec. 8

[7] A. Pope : *Essay on Man*, Ep. III, sec. 1.

[8] Plato : *Five Dialogues on Poetic Inspiration*, p. 50

[9] ibid. p. 54.

[10] ibid. p. 216.

[11] ibid. p. 230.

[12] ibid, p. 206.

[13] A. H. Armstrong : *Plotinus*, p. 51.

[14] G. Bullett : *The English Mystics*, p. 44.

[15] ibid, p. 126.

[16] J. Locke : *Essay on Human Understanding*, p. 5.

[17] ibid. p. 26.

[18] Sir C. Sherrington : *Man on His Nature*, pp. 215–16.

[19] ibid. p. 190.

[20] J. K. Huysmans : *Against Nature*, p. 29.

[21] J. Locke : op cit., p. 27.

[22] Cassirer : *Platonic Renaissance in England*, p. 192.

[23] J. Laird : *Philosophical Incursions into English Literature*, p. 51.

[24] A. Pope : op cit., Ep. I, sec. 8.

[25] ibid. Ep. II, sec. 3.

[26] ibid. Ep. IV, sec. 1.

[27] ibid. Ep. IV, sec. 1.

[28] Smollett : *Humphry Clinker*, p. 180.

[29] J. Boswell : *London Journal*, p. 119.

[30] E. Gibbon : *Memoirs*, p. 199.

[31] F. A. de Voltaire : *Oeuvres Complètes*, XXVIII, p. 535.

[32] D. Hume : *Treatise of Human Nature*, I, p. 18. The summary of relevant aspects of Hume and Hartley's philosophy is based on :

(a) Hume : op cit., Part III, sec. 14.

(b) ibid, Part IV, sec. 7.

(c) D. Hartley : *Observations on Man*, I, pp. 56–114.

[33] E. de B. de Condillac : *Traité des Sensations*, I, p. 1.

[34] Smollett : *Works of Voltaire*, XVIII, p. 141.

[35] ibid. XIII, p. 103.

[36] Smollett : *Peregrine Pickle*, ch. 36.

[37] E. S. Noyes : op. cit., p. 60.

Chapter IV

[1] E. S. Noyes : op cit., p. 100.

[2] *Humphry Clinker*, p. 36.

[3] *Travels*, p. 13.

[4] ibid. p. 96.

[5] *Humphry Clinker*, p. 15.

[7] ibid. p. 48.

[8] ibid. p. 47.

[9] First edition only of *Peregrine Pickle*. See the collation of the first and second editions in H. S. Buck : *A Study in Smollett*.

[10] *Peregrine Pickle*, ch. 70.

[11] See also the "characters" in the 2nd (1760) edition of *The Complete History of England*, Vols. VI–X.

[12] ibid. ch. 79.

[13] D. Hartley : op. cit., vol. I, p. 167.

[14] *Peregrine Pickle*, ch. 101.

[15] *Count Fathom*, ch. 40.

[16] *Peregrine Pickle*, ch. 100.

[17] ibid. ch. 95.

[18] F. A. de Voltaire : op cit., vol. XXII, p. 19.

[19] *Travels*, p. 74.

[20] *Humphry Clinker*, p. 98.

[21] *Peregrine Pickle*, ch. 44.

[22] *Roderick Random*, ch. 29.

[23] *Count Fathom*, ch. 67.

[24] *Peregrine Pickle*, ch. 76.

[25] *Essay on the External Use of Water*, p. 4.

[26] *Count Fathom*, ch. 14.

[27] *Peregrine Pickle*, ch. 56.

[28] *Roderick Random*, ch. 32.

[29] *Count Fathom*, ch. 30.

[30] *Travels*, p. 173.

[31] *Peregrine Pickle*, ch. 38.

[32] E. de B. de Condillac : *Essai sur l'Origine des Connaissances Humaines*, loc. cit.

[33] *Humphry Clinker*, p. 86.

[34] ibid. p. 112.

[35] ibid. p. 117.

[36] ibid. p. 119.

[37] *Count Fathom*, ch. 21.

[38] *Roderick Random*, ch. 56.

[39] *Peregrine Pickle*, ch. 63.

[40] *Count Fathom*, ch. 64.

[41] ibid. ch. 66.

[42] *Roderick Random*, ch. 55.

[43] *Peregrine Pickle*, ch. 86.

[44] *Roderick Random*, ch. 8.

[45] *Peregrine Pickle*, ch. 69.

[46] *Roderick Random*, ch. 6.

[47] *Count Fathom*, ch. 38.

[48] *Peregrine Pickle*, ch. 47.

[49] ibid. ch. 48.

[50] *Humphry Clinker*, p. 210.

[51] *Roderick Random*, ch. 64.
[52] *Essay on the External Use of Water*, p. 10.
[53] *Count Fathom*, ch. 51.
[54] ibid. ch. 53.
[55] ibid. ch. 49.
[56] *Peregrine Pickle*, ch. 90.
[57] *Count Fathom*, ch. 46.
[58] *Roderick Random*, ch. 22.
[59] *Peregrine Pickle*, ch. 96.
[60] ibid. ch. 104.
[61] *Roderick Random*, ch. 44.
[62] ibid, ch. 58.
[63] ibid. ch. 58.
[64] *Peregrine Pickle*, ch. 9.
[65] *Count Fathom*, ch. 33.
[66] *Peregrine Pickle*, ch. 28.
[67] *Count Fathom*, ch. 23.
[68] ibid. ch. 26.
[69] *Peregrine Pickle*, ch. 7.
[70] ibid. ch. 94.
[71] *Count Fathom*, ch. 49.
[72] ibid. ch. 60.
[73] *Peregrine Pickle*, ch. 86.
[74] *Travels*, p. 282.
[75] *Count Fathom*, ch. 29.
[76] ibid. ch. 25.

Chapter V

[1] *Humphry Clinker*, p. 212.
[2] *Peregrine Pickle*, ch. 87.
[3] *Humphry Clinker*, p. 23.
[4] *Peregrine Pickle*, ch. 70.
[5] *Roderick Random*, ch. 19.
[6] *Count Fathom*, ch. 12.
[7] ibid. ch. 30.
[8] ibid. ch. 30.
[9] ibid. ch. 34.
[10] ibid. ch. 43.
[11] ibid. ch. 8.
[12] *Peregrine Pickle*, ch. 77.
[13] ibid. ch. 67.
[14] ibid. ch. 75.
[15] *Roderick Random*, ch. 22.
[16] ibid. ch. 44.
[17] ibid. ch. 68.

[18] ibid. ch. 19.

[19] ibid. ch. 57.

[20] *Roderick Random*, ch. 42.

[21] ibid. ch. 49.

[22] ibid. ch. 50.

[23] ibid. ch. 23.

[24] *Peregrine Pickle*, ch. 87.

[25] ibid. ch. 79.

[26] *Advice*, lines 77–80.

[27] ibid. lines 88–90.

[28] ibid. Smollett's note to line 103.

[29] ibid. lines 95–98.

[30] *Roderick Random*, ch. 51.

[31] *Launcelot Greaves*, ch. 13.

[32] *Roderick Random*, ch. 64.

[33] ibid. ch. 59.

[34] ibid. ch. 65.

[35] *Launcelot Greaves*, ch. 21.

[36] *Peregrine Pickle*, ch. 73.

[37] *Count Fathom*, ch. 34.

[38] *Roderick Random*, ch. 67.

[39] *Humphry Clinker*, p. 223.

Chapter VI

[1] *Humphry Clinker*, p. 103.

[2] ibid. p. 104.

[3] Noyes : op. cit., p. 69.

[4] *Continuation of the History of England*, vol. II, p. 215.

[5] *Travels*, p. 30.

[6] *Launcelot Greaves*, ch. 20.

[7] *Humphry Clinker*, p. 412.

[8] *Peregrine Pickle*, ch. 101.

[9] J. Moore : *Life of Smollett* prefixed to his edition of Smollett, vol. I, p. 150.

[10] *Travels*, p. 173.

[11] ibid. p. 26.

[12] J. H. Plumb : *England in the Eighteenth Century*, p. 17.

[13] D. Marshall : *The English Poor in the Eighteenth Century*, p. 201.

[14] H. Walpole : *Letters*, p. 497.

[15] A. S. Turberville : op. cit., vol. I, pp. 314–16.

[16] *Continuation of the History of England*, vol. I, p. 125, and H. Walpole : *Letters*, p. 500.

[17] *Roderick Random*, ch. 60.

[18] *Humphry Clinker*, p. 181.

[19] ibid. p. 193.
[20] R. Bayne-Powell : *Eighteenth Century London Life*, p. 218.
[21] *Continuation of the History of England*, vol. IV, pp. 104–5.
[22] *Roderick Random*, ch. 46.
[23] J. Boswell : *London Journal*, p. 324.
[24] *Roderick Random*, ch. 23.
[25] ibid. ch. 23.
[26] ibid. ch. 21.
[27] ibid. ch. 23.
[28] ibid. ch. 49.
[29] *Travels*, p. 152.
[30] *Roderick Random*, ch. 46.
[31] *Humphry Clinker*, p. 52.
[32] *Count Fathom*, ch. 47.
[33] *Peregrine Pickle*, ch. 97.
[34] *Roderick Random*, ch. 47.
[35] *Peregrine Pickle*, ch. 87.
[36] ibid. ch. 36.
[37] ibid. ch. 41.
[38] *Count Fathom*, ch. 1.
[39] *Roderick Random*, ch. 44.
[40] ibid. ch. 60.
[41] *Travels*, p. 60.
[42] ibid. p. 58.
[43] ibid. p. 134.
[44] ibid. p. 339.
[45] *Count Fathom*, ch. 1.
[46] *Launcelot Greaves*, ch. 25.
[47] *Count Fathom*, ch. 10.
[48] ibid. ch. 20.
[49] ibid. ch. 21.
[50] ibid. ch. 67.

Chapter VII

[1] B. Williams : *The Whig Supremacy*, p. 140.
[2] *Count Fathom*, ch. 39.
[3] *Peregrine Pickle*, ch. 47.
[4] *Humphry Clinker*, p. 51.
[5] G. N. Clark : *The Wealth of England*, p. 192.
[6] T. S. Ashton : *Economic History of England in the Eighteenth Century*, p. 235.
[7] Smollett's note to *Reproof*, I, p. 126.
[8] Pope's note to *Moral Essays*, Epistle III, I, p. 20.
[9] H. Walpole : *Memoirs of the Reign of George II*, vol. III, p. 308.

10 ibid. vol. III, p. 306.
11 *Humphry Clinker*, p. 419.
12 ibid. p. 228.
13 W. Lecky : *History of England in the Eighteenth Century*, vol. I, p. 521.
14 H. Walpole : *Memoirs of the Reign of George II*, vol. I, p. 52.
15 H. Walpole : *Letters*, p. 523.
16 ibid. p. 491.
17 *Advice*, ll. 237–8.
18 J. H. Plumb : op. cit., p. 36.
19 ibid. p. 38.
20 J. Boswell : *London Journal*, p. 301.
21 *Peregrine Pickle*, ch. 85.
22 *Humphry Clinker*, p. 152.
23 V. H. H. Green : *The Hanoverians*, p. 243, and W. Lecky : op. cit., vol. I, p. 559 *et seq.*
24 T. S. Ashton : op. cit., p. 7.
25 H. Piozzi : op. cit., p. 147 and p. 105.
26 ibid. p. 74.
27 T. S. Ashton : op. cit., p. 203, and B. Williams : op. cit., p. 100.
28 T. S. Ashton : op. cit., p. 203.
29 *Reproof*, ll. 135–42.
30 *Launcelot Greaves*, ch. 21.
31 H. Piozzi : op. cit., p. 64.
32 *Humphry Clinker*, p. 104.
33 *Reproof*, ll. 171-80.
34 R. Bayne-Powell : op. cit., p. 329.
35 ibid. p. 136.
36 ibid. p. 309.
37 ibid. p. 333.
38 *Travels*, p. 47.
39 H. Walpole : *Letters*, p. 504.
40 B. Williams : op. cit., p. 127.
41 *Humphry Clinker*, p. 90.
42 ibid. p. 51.
43 ibid. p. 341.
44 ibid. p. 348.
45 ibid. p. 390.
46 ibid. p. 408.
47 *Ode to Independence*, ll. 93–120.
48 *Humphry Clinker*, p. 299.
49 ibid. p. 123.
50 *Launcelot Greaves*, ch. 9.
51 ibid. ch. 9.
52 *Continuation of History*, vol. II, p. 259.

[53] ibid. vol. II, p. 260.
[54] ibid. vol. II, pp. 260–1.
[55] H. Walpole: *Memoirs*, I, p. 235.
[56] H. Walpole: *Memoirs*, I, p. 383.
[57] ibid. I, p. 169.
[58] *Peregrine Pickle*, ch. 89.
[59] *Launcelot Greaves*, ch. 10.
[60] ibid. ch. 9.
[61] H. Walpole: *Memoirs*, I, p. 162.
[62] J. H. Plumb: op. cit., p. 39 *et seq.*
[63] ibid. p. 43.
[64] ibid. p. 45.
[65] *Humphry Clinker*, p. 122.
[66] ibid. p. 123.
[67] ibid. p. 138.
[68] V. H. H. Green: op. cit., p. 144.
[69] H. Walpole: *Memoirs*, I, p. 52.

Chapter VIII

[1] Motto from Juvenal prefixed to *Count Fathom*.
[2] *Travels*, p. 130.
[3] *Launcelot Greaves*, ch. 18.
[4] *Peregrine Pickle*, ch. 60.
[5] Henry Fielding: *Tom Jones*, Book II, ch. 14.
[6] H. Walpole: *Letters*, pp. 494–5.
[7] *Travels*, p. 241.
[8] E. Gibbon: *Memoirs*, p. 150.
[9] J. Boswell: *Boswell on the Grand Tour: Italy, Corsica and France*, p. 65.
[10] ibid. p. 116.
[11] ibid. p. 7.
[12] *Travels*, p. 253.
[13] ibid. p. 253.
[14] J. Boswell: *Italy, Corsica and France*, p. 6.
[15] *Works of Voltaire*, XV, p. 48.
[16] J. B. Bury: *History of Freedom of Thought*, p. 111.
[17] E. S. Noyes: op cit., p. 54.
[18] ibid. p. 60.
[19] B. Williams: op. cit., p. 76.
[20] J. Swift: *Poems*, II, p. 419.
[21] *Roderick Random*, ch. 34.
[22] *Ode to Independence*, ll. 17–24.
[23] *Humphry Clinker*, p. 218.
[24] *Works of Voltaire*, IX, p. 81.
[25] ibid. IX, p. 49.

[26] ibid. XI, p. 143.
[27] ibid. VIII, p. 24.
[28] ibid. XII, p. 24.
[29] J. B. Bury : op. cit., p. 115.
[30] ibid. p. 117.
[31] E. Gibbon : *Decline and Fall of the Roman Empire*, ch. 16.
[32] *Humphry Clinker*, pp. 235–6.
[33] *Works of Voltaire*, XVIII, p. 70.
[34] *Travels*, p. 266.
[35] ibid. p. 266.
[36] ibid. p. 229.
[37] ibid. p. 172.
[38] *Humphry Clinker*, p. 218.
[39] ibid. p. 217.
[40] *Travels*, p. 30.
[41] *Humphry Clinker*, p. 218.
[42] ibid. p. 218.
[43] *Travels*, p. 267.
[44] ibid. p. 241.
[45] *Humphry Clinker*, p. 50.
[46] ibid. p. 49.
[47] A. S. Turberville : op. cit., vol. I, p. 168.
[48] *Travels*, p. 6.
[49] *Travels*, p. 36.
[50] *Humphry Clinker*, p. 63.
[51] ibid. p. 62.
[52] H. Fielding : *Proposal for Making Effective Provision for the Poor*.
[53] *Humphry Clinker*, p. 85.
[54] *Roderick Random*, ch. 25.
[55] *Compendium of Authentic and Entertaining Voyages*, V, p. 329.
[56] *Travels*, p. 258.
[57] G. N. Clark : *The Wealth of England*, p. 192.
[58] A. S. Turberville : op. cit., I, p. 308.
[59] Pope's note to his *Moral Essays*, Epistle III, l. 100.
[60] H. Piozzi : op. cit., p. 64.
[61] ibid. p. 63.
[62] *Humphry Clinker*, p. 33.
[63] *Peregrine Pickle*, ch. 80.
[64] ibid. ch. 82.
[65] T. S. Ashton : op. cit., p. 6.
[66] V. H. H. Green : op. cit., p. 254.
[67] D. Marshall : *English Poor in Eighteenth Century*, p. 227.
[68] H. Walpole : *Memoirs*, vol. I, p. 176.
[69] *Humphry Clinker*, p. 216.

[70] *Launcelot Greaves*, ch. 12.
[71] ibid. ch. 12.
[72] *Humphry Clinker*, p. 67.
[73] Motto from Horace prefixed to *Roderick Random.*
[74] Preface to *Roderick Random.*
[75] *Launcelot Greaves*, ch. 22.

Chapter IX

[1] Edward Gibbon : *Memoirs*, p. 77.
[2] H. Piozzi : op. cit., p. 79.
[3] *Advice*, ll. 221–2.
[4] *Launcelot Greaves*, ch. 25.
[5] ibid. ch. 12.
[6] E. Gibbon : *Decline and Fall of the Roman Empire*, ch. 66.
[7] E. Gibbon : *Memoirs*, p. 55.
[8] ibid. p. 66.
[9] E. Gibbon : *Decline and Fall of the Roman Empire*, ch. 71.
[10] F. R. Cowell : *Everyday Life in Ancient Rome*, p. 44.
[11] *Travels*, p. 274.
[12] ibid. p. 247.
[13] Preface to *Roderick Random.*
[14] J. Addison : *An Account of the Greatest English Poets*, ll. 19–22.
[15] *The Spectator*, No. 62.
[16] ibid. No. 61.
[17] *Humphry Clinker*, p. 240.
[18] *Travels*, p. 112.
[19] *Travels*, p. 36.
[20] *Advice*, ll. 201–14.
[21] *Launcelot Greaves*, ch. 23.
[22] H. Piozzi : op. cit., p. 44.
[23] *Humphry Clinker*, p. 51.
[24] ibid, p. 69.
[25] *Joseph Andrews*, vol. I, ch. 3.
[26] ibid. vol. I, ch. 1.
[27] ibid. vol. III, ch. 5.
[28] L. Knapp : op. cit., p. 8.
[29] H. Fielding : *Tom Jones*, Book II, ch. 7.
[30] H. Fielding : *Joseph Andrews*, Book III, ch. 11.
[31] ibid. Book I, ch. 3.
[32] F. Cordasco : *Letters of Tobias George Smollett*, p. 22.
[33] *Roderick Random*, ch. 43.
[34] *Fathom*, ch. 40.
[35] *Roderick Random*, ch. 2.
[36] ibid. ch. 30.

Chapter X

[1] *Advice,* ll. 27–32.
[2] *Advice,* ll. 49–54.
[3] ibid. ll. 131–44.
[4] ibid. ll. 145–52.

Chapter XI

[1] *The Spectator,* No. 135.
[2] H. Piozzi : op. cit., p. 60.
[3] J. Locke : op. cit., xxiii.
[4] H. Piozzi : op. cit., p. 16.
[5] *The Spectator,* No. 409.
[6] H. Piozzi : op. cit., p. 48.
[7] *Count Fathom,* ch. 23.
[8] *Peregrine Pickle,* ch. 8.
[9] ibid. ch. 44.
[10] ibid. ch. 45.
[11] ibid. ch. 94.
[12] ibid. ch. 6.
[13] ibid. ch. 54.
[14] *Count Fathom,* ch. 30.
[15] G. M. Kahrl : *Tobias Smollett,* p. 111.
[16] *Count Fathom,* ch. 34.

Chapter XII

[1] J. Swift : *A Tale of a Tub,* p. 59.
[2] ibid. p. 33.
[3] ibid. p. 83.
[4] Lord Hervey : *Memoirs,* p. 38.
[5] ibid. p. 29.
[6] ibid. p. 71.
[7] ibid. p. 81.
[8] ibid. p. 269.
[9] *Works of Voltaire,* XVIII, p. 60.
[10] *Roderick Random,* ch. 33.
[11] *Count Fathom,* ch. 30.
[12] ibid. ch. 30.
[13] *Travels,* p. 251.
[14] *Continuation of Complete History,* IV, p. 131.
[15] J. Swift : *Poetical Works,* II, p. 86.
[16] ibid. II, p. 209.
[17] F. M. A. de Voltaire : *Candide,* p. 112.
[18] ibid. p. 120.
[19] J. Swift : *Tale of a Tub,* p. 54.

[20] J. Swift : *Gulliver's Travels*, III, p. 8.
[21] Lord Hervey : op. cit., p. 236.
[22] ibid. p. 73.
[23] Lord Hervey : op. cit., p. 58.
[24] ibid. p. 37.
[25] *Count Fathom*, ch. 37.
[26] *Peregrine Pickle*, ch. 83.
[27] *Roderick Random*, ch. 34.
[28] ibid. ch. 35.
[29] J. Swift : *Gulliver's Travels*, IV, p. 2.
[30] *Roderick Random*, ch. 23.
[31] *Count Fathom*, ch. 20.
[32] *Roderick Random*, ch. 44.
[33] J. Swift : *Poetical Works*, II, p. 342.
[34] ibid. I, p. 203.
[35] J. Swift : *Tale of a Tub*, p. 125.
[36] *Roderick Random*, ch. 33.
[37] J. Swift : *Prose Works*, XI, p. 353.
[38] ibid. XI, p. 309.
[39] Lord Hervey : op. cit., p. 299.
[40] ibid. p. 83.
[41] ibid. p. 97.
[42] ibid. p. 65.
[43] *Roderick Random*, ch. 42.
[44] *Peregrine Pickle*, ch. 91.
[45] See H. S. Buck : *A Study in Smollett*, p. 149.
[46] *Count Fathom*, ch. 5.
[47] *Roderick Random*, ch. 31.
[48] *Launcelot Greaves*, ch. 12.

Chapter XIII

[1] D. Hume : op. cit., Part IV, section vii.
[2] Earl of Shaftesbury : *Characteristics*, vol. II, p. 345.
[3] Roderick Random, ch. 27.
[4] *Travels*, p. 194.
[5] *Humphry Clinker*, p. 74.
[6] *Count Fathom*, ch. 60.
[7] ibid. ch. 67.
[8] *Peregrine Pickle*, ch. 50.
[9] *Travels*, p. 64.
[10] ibid. p. 107.
[11] *Count Fathom*, ch. 31.
[12] ibid. ch. 49.
[13] *Roderick Random*, ch. 34.
[14] *Humphry Clinker*, p. 221.

[15] *Essay on the External Use of Water*, p. 20.
[16] *Launcelot Greaves*, ch. 23.
[17] ibid. ch. 24.
[18] J. Boswell : *The Hypochondriac*, p. 27.
[19] T. Hobbes : *Leviathan*, Section I, ch. 3.
[20] ibid. Section I, ch. 4.
[21] ibid. Section I, ch. 1.
[22] D. Hume : op. cit., IV, vii.
[23] ibid. xxv.
[24] ibid. IV, v.
[25] D. Hume : op. cit., I, ii.
[26] ibid. I, i.
[27] ibid. II, xvi.
[28] ibid. II, i
[29] ibid. II, vii.
[30] A. E. Underwood, in *The Proceedings of the Royal Society of Medicine* (1937), XXX, p. 961.
[31] *Travels*, p. 23.
[32] ibid. p. 92.
[33] *Peregrine Pickle*, ch. 47.
[34] O. Goldsmith : *Present State of Polite Learning*, ch. 10.
[35] L. Knapp : *Smollett and Chatham* in MLN, Vol. 59 (1944), p. 250.

CHRONOLOGY

1721 Smollett born at Cardross, Dumbartonshire, the grandson of the local Whig statesman, Sir James Smollett, a member of the landed gentry of the county.

1728 Smollett enters Dumbarton Grammar School.

1735 Publication of *Gil Blas*.

1736 Smollett apprenticed to Dr. Gordon in Glasgow, where he attends lectures at the University.

1738 Smollett becomes "sometimes troubled with a cough" and is released from his contract with Dr. Gordon.

1739 In extravagant costumes for which he has borrowed the money, Smollett leaves for London, taking with him his tragedy called *The Regicide,* many letters of recommendation and otherwise empty pockets.

1740 Smollett embarks on H.M.S. *Chichester* as surgeon's second mate.

1741 Smollett witnesses the attack on Carthagena.

1744 Smollett, having married a West Indian heiress, sets up as a surgeon in Downing Street and spends recklessly.

1746 Smollett moves to a cheaper residence in Soho. In spite of Lord Chesterfield's intervention, the Drury Lane Theatre rejects *The Regicide*. *Advice* published.

1747 *Reproof* published. Smollett writes *Roderick Random* in eight months.

1748 Smollett's great year. *Roderick Random* and the translation of *Gil Blas* published. Moves to the Strand, where his daughter Elizabeth is born. Starts a translation of *Don Quixote* and projects a masque called *Alceste,* for which Handel is to write the music.

1749 Tours the Low Countries and corrects a translation of *Le Diable Boiteux*. Abandonment of his masque.

1750 Smollett obtains his M.D. from Aberdeen University, visits Paris and moves to Chelsea, where he resides for the next thirteen years. *Peregrine Pickle* published.

1751 Reviews medical works in *The Monthly Review* and sees Smellie's *Midwifery* through the press.

1752 *Essay on the External Use of Water* published.

1753   Publication of *Ferdinand, Count Fathom,* which contains much satire on the medical world which Smollett has tried strenuously to inhabit during the three past years. Smollett is successfully sued for assault on Peter Gordon. Revisits Scotland. Is in financial difficulties again. Contracts to compile volumes of travels and translations for booksellers.

1754   Smollett, overworked, shows first symptoms of tuberculosis.

1755   Smollett's translation of *Don Quixote* published.

1756   Smollett launches *The Critical Review.* Compendium of Voyages published under his direction. At work on the *History of England.*

1757   First three volumes of the *History* published. Smollett defends the Hunters against their medical detractors in *The Critical Review.*

1758   Fourth volume of the *History* published, bringing a measure of financial success. Second (considerably revised) edition of *Peregrine Pickle.* Smollett insults Admiral Knowles in *The Critical Review.*

1759   Smollett writes, "I have toiled myself into an habitual asthma . . . To tell you a secret, my constitution is quite broken".

1760   Starts *British Magazine,* with *Sir Launcelot Greaves* as a serial and Oliver Goldsmith as a regular contributor. At work on a *Universal History.* Starts publishing the *Continuation of the Complete History of England.* Visits Scotland. Imprisoned for three months for his libel on Admiral Knowles.

1761   Issue of first volumes of a translation of Voltaire supervised by Smollett.

1762   *Sir Launcelot Greaves* published in book-form.

1763   Death of Smollett's daughter Elizabeth. Smollett, seriously ill, leaves for the South of France.

1765   Smollett returns to England and stays at Bath.

1766   Last visit to Scotland. *Travels* published. Smollett settles in Bath.

1768   Completes labours on the compilations and returns to Italy.

1771   Publication of *Humphry Clinker.* Death of Smollett.

1773   Posthumous publication of *Ode to Independence.*

BIBLIOGRAPHY

Joseph Addison : *Poetic Works* (ed. G. Gilfillan). Edinburgh. 1862.
John Armstrong : *The Economy of Love*. London. 1736.
T. S. Ashton : *The Economic History of England in the Eighteenth Century*. London. 1955.
F. W. Boege : *Smollett's Reputation as a Novelist*. Princeton. 1947.
James Boswell : *The Grand Tour: Italy, Corsica and France*. London, 1955.
James Boswell : *The Hypochondriac*. London. 1928.
James Boswell : *The London Journal*. London. 1950.
H. S. Buck : *A Study in Smollett*. Newhaven and London. 1925.
G. Bullett : *The English Mystics*. London. 1950.
E. Cassirer : *The Platonic Renaissance in England*. Edinburgh. 1953.
G. N. Clark : *The Wealth of England from 1496 to 1760*. London. 1946.
J. Combrie : *A History of Scottish Medicine*. London. 1932.
E. de B. de Condillac : *Essai sur l'Origine des Connaissance Humaines*. Paris. 1746.
F. Cordasco : *The Letters of T. G. Smollett*. Madrid. 1950.
(N.B. Some of the letters in this supplement to the collection made by Noyes are forgeries, and these, of course, are not cited here.)
F. R. Cowell : *Everyday Life in Ancient Rome*. London. 1961.
A. F. Fergus : *The Origin and Development of the Glasgow School of Medicine*. Glasgow. 1911.
Henry Fielding : *Joseph Andrews* (Everyman's Library). London. 1931.
Henry Fielding : *A Proposal for Making Effective Provision for the Poor*. London. 1753.
Henry Fielding : *Tom Jones* (Everyman's Library). London. 1918.
F. H. Garrison : *An Introduction to the History of Medicine*. Philadelphia. 1929.
Edward Gibbon : *The Decline and Fall of the Roman Empire* (The World's Classics). London. 1903.
Edward Gibbon : *Memoirs* (The Carisbrooke Library). London. 1891.
S. R. Gloyne : *John Hunter*. Edinburgh. 1950.

Oliver Goldsmith : *The Present State of Polite Learning*. London. 1759.

V. H. H. Green : *The Hanoverians*. London. 1948.

D. Guthrie : *A History of Medicine*. London. 1945.

David Hartley : *Observations on Man*. London. 1749.

William Hazlitt : *Complete Works*. London. 1931.

Lord Hervey : *Memoirs* (ed. R. Sedgwick). London. 1952.

David Hume : *Treatise of Human Nature* (Everyman's Library). London. 1911.

G. M. Kahrl : *Tobias Smollett, Traveller-Novelist*. Chicago. 1945.

L. M. Knapp : *Tobias Smollett, Doctor of Men and Letters*. Princeton. 1949.

J. Laird : *Philosophical Incursions into English Literature*. Cambridge. 1946.

W. Lecky : *A History of England in the Eighteenth Century*. London. 1879.

John Locke : *An Essay on Human Understanding* (ed. R. Wilburn). London. 1947.

W. J. Maloney : *George and John Armstrong*. Edinburgh. 1954.

D. Marshall : *The English Poor in the Eighteenth Century*. London. 1926.

L. Martz : *The Later Career of Tobias Smollett*. New Haven. 1942.

G. R. Mather : *Two Great Scotsmen, John and William Hunter*. Glasgow. 1893.

Modern Language Notes LIX. Baltimore. 1944.

J. Moore : *Medical Sketches*. London. 1786.

J. Moore (ed.) : *The Works of Tobias Smollett*. London. 1872. (N.B. This is a corrupt text, and only Moore's introductory memoirs of Smollett have been cited.)

The Nineteenth Century V. London. 1879.

Plato : *Five Dialogues on Poetic Inspiration* (Everyman's Library). London. 1910.

Plotinus : *Works* (ed. A. H. Armstrong). London. 1953.

J. H. Plumb : *England in the Eighteenth Century*. London. 1950.

Alexander Pope : *Poems* (ed. Warburton). London. 1770.

R. Bayne-Powell : *Eighteenth-Century London Life.*. London. 1937.

Earl of Shaftesbury : *Characteristics*. London. 1732.

Sir Charles Sherrington : *Man on His Nature*. London. 1955.

Tobias George Smollett :
  (a) THE NOVELS
  In Hutchinson's Classic Novels. London. 1904 :
  Roderick Random
  Peregrine Pickle
  Ferdinand, Count Fathom

Sir Launcelot Greaves
Humphry Clinker
(N.B. Where other editions have been used for some special reason, reference is made to them, and they are listed here, under the names of the editors. The valuable collation of the editions of *Peregrine Pickle* in Dr. Buck's *Study in Smollett* (q.v.) has also been employed and referred to. Because of the multiplicity of editions of Smollett's novels, reference has been made to chapters rather than to pages, except in the case of *Humphry Clinker,* and in the hope that this will be helpful to the reader, the same practice has been adopted with a few other standard works.
(b) *Travels through France and Italy,* edited by Thomas Seccombe (The World's Classics). London. 1907.
(c) *The Poetical Works,* edited by G. Gilfillan. Edinburgh. 1862.
(d) OCCASIONAL PIECES
An Essay on the External Use of Water. London. 1752.
A Compendium of Useful and Entertaining Voyages. London. 1756.
The Works of Voltaire. London. 1761–9. (N.B. Smollett wrote the notes to the volumes which appeared before 1764.)
(e) *A Continuation of the Complete History of England.* London. 1841.

* * *

The Spectator, ed. G. G. Smith (Everyman's Library). London. 1907.
B. de Spinoza : *Ethics* (Everyman's Library). London.
Jonathan Swift : *The Prose Works* (ed. Temple Scott). London. 1907.
The Tale of a Tub, the Battle of the Books and Other Satires (Everyman's Library). London. 1909.
Gulliver's Travels (The Novel Library). London. 1947.
Poetical Works (Aldine Edition). London. 1833.
Collected Poems (ed. J. Horell). London. 1958.
A. S. Turberville (ed.) : *Life in Johnson's England.* Oxford. 1933.
J. Thomson : *An Account of the Life, Lectures and Writings of William Cullen.* Edinburgh. 1859.
Voltaire : *Oeuvres Complètes* (ed. L. Moland). Paris. 1883.
Voltaire, F. M. A. de : *Candide and Other Tales* (a revised version of Smollett's translation). London. 1937.
Horace Walpole : *Selected Letters* (Everyman's Library). London. 1926.
Horace Walpole : *Memoirs of the Reign of George II* (ed. Lord Holland). London. 1847.
Basil Williams : *The Whig Supremacy.* Oxford. 1949.

INDEX